KV-575-283

INTELLIGENT
KNOWLEDGE-BASED
SYSTEMS
AN INTRODUCTION

Series in Information Technology
Editor: Tim O'Shea

INTELLIGENT KNOWLEDGE-BASED SYSTEMS
An Introduction

edited by

TIM O'SHEA
Institute of Educational Technology
The Open University

JOHN SELF
Department of Computing
University of Lancaster

GLAN THOMAS
British Broadcasting Corporation

WATERFORD REGIONAL
TECHNICAL COLLEGE
LIBRARY

CLASS :
ACC. No. 02806-8

Harper & Row, Publishers
London

Cambridge
Mexico City
New York
Philadelphia

San Francisco
São Paulo
Singapore
Sydney

Copyright © 1987 Harper & Row
All rights reserved.

First published 1987

Harper & Row Ltd
28 Tavistock Street
London WC2E 7PN

No part of this book may be reproduced in any manner whatsoever without written permission except in the case of brief quotations embodied in critical articles or reviews.

British Library Cataloguing in Publication Data
Intelligent knowledge-based systems: an introduction
　1.　Artificial intelligence
　I.　O'Shea, Tim　II. Self, John
　III. Thomas, Glan
　006.3　　Q335

ISBN 0-06-318366-8

Typeset by Burns and Smith
Printed and bound by The Bath Press, Bath

CONTENTS

Contributors   vii
Foreword   x

1 IKBS — Setting the Scene   1
Jim Howe

2 Artificial Intelligence Languages   15
Aaron Sloman

3 An Expert System for Medical Diagnosis   36
Alan Bundy

4 Dealing with Uncertainty   52
John Fox

5 An Introduction to Production Systems   68
Richard M. Young

6 Logic Programming in Artificial Intelligence and
Software Engineering   83
Robert Kowalski

7 Expert Systems — Some User Experience   97
Stuart Moralee

8 Artificial Intelligence: Next Generation Solutions   110
Arnold Kraft

9   Image Understanding   122
    John Frisby

10 Machine Learning   155
    Tim O'Shea

11 Natural Language Processing   175
    Karen Sparck Jones

12 Proving the Correctness of Digital Hardware
    Designs   197
    Harry Barrow

Index   229

CONTRIBUTORS

Dr. Harry Barrow received his first degree in Mathematics and Physics from Cambridge University in 1965, an M.Sc. (1966) and Ph.D. (1969) in Communication from Keele University where he investigated the human tactile sense. From 1968 to 1975 Dr. Barrow was a Research Fellow in the Department of Artificial Intelligence, Edinburgh University. During that period he worked on the design and construction of the FREDDY 1 and FREDDY 2 robot systems, and conducted research on computational vision and robotics. He was a major contributor in the development of the Versatile Assembly system which pioneered the intensive use of A.I. techniques in automated assembly operations. Dr. Barrow joined the Artificial Intelligence Center at Stanford Research Institute (SRI), Menlo Park, California in 1975. At SRI he continued to lead research in computational vision, formulating the Intrinsic Image model of early visual processing, and developing intelligent aids for cartographers. In 1980, Dr. Barrow left SRI to become one of the founders of the Schlumberger Palo Alto Research Artificial Intelligence Laboratory, initially called FLAIR — the Fairchild Laboratory for Artificial Intelligence Research. At Schlumberger, he is involved in a broad range of research activities, from expert systems for diagnosis, to intelligent aids for designers. Currently his main activity concerns automating formal proofs of correctness of digital hardware designs.

Dr. Alan Bundy was educated as a mathematician, obtaining a B.Sc. degree in Mathematics in 1968 from Leicester University and a Ph.D. in Mathematical Logic in 1971, also from Leicester. Since 1971 he has been a member of the Department of Artificial Intelligence at Edinburgh University, first as a research fellow, but becoming a lecturer in 1974 and a reader in 1984. During this period he has built a number of problem solving programs for different branches of mathematics, e.g. Number Theory, Algebra and Mechanics, and an intelligent front end for ecological modelling. He is also researching into methods of teaching PROLOG. He is the editor of three books on Artificial Intelligence and the author of a book on the automation of mathematical reasoning. He has been sole or joint holder of seven SERC grants and one ESRC grant. He has held the offices of newsletter editor and treasurer of the AISB, the European Artificial Intelligence Society. He was programme chairman for IJCAI-83 and will be conference chairman of IJCAI-87.

Dr. John Fox is Head of the Biomedical Computing Laboratory of the Imperial Cancer Research Fund, London. He has been a visiting worker at Edinburgh, Stanford and Carnegie-Mellon Universities; a consultant on applied artificial intelligence to academic, commercial and government bodies, and is a member of the Knowledge Based Systems Advisory Group of the Department of Industry's Alvey Directorate. He was programme chairman of Expert Systems 83 in Cambridge, and has lectured on knowledge engineering to many bodies, most recently delivering the Annual Lecture of the Science, Education and Technology Division of the Institution of Electrical Engineers. His present research is primarily concerned with theories of decision-making and biomedical applications of knowledge based concepts.

Professor John Frisby is the joint founder (with Dr. J.E.W. Mayhew) of the Artificial Intelligence Vision Research Unit at the University of Sheffield. He is an Honorary Fellow of the British College of Ophthalmic Opticians and the author of the book *Seeing: Illusion, Brain and Mind* (Oxford University Press, 1980). His main research interest lies in combining psychophysical and computational studies of stereoscopic vision. He is the joint coordinator of Alvey's IKBS image interpretation research theme, a large multi-site research programme involving four major industrial companies and five university groups in providing enhanced visual guidance for autonomous vehicles and industrial assembly workstations.

Professor Jim Howe is Head of the Department of Artificial Intelligence at Edinburgh University. He is also founder of the University's AI Applications Institute set up in 1984 to transfer AI/IKBS skills and techniques to industry/commerce. After carrying out postgraduate research at Cambridge University, Dr. Howe came to Edinburgh in 1966 as a founder member of the AI Department. His research interests are broad, including image understanding, intelligent signal processing, and novel applications of computers in school learning. He has published about 100 scientific papers, and has lectured throughout Europe, in North America, and in Australia. He is Chairman of the Alvey Directorate's IKBS Advisory Group. He is also a member of the Science and Engineering Research Council's Information Engineering Committee, its Computing Science Sub-Committee and its Single User System Steering Group. Other interests include Chairmanship of the UK professional society, AISB.

Professor Robert Kowalski is Head of the Logic Programming Group at Imperial College, London. The Group is investigating the implementation and application of PROLOG in such areas as expert systems, intelligent databases and operating systems, and is studying more long term highly parallel implementations and extensions of logic programming. He studied at the Universities of Bridgeport, Stanford and Edinburgh, and from 1967 to 1975 was a Research Fellow in the Department of Computational Logic at the University of Edinburgh. He came to Imperial College in 1975 as Reader in Theory of Computing. In October 1982 he was appointed Professor of Computational Logic. His early research was in the field of automated deduction. This led in 1972 to the development with Alain Colmerauer at the University of Aix-Marseilles of the use of formal logic as a programming language.

Arnold Kraft has been since 1980 a member of the group that develops artificial intelligence based applications for use within Digital Equipment Corporation. Currently, he is a senior member of the AI Marketing Group. Prior to that, he managed the group that developed XCON and XSEL, the computer configuration programs, and then managed the External Resources requirements for the Intelligent Systems Technologies Group, in Hudson, MA. Previously, he was MIS Manager for the Commercial Group and the Industrial Products Group, having joined Digital Equipment Corporation in 1977.

Stuart Moralee is head of the group which develops Knowledge Engineering applications for use within the Unilever Research Port Sunlight Laboratory. He has been working with Knowledge-Based Systems since 1980. He is an honorary Professorial Fellow at the Department of Computer Science, University of Liverpool.

Dr. Tim O'Shea was trained at the Universities of Sussex and Leeds. He has carried out research on the educational applications of artificial intelligence at the Universities of Texas at Austin, Edinburgh and California at Berkeley and also at the Xerox Palo Alto Research Centre. He is currently employed as a senior lecturer in the Information Technology Centre of the Open University Institute of Educational Technology. He is a past Chairman of AISB (the Artificial Intelligence Society) and was a member of the Alvey Advisory Committee on Intelligent Knowledge Based Systems. His publications include *Learning and Teaching with Computers* (co-authored with John Self, Harvester Press) and *Artificial Intelligence: Tools, Techniques and Applications* (co-edited with Marc Eisenstadt, Harper & Row). He wrote and presented the BBC series 'The Learning Machine'. He lives mostly in Stony Stratford, Buckinghamshire and partly in Balleen, County Kilkenny with his wife Eileen Scanlon and children Catherine and Philip.

Professor Aaron Sloman is Professor of Artificial Intelligence and Cognitive Science at the University of Sussex. He is a member of the SERC/DTOI Study Group on architectures for intelligent knowledge-based systems. He was co-founder of the Cognitive Studies Program at Sussex; has been invited speaker at many AI meetings and conferences, world-wide; and is the author of the book *The Computer Revolution in Philosophy: Philosophy, Science and Models of Mind* and co-author of *Pop-11: a Practical Language for Artificial Intelligence*. He was co-developer and project leader for the POPLOG AI software development environment, now used for teaching and research in many universities and commercial organisations.

Dr. Karen Sparck Jones is a GEC Research Fellow and Senior Research Associate at the Computer Laboratory, University of Cambridge. She has worked in automatic language and information processing since the late fifties, and is the author of numerous publications in these areas. She has recently been a member of groups working on the UK's programme for R&D on Intelligent Knowledge-Based Systems, and has special responsibility for natural language work under the programme.

Dr. Richard Young dabbled in Engineering, Computer Science, and Artificial Intelligence before gaining his Ph.D. in Psychology from Carnegie-Mellon University in 1973. Since then he has worked at the Artificial Intelligence Department at Edinburgh University and the Medical Research Council's Applied Psychology Unit in Cambridge. His research interests are in the use of artificial intelligence for the computer simulation of adults' and children's thinking, problem solving, and mathematical skills. He is interested in human-computer interaction and has carried out work on users' mental models of interactive devices. He has recently been working on techniques for knowledge elicitation and the human interface of expert systems. He is a member of the Alvey Directorate's IKBS Advisory Group.

FOREWORD

The launch of the Alvey Programme by the UK Government in mid-1983 created a great deal of interest in both industry and universities in advanced research in information technology and particularly in Intelligent Knowledge-Based Systems, the newest subject included within the programme. One manifestation of this interest was the tremendous demand placed on the small band of experts in this country to give lectures on their IKBS specialisms, a demand so great that it could not reasonably be satisfied. The solution adopted was to have the lectures video-taped and placed on general sale. This has turned out to be a successful approach judging by the number of tapes sold. I anticipate that the present 'book of the film' will be equally successful.

   I would like to place on record my thanks to the lecturers, to Dr Tim O'Shea of the Open University who organised the series and to the BBC Open University Production Centre which made the videos, particularly the Producers, Mr John Jaworski and Dr Glanffrwd Thomas. Last but not least I would like to thank the lecturers for contributing written versions of their talks, and to the Editors for moulding these into the present text. Without their willing cooperation the venture could not have gone ahead.

D.B. THOMAS
Alvey Directorate
London
August 1986

INTELLIGENT
KNOWLEDGE-BASED
SYSTEMS
AN INTRODUCTION

1

IKBS — SETTING THE SCENE

JIM HOWE

UNIVERSITY OF EDINBURGH

In late 1981, the Japanese Government startled the international computing community by announcing its Fifth Generation Computing Systems project. The objective of this project is to build by 1990 prototype computing systems that can converse with their users in their natural way, through human language, speech and visual images.

An example of a specific system proposed by the 5G programme, as it has come to be called, is a machine translation system. Such a system would combine two capabilities, namely, automatic natural language interpretation and automatic language production, within a single system, in order to achieve, first, multilingual translation, secondly, a capacity of at least 100 000 words, and thirdly, translations of 90 per cent accuracy or greater. All this would be at a cost saving of at least 30 per cent over the use of a human translator.

A second project, and a second example of the kinds of objective set by this programme, is a question-answering system which would combine automatic speech or language interpretation capabilities with an ability to reason about knowledge stored in very large commercial and industrial databases. As before, the criteria would be to be able to answer questions in a whole variety of different professional fields and to be able to do this with a word capacity of at least 5000 words for databases which contain at least 10 000 rules.

A third project concerns applied speech understanding systems. Like the machine translation system, it would combine natural language interpretation and production capabilities, to which would be added speech signal processing and speech synthesis capabilities to achieve, for example, a speech-driven typewriter with a capacity of 10 000 words. A second example of an applied speech understanding system is a speech response system with a vocabulary of 10 000 words and capable of carrying on a natural conversation with a person. A third example is a speaker identification system which would be capable of recognizing one out of a few hundred speakers.

The fourth main project is an image understanding system capable of storing 100 000 pieces of information in image form. In this case, it would combine a picture and image interpretation capability, so that it could cope with handwritten sketches, TV images, satellite photographs or X-ray images. It would combine this picture interpretation capability with a picture generation facility capable also of representing a wide range of complex visual patterns.

The financial rewards from all this are really very clear. One of the current estimates of the size of the North American market sets it at the order of $128 million in 1984 for the advanced IT projects, rising to $2500 million in 1990 (see Table 1.1). The table shows the steep predicted growth, particularly in the areas of language interpretation and visual recognition systems, where the market by 1990 is estimated to rise to about $1000 million in both cases. In the case of voice recognition and expert systems there is a rather more modest growth, to about $250 million by 1990. In part, the shape of these curves represents the difficulty of the problems that have to be resolved in building practical systems.

TABLE 1.1   Estimates of the North American market for advanced IT projects (from Manuel and Evanczuk, 1983)

Product category	Market estimate ($ millions)							
	1983	1984	1985	1986	1987	1988	1989	1990
Knowledge systems	10	16	25	40	60	90	145	220
Natural-language software	18	32	60	105	190	335	600	1,090
Computer aided instruction	7	11	15	20	30	45	70	100
Visual recognition	30	55	100	150	230	360	555	860
Voice recognition	10	14	20	30	50	80	130	230
Total	75	128	220	345	560	910	1,500	2,500
Source: DM Data Inc.								

THE NEED FOR KNOWLEDGE REPRESENTATION

Achieving these targets would imply a successful development of a computing technology that is radically different from the computing technology available today, where the user communicates with a system via a formal programming language or a query language, and the underlying machine works in a serial fashion. At the software level, what is critically required is the skilled deployment of existing and new computing techniques for representing and manipulating knowledge, complemented at the hardware level by the invention of new parallel processing computing regimes to provide the additional computational power and speed that the knowledge-related techniques will require to achieve the natural rhythm of dialogue between participants.

Now, the man in the street can readily understand that greatly increased processing power will be needed to handle tasks of such complexity, but the suggestion that knowledge representation techniques are crucial is probably quite mysterious. After all, if I asked what a computer is, the same man in the street will tell me that it is a machine that processes data, probably numerical data, by blindly applying instructions given by human beings. To try to show why knowledge representation techniques are so crucial I will consider briefly some aspects of the problem areas selected by the Japanese programme, beginning with machine translation.

Early interest in machine translation evolved in wartime work on code-breaking by computers, which made use of tables of information about letter and word frequencies. By and large, machine translation programs built during the 1950s and 1960s were based on the notion that translation is done by looking up words in a language synonym dictionary. However, as every dictionary user knows, most words have more than a single synonym. This point is made quite well by some sample English output text translated from Russian by Oettinger's machine translation program:

[In, At, Into, For, On] [last, latter, new, latest, lowest, worst] [time, tense] for analysis and synthesis relay contact electrical [circuit, diagram, scheme] parallel-[series, successive, consecutive, consistent] [connection, junction, combination] [with, from] [success, luck] [to be utilize, to be take advantage of] apparatus Boolean algebra.

What the user was supposed to understand from that output was:

In recent times Boolean algebra has been successfully employed in the analysis of relay networks of the series-parallel type.

A more famous, if apocryphal, example is the sentence

The spirit is willing but the flesh is weak.

which, when translated into Russian and back into English again, is said to have come out as

The vodka is strong but the meat is rotten.

The entertainment value of these outputs tends to obscure a vital point — these early machine translation programs expressed expert linguists' understanding of the translation process at the time. The programs' poor performance was not due to a failure of technology; it was due to the weakness of the prevailing linguistic theory which the technology had put to work.

In the early 1970s, encouraged by advances in linguistic theory and the availability of more powerful computing techniques, attention in the natural language area switched from machine translation to language understanding. After all, if the machine could understand the meaning of a sentence it could presumably paraphrase it, or answer questions about it, or translate it into another language. But what does understanding the meaning of a sentence mean?

One answer is that something is understood when it is transformed from one representation, the source representation (in this case, a sentence in English), into another representation, the target representation, which is some kind of computer-manipulable formalism. The target representation chosen must provide a set of actions that could be performed. Also, the mapping between representations must be designed so that for each event in the source representation, an appropriate action will be performed by the target representation. In practice, three problems stand out:

(i) the complexity of the target representation into which the mapping is being done;
(ii) the type of mapping: one-to-one, many-to-one, one-to-many, or many-to-many;
(iii) the interactions between components in the source representation.

The first of these problems, the complexity problem, can be illustrated by comparing the type of representation needed when English sentences are used to access a keyword database system with the type of representation needed to enable a system to answer a variety of questions about the events and relationships within a story. If we take the former case of the keyword-driven system, then a sentence such as

I want to read all about the last presidential election.

might be represented simply by the pair of keywords 'election' and 'president'. The mapping between the input sentence and the database would be done on the basis of those two keywords.

On the other hand, if we take the story

Bill told Mary he would not go to the movies with her. Her feelings were hurt.

then clearly a much more complicated formalism is required to represent the concepts in this story and the relationships between the concepts. One such formalism is Schank's 'conceptual dependency', which represents the actions and events of the situation as a network of primitive conceptual elements (see Figure 1.1).

FIGURE 1.1   Example of Schank's 'conceptual dependency' formalism (from Rich, 1983)

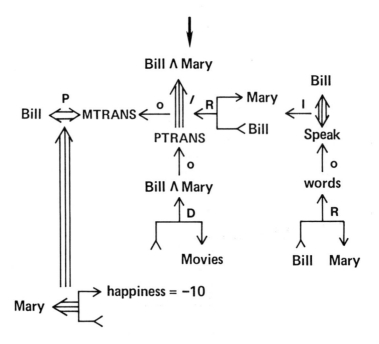

The story is represented by that formalism in the following way. First, the mental transfer of information from Bill to Mary is represented in the formalism by the primitive element MTRANS at the top left-hand side of the network. The physical action of going to the movies is represented by the PTRANS conceptual unit in the centre of the network, and in this case it is negated by the small, angled dash at the top right-hand side of the PTRANS unit. The method of transferring the information between Bill and Mary is represented at the right-hand side through the action Speak and its relationships. And, finally, Bill's effect on Mary is represented by the relationship at the lower left-hand side of the network.

Building such a complex representation is difficult because a great deal of information must be extracted from the input sentences. Often, our ability to extract that information requires the use of non-linguistic knowledge about the world described by the sentences in the story; for example, knowledge about the participants' intentions, their feelings and their emotions.

I'd like to turn now to the second problem — the type of mapping. One-to-one mappings are rare in English, many-to-one mappings being much more common. For example, if we go back to the keyword-driven database system, then a number of apparently different sentences have a single mapping. The sentence

Tell me all about the last presidential election.

would access the database with the keywords 'election' and 'president'. Similarly, the sentence

Show me all the stories about the last presidential election.

also maps on to the keywords 'election' and 'president'. And yet again, the statement

I am interested in the last presidential election.

would also map on to the same keywords. In the case of many-to-one mappings, of which this is an example, the understanding system must know about all the ways that a target representation can be expressed in the source language.

One-to-many mappings, however, usually require a great deal of non-linguistic knowledge so that the correct target representation can be made. If we take the sentence

They are flying planes.

then that sentence might be interpreted as

(They are (flying aeroplanes)).

that is, they are aeroplanes that can fly, not toy aeroplanes. On the other hand, the sentence could be interpreted as

(They (are flying) aeroplanes).

in which case the conversation is probably about pilots flying aeroplanes. Alternatively, the sentence might be nothing to do with aeroplanes: it could be about carpenters' planes:

(They are (flying carpenters' planes)).

Finally, it could be interpreted as

(They (are flying) carpenters' planes).

meaning, perhaps, that some company is shipping some supply of carpenters' planes to some other country. There are a number of other interpretations that one can make on that simple sentence, and so this is an example of the one-to-many mapping.

The problem with English is that it has the properties of both these examples. It involves many-to-many mappings. In other words, there are many ways of saying the same thing, and a given statement may have many meanings. To implement many-to-many mappings in a program, as we have seen with these short examples, requires a great deal of non-linguistic knowledge about the task domains in the framework of linguistic knowledge about language structure.

So far I've only talked about representation at the sentence level, since it's received probably most attention from linguists. If you think about the paragraph level, where relationships between sentences must be recognized, of course the complexity is going to increase significantly. Indeed, complexity explodes when we turn to consider dialogues between participants, since any understanding system has to cope with implicit presuppositions, indirect speech acts and participants' beliefs about the world. Indeed, it is these issues which are at the heart of current language research. So the linguistic theory needed to underpin computation systems is still comparatively undeveloped.

The third problem, the interaction between components, can be illustrated first by considering speech understanding. In addition to the linguistic problems that we have just discussed, a speech system has to chop the continuous speech waveform into chunks which correspond to linguistic units. At face value, one might imagine that this task is straightforward, involving a simple matching process between features in the source and target representations, and essentially that is what happens in word recognition systems. However, when speech is continuous, the acoustic representations of speech units are continually modified through the operation of the vocal tract. For example, the simple sentence

You gave the cat your dinner.

may sound like

You gave the catcher dinner.

Speech understanding systems are faced with the fundamental problem of how to break down a continuous speech waveform into units which can then be handled in the way in which one would handle text in natural language understanding.

It's not just the fact that the speech is generated by a mechanical device, the vocal tract: a number of the complications in speech processing are produced by the fact that variations in the sound of a word result from its position in a phrase, from its degree of emphasis, and from the rate at which it is pronounced. Also, the size and shape of the vocal tract differs widely from one individual to another. And, of course, habits of speech differ according to age, sex, geographic region and social background. In addition to the sounds made by the speaker, the signal that reaches a speech recognition device is influenced by other circumstances such as the room acoustics, the background noise and the characteristics of the transmission channel.

From a theoretical point of view, one crucial unknown is the extent to which general and/or specific knowledge of the topic of conversation must be made use of within the speech segmentation process. For example, the Bell Laboratories' airline ticket booking system, with which a user communicates by telephone, knows about such concepts as 'destination', 'departure times' and 'departure dates' and can assign values to them in a particular context. The transcript (Figure 1.2) is a fragment of a telephone conversation that illustrates the competence of this particular system.

FIGURE 1.2   Part of a telephone conversation with the Bell Laboratories' airline ticket booking system (from Levinson and Liberman, 1981)

U: I want one first-class seat on flight number three one to Denver on Sunday
M: I am sorry the flight is not available on Sunday
U: I would like to leave on Saturday
M: Flight number three leaves New York at . . .
U: What is the flight time?
M: The flight time is five hours and twenty five minutes
U: How many stops are there on the flight?
M: This flight makes one stop
U: I want a non-stop flight

.
.
.
.
.

It begins with a user saying over the phone to the system, 'I want one first class seat on Flight 31 to Denver on Sunday'. In the same time as it would take a human being at the end of the phone to respond, the system comes back with the information from its database of knowledge about flights: 'I am sorry the flight is not available on Sunday.' The user then thinks and says, 'I would like to leave on Saturday'. The system, again in real time, is able to interpret that utterance and come back with the response that Flight No. 3 leaves New York at a particular time on that day. The user then goes on to ask what is the flight time, and again the system is quickly able to come up with the information that the flight time is five hours and twenty-five minutes. And so the conversation continues.

Now, difficult though speech understanding is, image understanding presents even greater problems. Image data is usually acquired by measuring the light intensities at a rectangular array of positions within an image. Each cell in this array, called a picture element, or pixel for short, takes a numerical value. That value represents the compounding of many factors. For example, the appearance of an object is influenced by its surface material, the atmospheric conditions, the angle of the light source, the ambient light, the camera angle, the camera transmission characteristics, and so on. It is extraordinarily difficult to determine the contribution of each of these factors to a pixel value. Furthermore, an image collapses three dimensions into two, introducing ambiguities that cannot be resolved from the input data alone. Many of these ambiguities are because objects in the foreground of an image obscure parts of objects in the background. This would be analogous to speech or language processing with parts of utterances or parts of sentences removed from the input. Not surprisingly, perhaps, the current state of the art in image understanding lags behind speech and language understanding, despite its commercial significance.

EXPERT SYSTEMS

Perhaps one of the key problems in image understanding is our own inability to think about how we see. For many other complex intellectual tasks that are as underdetermined as image understanding, we can articulate at least a partial explanation of the way in which we tackle that task. We can think of that explanation as a set of rules which describe what we do under differing circumstances when tackling problems in some specific domain. Programs which automate the application of these rules are known popularly as *expert systems*.

One example of a domain where the input data is very underdetermined is the analysis of geological measurements taken from oil wells. A measuring device, which may irradiate the bore, is lifted from the bottom to the top. As it traverses the wall of the bore hole, the measurements made are encoded and are reproduced on a record which is known as a log (Figure 1.3).

This output has to be interpreted by the expert who is trying to determine the characteristics of the substrata through which the bore hole has been drilled. The measurements would be physical properties of the underground rock such as density, electrical resistivity, sound transmission and radioactivity. When interpreting these measurements geologists use various sorts of knowledge. They have to take into account qualitative data; for example, if the rock is Cambrian, it has the connotation of being 'very old' and therefore suggests 'a very compacted rock'. So qualitative data is required, as well as quantitative data about such things as the permeability, the porosity, the percentage of calcite, and so on. Interpretation of this quantitative data is further complicated by the fact that some rocks, for example chertz and quartzites, have similar log responses, and so can only be distinguished in the context of knowledge about their geological environments.

FIGURE 1.3   A geological 'log' of a bore hole (from Barstow, 1983)

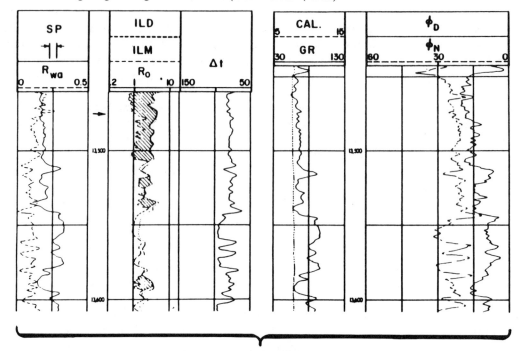

(A) MEASURED

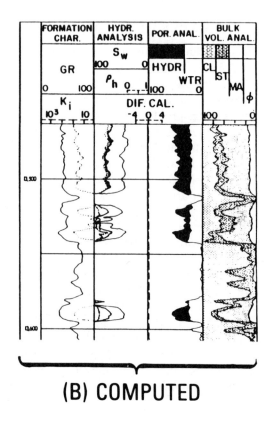

(B) COMPUTED

The LITHO program, which is under development in France, represents part of the knowledge of an expert geologist, and has been checked out on different wells in Europe and the Middle East. The transcript (Figure 1.4) shows the start of a dialogue between a geologist and the LITHO system.

FIGURE 1.4   The start of a dialogue with the LITHO program (from Bonnet and Dahan, 1983)

```
M   :   NAME OF WELL?
U   :   DIDI-7
M   :   WHERE ARE YOU?
U   :   IRAQ-NORTH
        THE GEOLOGICAL PROVINCE
        IS ZAGROS-FOLD-BELT
        THE CONTINENT IS
        MIDDLE-EAST
                 :
                 :
                 :
M   :   WHAT IS THE GEOLOGICAL
        AGE OF DIDI-7?
U   :   UNKNOWN
M   :   PLEASE ENTER THE PALEONTOLOGY
        WORDS YOU KNOW FOR ZONE
U   :   FORAMINIFERA OSTRACODS
        THE PALEONTOLOGICAL CLASSES ARE:
        FORAMINIFERA ARTHROPODS
        THE PALEONTOLOGICAL ORDER IS:
        OSTRACODS
                 :
                 :
                 :
```

First, the system asks the user to identify the well. The user types in 'Didi-7'. The system then wants to know where this well is located, so it outputs 'where are you?' to the user, and the user feeds back the information that it's located in north Iraq, in the geological province of Zagros-fold-belt in the Middle East continent. The system then decides that it needs to know something about the geological age of Didi-7. The user, of course, knows nothing about this and has to tell the system, 'unknown'. The system then has to find other ways of getting the information it requires. It asks the user to enter the paleontology words which he knows for the zone. The user responds with the information 'Foraminifera Ostracods. The palaeontological classes are Foraminifera Arthropods. The palaeontological order is Ostracods.'

The dialogue proceeds in this vein, moving on to the stage where the system wants to have not just qualitative information about the zone but also some information about the measurements in the logs (Figure 1.5). In this case the particular log measurements it's interested in are gamma-ray log measurements, and so it asks the user, 'Please enter the characteristic features of the gamma-ray log in this zone', and it prints the word 'plateaus'. The user responds that there are no plateaus, and, in answer to the subsequent prompts, that there are no massive beds, megaramps are absent, mesoramps are absent, and so on.

The machine reasons on the basis of the information given, and tries to discover what information it needs to come to a decision about the geological structure. It reaches the stage where it decides that it needs to know something about the tectonic structure of the zone (Figure 1.6). In this case the user is puzzled about the request and says 'Why?' This shows that the

FIGURE 1.5 Further dialogue with the LITHO program (from Bonnet and Dahan, 1983)

```
                        :
                        :
        M   :   PLEASE ENTER THE
                CHARACTERISTIC FEATURES
                OF THE GAMMA-RAY LOG
                IN ZONE
                PLATEAUS      :  (U) NO
                MASSIVE BEDS  :  (U) NO
                MEGARAMPS     :  (U) ABSENT
                MESORAMPS     :  (U) ABSENT
                MEDIUM BEDS   :  (U) NO
                MEDIUM RAMPS  :  (U) RARE
                        :
                        :
```

FIGURE 1.6 Next stage of the dialogue with LITHO (from Bonnet and Dahan, 1983)

```
                        :
                        :
        M   :   WHAT IS THE TECTONIC
                STRUCTURE OF ZONE?
        U   :   WHY?

        M   :   THIS WILL AID IN DETERMINING
                THE PALEOENVIRONMENT OF
                DEPOSITION ON ZONE.   IT HAS
                ALREADY BEEN ESTABLISHED THAT
                THE MAIN LITHOLOGIC TYPE OF
                ZONE IS BIOLOGICAL, THEREFORE
                IF FRACTURE IS ONE OF THE
                TECTONIC STRUCTURES OF ZONE,
                THEN THERE IS WEAKLY SUGGESTIVE
                EVIDENCE (.3) THAT THE PALEOENVIRONMENT
                OF DEPOSITION OF ZONE IS REEFAL
                (ALSO THERE IS WEAKLY SUGGESTIVE
                EVIDENCE (.3) THAT THE GEOLOGICAL
                FORMATION IS GLOBALLY COMPACTED. )
                        :
                        :
```

system has a capability of explaining its reasoning at this stage, for it tells the user that this will aid in determining the paleoenvironment of the deposition on zone. It points out to him that previously it had already been established that the main lithologic type of the zone is biological. Therefore, if fracture is one of the tectonic structures of zone, then there is weakly suggestive evidence (and it puts a numerical value on the strength of that evidence of .3) that the paleoenvironment of the deposition of the zone is reefal. Also there is weakly suggestive evidence, again at the .3 level, that the geological formation is globally compacted.

Finally (Figure 1.7), the system produces its conclusion that the paleoenvironment of the deposition is coastal or lagoonal, the main lithologic type is biological, and the most plausible lithofacies are well cemented Dolomitic limestone, well cemented Dolomite, moderately cemented Dolomitic limestone, anhydritic Dolomite, and argillaceous limestone. This is the kind of information that the geologist needs so that he can decide about the worthwhileness or not of carrying on with drilling activities in this particular location.

FIGURE 1.7   The LITHO program's conclusions (from Bonnet and Dahan, 1983)

```
                    :
                    :

        HERE ARE MY CONCLUSIONS:
        THE PALEOENVIRONMENT OF DEPOSITION
        IS COASTAL OR LAGOONAL
        THE MAIN LITHOLOGIC TYPE IS BIOLOGICAL
        THE MOST PLAUSIBLE LITHOFACIES ARE:
        WELL CEMENTED DOLOMITIC LIMESTONE
        WELL CEMENTED DOLOMITE
        MODERATELY CEMENTED DOLOMITIC LIMESTONE
        ANHYDRITIC DOLOMITE
        ARGILLACEOUS LIMESTONE
```

ARTIFICIAL INTELLIGENCE AND THE ALVEY PROGRAMME

Thirty years ago, the challenge of modelling by machine these kinds of problems — the problems of machine translation, natural language understanding, image understanding and so on — invoked a new discipline called Artificial Intelligence. From the start, knowledge representation and knowledge use have been key issues in AI research. Various techniques have been devised for dealing with the problem of storing large bodies of knowledge and data structures for the purposes of symbolic computation. These include production rule systems, semantic nets, frames and predicate logic. Various knowledge handling and system organization techniques have also been implemented for knowledge use. These include data-driven and goal-driven control regimes, the blackboard, the chart, and so on.

Besides a common interest in representation and control, AI practitioners share a common methodology. I think it's fair to say that the methodology of AI rests on the assumption that all cognitive activity can be described as symbol manipulation. The need for a new kind of notation for representing knowledge and knowledge-handling mechanisms symbolically by machine prompted the development of the AI programming languages; languages like LISP, POP-2 and PROLOG.

These languages differ from conventional programming languages such as FORTRAN and PASCAL in a number of important respects. First, they have a richer set of data structures for non-numerical computations; for example, lists, arrays, strings, words, procedures, processes, and so on. Secondly, their data structures are type-free. So, for example, lists can contain arbitrary objects, and code can be treated as data. Thirdly, they are extensible, which allows the user to add new syntactic constructions defined in terms of existing primitives.

Over the last decade a great deal of effort has gone into the construction of AI program support environments that integrate an AI language with an editor, a compiler, a run-time system, debugging tools and an on-line documentation system. The best-known examples of these environments are the INTERLISP environment, which has been developed in the USA over the last 10 years or so, and, in the UK, the POPLOG environment, which has been developed at Sussex University.

These environments have two advantages. The first advantage is that they facilitate a particular style of programming that has been called 'structured-growth'. The phrase 'structured-growth' characterizes programming that is done incrementally. The programmer starts out with a simple initial program which is allowed to grow by increasing the complexity of the individual modules to represent his growing understanding of the problem. This bottom-up, perhaps piecemeal, approach reflects the absence of a detailed formulation of how to solve the problem, more often than not the case when starting out to build a complex AI system. The AI approach stands in marked contrast to the conventional software engineering methodology which is predicated on two assumptions: (a) that the design is decided upon at the start of a project, and (b) that the subsequent programming activity is a straightforward development task.

The second advantage of the AI programming development environment is that it speeds up program building compared to a traditional programming system, which separates the activities of building, compiling, editing and documenting a program. For example, in the POPLOG system, new commands can be given at any time, procedures can be edited and recompiled without a relinking process (because only the altered code has to be recompiled), temporary procedures can be defined at run time to interrogate the data structures, and so on.

In summary, the AI programming environment provides the user with extremely powerful facilities for carrying out experiments concerned with mechanizing ideas. It is in this sense that AI programming is experimental programming.

In the United Kingdom, AI gained a firm foothold when Edinburgh University set up an AI department in the mid-1960s. In the early 1970s the level of investment in academic AI plummeted, due to Sir James Lighthill's adverse review of the subject. Having lived through the aftermath of the Lighthill report, I'd like to quote an observation made by Lady Lovelace more than a hundred years ago. She said:

> In considering any new subject, there is frequently a tendency first to overrate what we find to be already interesting or remarkable: and, secondly, by a sort of natural reaction to undervalue the true state of the case when we do discover that our notions have surpassed those that were really tenable.

When she wrote those words, she was talking about Babbage's Analytical Engine, but in fact she could have been describing AI in this country in the 1970s!

Now I think it's fair to say that the Alvey programme is giving AI the 'kiss of life' through its Intelligent Knowledge-Based Systems programme. The name 'IKBS' has been coined to describe systems of limited intelligence that can be built and sold as products during the next decade. In this context, the role of the Alvey IKBS programme is to encourage the development of new representational techniques and new modelling tools — the so-called IKBS 'enabling technology'. It is a directed programme, organized by themes, with a very strong market pull.

The work within the programme is organized by 'research themes'. In fact, the IKBS programme is slightly wider than a software programme, for it also includes some of the research required to develop the infrastructure, the computing engines, the hardware knowledge stores, and the parallel processing languages needed to support the operation of the complex software systems which will produce the behaviour that I have described.

Within the research themes we have expert systems and intelligent front ends, which are programs that try to ease the transaction between the user and some complex program like a finite analysis program. We have research themes on knowledge representation, inference and planning — recognizing that the organization of the search through the database of knowledge is a critical issue with the large complex systems which we are starting to build. We've already touched on the problems in natural language and image interpretation. There is also a research theme on intelligent computer-aided instruction. With the rapid pace of technological change, it's rather regrettable that we don't have any good intelligent computer-aided instruction systems capable of doing something about some of the training problems that we have in the programme today.

It is also interesting to note that three of the four recently announced Alvey large-scale demonstrator projects have significant IKBS content. Over the next five years they will push AI technology to the limit, to achieve prototype systems at least the equal of the Fifth Generation Systems projects. As we saw earlier, the stakes are very high.

QUESTIONS

Q.   You've referred to the efforts in the UK and also made some reference to research going on in Japan. What other countries are leading in this race, if it is a race?

A.   Well, I don't know if one should characterize it as a race or not. I think that perhaps I should have made it clear that the main body of work in AI is being carried out in North America, particularly the United States. A number of US companies are putting together an organized programme of work which is in principle somewhat similar to the Alvey programme. But it is behind the Japanese and Alvey programmes, and is still being put into place and still being recruited. The Americans, like us, suffer from enormous problems of lack of trained personnel. Although a great deal of money is available, they have the same problem of actually finding people who can build these complex systems. So although there is more money in the USA, it is not clear really that in terms of know-how and ability to exploit it they are necessarily out of sight.

Q.   You mentioned this lack of skilled manpower. Does the Alvey project actually include the idea of promoting the teaching of these skills in universities?

A.   Yes it does. This lecture is, after all, part of Alvey's IKBS awareness programme, and the awareness programme extends from awareness through to education. Really it is SERC (the Science and Engineering Research Council), together with the UGC, that is responsible for the teaching programmes in the universities. A number of new M.Sc. courses have been begun. One began at Edinburgh last year, and we took in 10 students; next year it goes up to 20. A new course will start at Cambridge University next year, an M.Sc course; and also at the same time a new course ought to start at Imperial College. Besides that, I believe that there is some hope that the programme may be able to make use of distance learning methods to try to get to much larger audiences. The problem about the formal M.Sc. courses is that, at best, they can probably only cope with relatively small numbers, perhaps 50 students. If you talk to one of the larger British companies, the personnel officer will say, 'We'll hire the lot.' That's the extent of the shortage.

Q.   The attraction of an expert, Dr Howe, is that he is always bang up to date, like yourself. But the system is so complex (when we come to intelligent knowledge-based systems) that one has the feeling that it's best for conservative knowledge.

A.   Probably, as things stand at present, that's a good strategy. But in the long run a good expert system, as I tried to show you with the oil well example, ought to be capable of interrogation. So it ought to be able to explain to the user the basis for its decision making. More importantly, it ought to be in a position to explain its decision making in terms which are really understandable by him. Now, at present the systems we are building are expert systems for experts. But we can expect to build expert systems which can be used by a non-expert, and then that does put a premium on having the kinds of representation which can explain things to him in the way in which he understands. And that raises huge problems, because we all have 'intuitive' rather than 'formal' models about the things that happen around us, and we really don't have very good ways of representing that sort of intuitive model of the world, with all its contradictions and gaps, in the machine. So, because of that, I think, probably, to some extent you're right: it's probably best to be conservative.

Q. You visualize then that this work will help computer-assisted instruction, do you?

A. Yes, it should do, because at present computer-assisted instruction tends to be very much people controlled by machines; the material is pre-programmed into the machine. The machine has no detailed knowledge about the user who's interacting with it. It doesn't know anything about how much knowledge he's got or how it's organized. And so it can't really adapt the teaching to that person. Building a dynamic model of the user's knowledge is perhaps the key issue that needs to be tackled in this area, and it is being tackled within the programme.

Q. Traditionally, new technologies have gone from the academic world into general use via their military application. Is the Alvey programme a military one?

A. I would like to believe that the Alvey programme is a non-military programme, and its objective is to achieve a technology transfer. We know of examples in the United States where AI techniques are being used by the military — that's inevitable, and probably inevitable in this country. The military research budget is much larger than non-military research budgets. I think that inevitably AI or IKBS is going to be partly driven by military funding and partly by non-military. And if you want to try and control that, then I don't know how you do it.

FURTHER READING

Barstow, D. (1983) A perspective on automatic programming, *AI Magazine*, Vol.5, pp 5–27

Bonnet, A. and Dahan, C. (1983) *Oil-well interpretation using expert system and pattern recognition techniques*. In A. Bundy (Ed.) (1983) Proceedings of Eighth Joint Conference on Artificial Intelligence, Kaufman, Los Altos, California

Levinson, S.E, and Libermann, M.Y. (1981) Speech recognition by computer, *Scientific American*, Vol.244, No.4, pp 56–68

Manuel, T. and Evanczuk, S. (1983) Commercial products begin to emerge from decades of research, *Electronics*, 3 Nov. 1983, pp 127–131

Moto-oka, T. *et al.* (1982) *Keynote speech*. In T. Moto-oka (Ed.) (1982) Fifth Generation Computer Systems, North Holland, Amsterdam

Rich, E. (1983) *Artificial Intelligence*, McGraw-Hill, Tokyo

SERC/DoI (1983) *Intelligent knowledge based systems: a programme for action in the UK*, Institution of Electrical Engineers, Hitchin, Herts.

2

ARTIFICIAL INTELLIGENCE LANGUAGES

AARON SLOMAN

UNIVERSITY OF SUSSEX

I hope to give you a brief taste of these languages, and perhaps give you an answer to the question, 'Why should we use artificial intelligence languages such as LISP, POP-11 and PROLOG, rather than more conventional languages like PASCAL, ADA, BASIC or COBOL?' For anyone who wants to pursue the matter further, there happens to be a very good book, edited by Tim O'Shea and Mark Eisenstadt of the Open University, called *Artificial Intelligence; Tools, Techniques and Applications* and published by Harper and Row, 1984. It's the only book I know that has a reasonable introduction to all three languages — in fact, has *any* introduction to all three languages.

Now, why should we use artificial intelligence languages? As you'll see, part of my answer will be that as well as having features as languages, they are also embedded in environments, and these language features and their environments together help the programmer to cope with complexity. Many of the tasks that we're concerned with are very difficult, and therefore we need as much help as possible from the computer. AI languages take advantage of the fact that, as manpower costs are going up, hardware costs are falling, for the languages certainly need powerful computing systems, for reasons that will become apparent.

With the languages and the environments taken together, one can use the technique of rapid prototyping (sometimes called 'structured program development') to explore a problem domain. The reason why this is needed is that many of the tasks that we're concerned with are not well defined at the start. If I were to ask you to write a program to encode some algorithm that mathematicians or physicists have already worked out, you would know in advance what the task would be. If, however, the task were to define a natural language system then it would be very ill-specified in all sorts of ways: we don't know many of the rules of our language and we don't necessarily know what kind of interaction is required. In this sort of case, we need to be able to produce experimental systems, to test our ideas.

The conventional idea is that program development (illustrated in Figure 2.1) goes in something like these stages: you formulate the requirements for the system; you then design your program; you write the program, perhaps in various modules; you compile the modules; you link the modules; and then you eventually run your program. If you're lucky the program works, and you can sell it or use it. Later you have the problems of maintaining and developing the program, of solving problems that arise in use, and so on.

FIGURE 2.1   Conventional program development

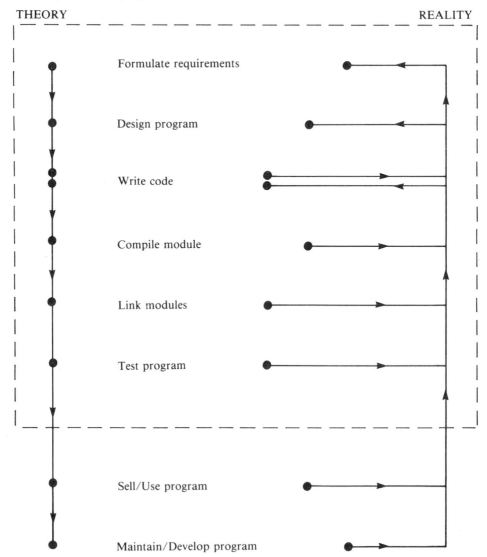

THEORY   REALITY

Formulate requirements

Design program

Write code

Compile module

Link modules

Test program

Sell/Use program

Maintain/Develop program

   With complex problems, this is not a straightforward process. Errors, difficulties and new ideas emerge at every stage, so that you have to go back to an earlier stage, change your requirements, change your design, or change some of the programs. If these different stages are done using different technologies, like pencil and paper for the requirements and the design, an editor perhaps for writing code, and then switching between various different programs for compilation, linking and running, then this process can be very slow and time-consuming.
   Artificial intelligence languages, and environments in which they are embedded, enable you to work in a different mode. There is one process in which the editor, compiler, the user's

programs and a whole range of utilities are all integrated. In this one process you can create programs, you can modify them, you can test them, you can document them and you can extend them. We'll see some of the advantages of this later, but one of the main advantages which should be obvious is that you can get considerably faster program development if you're not having to switch systems whenever a mistake is detected.

AN OVERVIEW OF LISP, POP-11 AND PROLOG

The three main languages that I'm going to discuss are LISP, POP-11 and PROLOG. These are often used as low-level implementation languages for the design of more specialized higher level languages, because one of the things that emerges from working in artificial intelligence is that there isn't a universal formalism (although that's a matter for some debate) but often people find that for particular problems you need particular languages. LISP, POP-11 and PROLOG can provide the basis for extending themselves, and that's an important point. You don't use one of these languages to produce a new language which is totally different. The extended language can be embedded in the original language, so that one can mix programs as required.

LISP comes in many dialects, of which one of the best-known is INTERLISP, which itself includes the whole programming environment. There are many others, including some very small LISP systems which will run on microcomputers but do not have most of the environmental features that I'll be discussing.

POP-11 is the latest version of a series of languages developed in Britain. POP-2, and before that POP-1.5, came from Edinburgh University, as did WONDER POP and POP-10, which was developed to run on a DEC-10 by Julian Davies, who has now moved to Canada. POP-11 was developed by Steve Hardy at Sussex University, orginally on a PDP-11, hence the name. It was then moved onto larger machines and became part of the POPLOG system, which I'll mention later.

LISP and POP-11 have a lot in common, but first I'll demonstrate some of the differences. I shall give most of my examples in POP-11, partly because that is the language I use most and partly because it is often found to be easier to read.

In artificial intelligence languages, list structures play a major role, for they have a great deal of flexibility and power. Unfortunately, lists are represented by different notations in the three languages (Figure 2.2). In LISP you use round brackets and put a quote mark in front to say, 'Don't treat A as a procedure to be applied to arguments B, C and D — treat (A B C D) as a

FIGURE 2.2   Examples of differences of notation in LISP, POP-11 and PROLOG

```
LISP:
    (a  b  c  d)

POP-11
    [a  b  c  d]

PROLOG
    [a,b,c,d]
```

list'. In POP-11 you use square brackets to say, 'That's a list of things'. PROLOG also uses square brackets, but the entries are separated by commas, alas. We will see some other differences in later examples.

We can use list structures to represent the features of a language (as shown in Figure 2.3), in this case a very simple subset of English, which is divided into a grammar and a lexicon. The grammar has a collection of rules which are expressed as lists of lists — in fact, lists of lists of lists, if you look carefully at how the brackets are nested. So, for instance, the first rule says that a sentence (S) can be made of a noun phrase (NP) followed by a verb phrase (VP). The second rule says that a noun phrase has three different forms: determiner followed by a noun, determiner followed by adjective followed by noun, and noun phrase followed by prepositional phrase. The third rule says what a prepositional phrase is, and so on. The details do not matter, only the general idea; you have a list of rules which represents a grammar. Then we can have a list of lexical entries saying what the words are that correspond to different grammatical categories. So the first list, N for noun, says you can have 'firm', 'order', 'client', 'price', 'product'; and obviously in a real example there would be a much longer list of nouns. Similarly, for verbs, prepositions, determiners and adjectives.

FIGURE 2.3   List structure of a language

```
[
 [s [np vp]]
 [np [det n] [det adj n] [np pp]]
 [pp [prep np]]
 [vp [verb np] [verb np prep np]]
] -> gram;


[
 [n      firm order client price product]
 [verb   sold paid bought used]
 [prep   in into on for at to]
 [det    the a every each one some]
 [adj    high low cheap efficient rich]
] -> lex;
```

There are various things one can do with such a representation of the structure of a language. One can use it to generate sentences, or one can use it to analyze sentences. Within the POP-11 library system there is an interactive program that will enable you to generate example sentences, more or less at random, which are consistent with your grammar and lexicon. That's sometimes a good way to check out your grammar, because when you get sentences generated at random you may well find surprising consequences of your grammar, and you may want to go back and change it. With the kind of environment that I'm talking about you can do that very quickly. You just switch into editor mode, change one of the lists, recompile a portion of what's on the screen by marking it, switch back immediately to program running mode, and test your program — giving commands in the same language.

If I give a command (Figure 2.4) which says, 'Repeat 5 times, generate', that is, apply the procedure 'generate' to the grammar and the lexicon and print out the result, then we get a number of sentences which don't necessarily mean very much but just show what the grammar can cope with. This turns out to be an extraordinarily powerful learning device. People who think they've understood something about a language can, by generating the consequences of their theories, discover the need for much finer distinctions of syntactic categories.

We now move on to an example of the use of the grammar to analyze sentences (Figure 2.5). The three hyphens introduce an example that I typed in — 'The firm sold a cheap product'. The

FIGURE 2.4   Using the grammar to generate sentences

```
repeat 5 times
    generate(gram,lex) ==›
endrepeat

**  [one efficient firm paid some low order]

**  [some rich firm in every efficient
         price bought the firm]

**  [some cheap product sold some price]

**  [the cheap firm for some
         order used the rich client]
```

FIGURE 2.5   Using the grammar to analyze sentences

```
--- the firm sold a cheap product

[s [np [snp [det the] [n firm]]]
   [vp [verb sold]
       [np [snp [det a]
           [adj cheap]
           [n product]]]]]



--- the firm sold a cheap product to a rich client

[s[np[snp [det the] [n firm]]]
   [vp[verb sold]
       [np [snp [det a]
               [adj cheap]
               [n product]]]
       [prep to]
       [np [snp [det a]
               [adj rich]
               [n client]]]]]
```

system analyzes that in relationship to the grammar and the lexicon, and says that it is a sentence which is made of two components, a noun phrase and a verb phrase, and then says how those are broken up, by using lists and sub-lists. The more complex example, 'The firm sold a cheap product to a rich client', also has a noun phrase followed by a verb phrase, but the verb phrase has a somewhat more complex structure ending in a prepositional phrase.

These structures, these lists of lists of lists of symbols saying what the components of the sentence are, can play an important role as an intermediate stage in the process of understanding some input typed in using a natural language.

Next (Figure 2.6) we have an example of the use of list structures to illustrate how these languages are good for symbolic computations. This shows how you would define in LISP, or one dialect of LISP, a procedure called 'join', which, when given two lists, will create a new list which contains all the elements of the two lists; e.g., by joining list (A B) to a list (C D E) you get a new list (A B C D E). In LISP we say we're defining a procedure called 'join' which takes two arguments, l1 and l2. The 'cond' introduces a conditional instruction. The first condition is that if the first list, l1, is null (i.e. there's nothing in it), then when you join the two together, you just get the second list. So if l1 is null then the result of join is l2. The 't' stands for

FIGURE 2.6   Defining a procedure in LISP

```
LISP

(define (join l1 l2)
   (cond ((null l1) l2)
      (t (cons (car l1)
         (join (cdr l1) l2)))))
```

'otherwise' in LISP; so, otherwise (if l1 is not null) construct two things. Now what are the two things? Well, first you join (using the same procedure recursively) the tail of l1 ('cdr' is the LISP jargon for the tail of the list), i.e. everything except the first element, to l2. That recursion will terminate because the lists are getting smaller, and it will eventually come to a null case. When you've joined them up, put the front of l1 (car l1) onto the front using a procedure 'cons', which constructs a new list. There is no need to worry about the details — the point is that you can do that kind of thing, you can talk about how to build lists out of other lists. LISP procedure definitions have lots of round brackets at the end to match things up. Some of the other languages have a richer syntax by comparison.

In LISP, if you want to test your procedure and join the list (a b c) to the list (d e f), you type

(join '(a b c) '(d e f))

and LISP will print out

(a b c d e f)

as the result.

LISP and POP-11 are very similar in function but different in appearance. To define the same procedure in POP (Figure 2.7), the name 'join' comes outside the brackets instead of inside as in LISP. If L1 is null then the result is L2, otherwise ('else' in POP) we join the tail of L1 (i.e. all except the first element of L1) to L2 and then put the head of L1 on the front of that, which is what the : : means. The 'endif' is just a closing bracket for 'if', and the 'enddefine' a closing bracket for 'define'. People who are familiar with conventional languages find POP

FIGURE 2.7   Defining a procedure in POP-11

```
POP-11

define join(L1, L2);
   if    null(L1)
   then L2
   else
         hd(L1)::join(tl(L1), L2)
   endif
enddefine;
```

somewhat more readable, although it is, of course, much less elegant than LISP. To test that procedure in POP, you write

join ([a b c],[d e f])

where the arguments have square brackets to distinguish them. I think that aids readability, instead of using round brackets for everything, but that's a detail. The POP system prints out the list

[a b c d e f]

in response.

POP-11 is often preferred by non-AI programmers and it's most widely used in the United Kingdom, although it is beginning to spread, for instance in Canada and even the USA. LISP, however, is much more widely used and it has some features which make it easier for programs themselves to manipulate programs in LISP. Its syntactic simplicity and mathematical elegance mean that it is amenable to more automatic analysis by programs. But that can be taken just as a challenge to the people designing program-analyzing programs: make them more intelligent and able to cope with things *people* find readable.

PROLOG is a very different language. Much of what you can do in LISP and POP you can do in PROLOG, although sometimes it is a bit clumsy. But there are some things you can do in PROLOG which are much harder to do in LISP and POP, and I will illustrate that with this very same procedure (Figure 2.8). In PROLOG, a procedure doesn't produce a result; instead it specifies a relationship between (in this case) the two inputs and the output. So, we can tell PROLOG that if you want to join the empty list ([]) to a list L2, then the resulting list is L2, the same as the second list. (Capital letters are used to indicate variables in PROLOG, at least in DEC-10 PROLOG.) That's part of the definition — the other part tells PROLOG how to join a list that isn't empty onto something else. If it isn't empty then it has a first element (X) joined onto something else (L1), which we previously called the tail of the list or the 'cdr' in LISP. The result of joining a non-empty list to L2 will be a new list whose first element is X and the rest of it, L3, is what you get by joining L1 and L2 together.

FIGURE 2.8   Defining a procedure in PROLOG

WATERFORD REGIONAL
TECHNICAL COLLEGE
LIBRARY

CLASS : 006. 33
ACC. No. 02806 - 8

```
PROLOG

join([ ], L2, L2).

join([X|L1], L2, [X|L3])
    :-
        join(L1,L2,L3).
```

Although you can treat that as a definition of a set of instructions to do something — in other words, it has a procedural interpretation — it also has a logical interpretation as a collection of assertions; namely that the empty list joined to something is that thing, and a non-empty list [X|L1] joined to L2 is [X|L3] provided it is true that L1 and L2 joined together is L3. In fact, PROLOG is inspired in part by predicate logic. The definition of join is an example of rules with variables in them and conditions under which things apply. You can also assert particular facts: for instance, if there were a particular pair of lists you often wanted to join, you could actually store the information that this list joined onto that one gives you a third, which is quite useful in some cases.

Now, in PROLOG, if you want to test that procedure you can ask a question by typing

join ([a,b,c], [d,e,f], New).

which says, 'What do you get if you join the list [a,b,c] and [d,e,f] to produce something called New (capital N for a variable)?' PROLOG would treat that as a question and it would print out

New = [a,b,c,d,e,f].

However, PROLOG also has the following interpretation of the procedure for 'join'. Besides constructing a new list given two input lists, as you can with LISP and POP, that very same definition of join can also be used for checking a relationship between some lists, and also for decomposing a list into smaller parts. Here's how you use it to check relationships. You can type in the question

join ([a,b],[b,c],[a,b,c]).

i.e. 'Is it true that if you join [a,b] and [b,c] together you get the list [a,b,c]?'. PROLOG will respond

no.

Or you could type

join ([a,b],[c],[a,b,c]).

and, in this case, PROLOG will produce the response

yes.

So far, we've seen how to use the PROLOG version of join for constructing lists and checking constructions. You can also use the very same definition to decompose a list, and I will give you two cases, a simple case and a more complicated one. In the simple case, we ask

join (L,[c,d],[a,b,c,d]).

i.e. 'How would we have to decompose the given list [a,b,c,d] into two parts, one of which (L) we don't know, the second of which is [c,d]?'. PROLOG responds that

L = [a,b].

In other words, you can give PROLOG either the first part or the second part of the list and, using join, it will find out what the remainder is.

If, however, you give it two unknowns and say

join (L1,L2,[a,b,c]).

i.e. 'How can you decompose the list [a,b,c] into L1 and L2?', then PROLOG will work out all the possible solutions, and in fact it will allow you to step through them one at a time. It will tell you that the first possibility is that L1 is [], the empty list, and L2 is [a,b,c]. The second possibility is that L1 is a list of one element, [a], and L2 is the remainder, [b,c]. Further possibilities are that L1 is [a,b] and L2 is [c], and L1 is [a,b,c] and L2 is [].

One of the important things about PROLOG is that it doesn't produce all the results at once, when you run the procedure join or ask it a question about joining. It produces a result which can then be used in some problem, but if that result turns out not to be a satisfactory one you can ask PROLOG to go back to the stage it got to and try again to see if there's another answer. PROLOG will do all the bookkeeping for you. That is why for many problems the programs can be written much more easily in PROLOG than in other languages.

In this kind of situation you can have what is called an Or-Tree. The Or-Tree (see Figure 2.9) is one where you have a question, or a problem, or goal to be achieved, and there may be (as in the Figure) three possible ways of solving it. When you try the first way you may find that one PROLOG rule invokes another, which in turn has three possible ways of doing it, of which the first has two possible ways, one of which gets an answer (Ans1) pretty quickly. If that answer turns out to be no good, it might branch into two other alternatives (Ans2, Ans3), and so on. If you have a program which needs to be able to explore a tree of possible answers, then the PROLOG inference mechanism provides a very powerful tool to enable you to write your programs with little effort. Unfortunately, if the answer you wanted was Ans6, say, you might have wasted a lot of time doing a depth-first search before you got to that. One of the research problems is how to extend the language so as to give people or programs more control over the order in which things are done, because sometimes you might find clues half-way down that suggest you should really switch to another branch, and it's not too easy to do that in PROLOG. That's an example of a research issue on which I expect interesting progress to be made, and there are already some ideas in the literature.

FIGURE 2.9 An OR-Tree

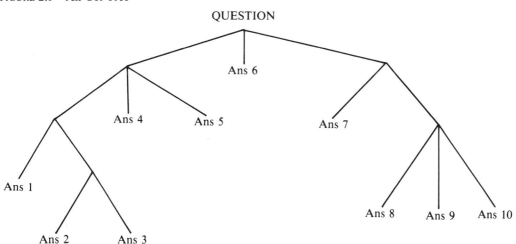

Now, if you listen to experts you will be aware that there are different ideologies. Some people say that we should be moving towards declarative languages, which are contrasted with the conventional procedural languages. In that dichotomy, LISP and POP-11 tend to be more like the conventional languages; that's to say, they're more procedural. This means that in those languages you have to say how to solve a problem, what steps to go through. You can be fairly structured about it, by breaking it down into various modules and so on, but it is still a case of saying 'how', in general. Whereas there is an interpretation of PROLOG in which you are stating relevant facts, and you're saying what your problem is by asking a question, and then the system works out for itself how to solve it. In fact, when you look closely, all these languages are hybrids: LISP and POP-11 can have declarative elements when you build information in list structures, and PROLOG can be interpreted procedurally, and often it is used procedurally. For instance, the order in which you put the rules into the system will affect the order in which things are tried out.

Some of us believe that having great debates about which language you should use is a bit pointless, because what you need are different systems for different purposes, and so one should go for some kind of hybrid. An example of an area where people are exploring the use of hybrid systems is in image understanding programs, where you may start off initially with digitized images, where you have a two-dimensional array of numbers representing image intensities. Then you might have a LISP or POP-11 program which is very procedural in its form, looking through those numbers and producing low-level descriptions of the image structure. Then those descriptions might be analyzed by a PROLOG program which produces high-level descriptions in terms of known structures.

These three languages, despite their differences, have a number of features that make them useful for dealing with complex problems. Some of them have to do with the availability of lists, as I've already mentioned. Others have to do with the languages being interactive in a way that I'll discuss later. One of the features that is fairly unusual is that these languages do not have typed variables. That is to say, when you have a variable it can be used sometimes to refer to a list, sometimes to a number, sometimes to a string, sometimes to a procedure, and so on. This has a number of good results and bad results. In particular, one unfortunate result is that at compile time, when your program is being read in, there is less information for the compiler to use to check that you've been totally consistent. In PASCAL, for example, if you say that x is going to be used for integers and then in another context you assume that it's not an integer, then the PASCAL compiler will tell you that you've made a mistake. In LISP, POP-11 and PROLOG you will only discover that at a later stage, when the program runs and gets into trouble. However, the absence of types means that the compiler isn't doing so much consistency checking and therefore it goes faster, which can help with program development and testing. That is important where your most likely errors are not of that simple type anyway, but are deep logical errors. In this case you need a rapid interaction with running programs rather than expecting the compiler to tell you what your mistakes are.

Because a variable may sometimes be a list, sometimes something else, and so on (for instance, in the definitions of join for LISP, POP-11 and PROLOG I didn't say anywhere that the variables were restricted to lists), tests have to be done at run time, and as a result things can run more slowly. However, in a language like PASCAL you would not be able to write the same procedure to join a list of integers, a list of real numbers, a list of lists, a list of procedures, a list of anything. So in LISP, POP-11 and PROLOG you have a module which is very general and very flexible.

PATTERN-MATCHING

I'm now going to move up to a higher level to illustrate some of the things that can be provided. These languages give you special syntax for constructing data structures using a pattern which shows the structure you want to build, as opposed to having to proceed in a procedural form. So in POP-11, for instance, I could have a list called 'adjs' with [big, young] in it, and another called 'props' with [very, clever] in it, and so on. Then I could say

[the ^adjs man is ^props]

to build a list which contains the word 'the', the contents of the variable 'adjs', then the words 'man is' and the contents of the variable 'props'. POP-11 will merge those lists and produce

[the big young man is very clever].

The point is that the pattern indicates the structure to be built, in something like the form in which you or I might think of it. In a conventional language you'd have to have some sort of loop to build up the whole list and for each of the two things in 'adjs' and 'props' you'd have to have a loop in which you would take elements from the component lists and put them into the list you're constructing.

So pattern-directed list construction can be very useful, as can the converse, pattern-directed structure decomposition. The illustration (Figure 2.10), again using POP-11, shows how you might do some searching for things stored in a simple kind of database made of a list of lists. Here, the lists [a b c d e] and so on to [r s t u] are collected together and assigned to a variable called 'info'. The task might be, 'Find an embedded list containing both l and p and make a list of the items between them'.

FIGURE 2.10   Pattern-directed structure decomposition

```
vars info;

[[a  b  c  d  e]  [f  g  h  i  j]  [k  l  m  n  o  p  q]  [r  s  t  u]]

    -> info;

Find  an  embedded  list  containing  l  and  p  and
make  a  list  of  the  items  between  them.
```

We can see the l and the p in the third list and we would just make a list of the things in between. To do that in a conventional language you would have to have a number of loops: one loop running down the lists; then, within each list, you'd have a loop looking for l; then, if you found it, another loop looking for p, and so on.

To do it in POP-11 we define a procedure called 'find', which takes two items 'x1', 'x2', and a 'list' like the one I've just described, and which produces a result called 'xxx' (see Figure 2.11). In POP-11 the pattern-matching arrow '_ _>' is used to decompose a list in accordance with a pattern indicating the structure that we are looking for. We can see that we're looking for an embedded list: we don't care what comes before it (that's what = = means) and we don't care what comes after it. Within the embedded list we want to find something which has the

FIGURE 2.11   List decomposition in POP-11

```
define find(x1, x2, list) -> xxx;

    list -->

        [ == [ == ^x1 ??xxx ^x2 ==] ==]

    enddefine;
```

value of x1 (we don't care what comes before) followed by something else (which I'll come back to) and then the value of x2 (and we don't care what comes after). The items that come between x1 and x2 we want to assign to the variable 'xxx' (that's what the ?? means). The syntax is slightly nasty, but the important point is the correspondence to the structure which you can visualize. You are much more likely to get your program right first time in this way than if you have to write it with lots of nested loops.

To test the procedure you could say

find ('l', 'p', info)

and POP-11 will produce a list of intervening items:

[m n o].

Once again, because it's a type-free language, the procedure will work on lists of lists of words, lists of lists of numbers, lists of lists of anything. Of course, one can define other procedures in terms of it. One of my colleagues used the pattern-matcher to write a compiler for LISP and he found that it enabled him to get most of his programs right first time. Of course, there is a cost — the pattern-matcher slows things down because it is essentially an interpreted data structure. So having got it all working, he then translated it into a lower level procedural form, also written in POP, to get the speed. But that's typical of what one does in this kind of environment: you first use the highest level tools to work out your algorithm and then you worry about efficiency.

AI ENVIRONMENTS

Ideally, these language features are made available in environments that provide a combination of features which are built on the language features. For instance, an AI environment will have an interactive language, such as LISP, POP, PROLOG, or some other language or derivative of one of those. The environment might actually include more than one language; for instance, POPLOG includes three languages. It would have an integrated editor, which is typically written in one of those languages. The compiler is also part of the run-time system, and therefore you don't have that switching between editing, linking, compiling and so on which I mentioned earlier. There can be a large collection of library packages, which can be linked in at any time because of the incremental nature of the compiler. There may be an on-line help facility, as there is in POPLOG and some of the LISP environments, and various debugging aids, also written in the same language. In fact, the language itself is a debugging aid, because at any time you can interrupt your program and give commands in that language to interrogate structures. You don't have to have a separate and usually very low-level debugging language. Some of these systems have built-in teaching facilities, as the POPLOG system does, with a large collection of teaching files and demonstration programs. When you put all these features together you get a whole which is more than the sum of its parts: you get something which is much more powerful as a program development environment or tool than you might expect.

Yet more advanced systems are based on special purpose hardware. What I've discussed so far is in principle possible in any portable environment, but there are LISP machines of varying prices and speeds, which will enable your AI programs to run much faster. They are single-user systems, with a very high resolution screen with a window manager (so you can have a lot of different things happening on the same screen in different windows), and some sort of pointing device, which you can move round to indicate which window you want to work in or which part of the screen you want to do something to. These machines will often be linked together in some kind of network, perhaps with a large computer providing a file store, printers, and so on.

An example of an AI environment is POPLOG, which has been adopted for the Alvey programme as part of the Intelligent Knowledge-Based Systems infrastructure. It is, unlike some of the others, reasonably portable. Most of it is written in POP, and there is a small portion that has to be rewritten for each new machine. It runs on VAXs under VMS and UNIX. It runs on an M68000 computer made by Bleasdale, a British firm. It runs on a SUN-2 workstation and a Hewlett Packard UNIX workstation.

It includes the three languages I have already mentioned. Like other environments, it's highly tailorable because nearly all of the system is written in the language that the programmer is using, and much of it can be redefined. This doesn't necessarily interfere with portability, because the tailoring programs can be part of a package that you send to another place. It has turned out to be extremely powerful both for beginners — at Sussex University we use it for teaching first year Arts undergraduates — and the most sophisticated research workers. Some of the beginners who are using it now are in industry, where they don't have teachers as readily available, and so they use the teach files that come with it. It's produced by Sussex University and marketed by Systems Designers Ltd.

Other environments, some of which are in some ways more powerful, are based on LISP machines. For instance, probably the two most powerful systems are the Symbolics 3600 and the LMI Lambda. They are, of course, quite expensive single-user systems, and you have to think in terms of about one hundred thousand pounds per system, though prices are falling. Versions of PROLOG embedded in LISP are becoming available. Some of these LISP machines have special microcode or other features that enable them to run faster. However, one thing that puts some people off is that they tend to have their own operating system, usually written in LISP, or a mixture of LISP and a low-level language, whereas the POPLOG environment goes on a variety of operating systems.

There will fairly soon be PROLOG workstations, which will run PROLOG programs very fast. The Japanese are certainly working to produce PROLOG work-stations. The development of PROLOG was done, after some initial ideas from Marseilles in France, in Edinburgh and Imperial College in the United Kingdom, but computer manufacturers in this country missed the opportunity to win the race to produce good PROLOG machines.

To summarize, AI languages tend to be available within integrated environments with the features that I've mentioned. These give very rapid testing of modules because switching between editing, compiling and testing is so fast that you are encouraged to thoroughly test each little bit before you move on. As a consequence, you can discover bad design features, cases that you hadn't thought of, or possibilities that enable you to generalize your design, very rapidly, and so you get rapid feedback to the design stage. You can also, I think, get greater reliability because of the encouragement to do this exhaustive testing. You can, of course, fall into the temptation of just messing around because you get this nice interactive tool. But there is a discipline that one has to learn in these environments, as with any other powerful tool. You'll also get a powerful debugging environment for the reasons I mentioned earlier, and I like to think of this as a case where we are using the computer not as an intelligent system in itself, yet, but as an intelligence amplifier.

Another feature that we didn't plan but which emerged in the POPLOG system is that the editor, because it is itself written in the language that people are using, is essentially a collection of subroutines which the user can use in his programs. The editor therefore provides a general purpose interface. All of these features, and others such as on-line help (where you just press a key to get a help file on a particular word that's bothering you, say), can contribute to greatly reduced development costs. My own guess is that, in principle, this could have, in the short run, a far greater impact on conventional non-AI programs than even on artificial intelligence work, because you can use these environments for any sort of programming. Previously it was too extravagant to do that, because you needed lots of computer power, because the languages were less efficient and because the environments were big. But now computer power is becoming more cheaply available, and so we can use such tools to save on manpower costs.

AN ILLUSTRATIVE INTERACTIVE SESSION

I'd now like to give you a feel for an interactive session in which we use a number of different features of one of these environments, in this case POPLOG. Figure 2.12 shows an artificially produced, two-dimensional array of numbers which represents a simulated image that might have been produced by camera, an image of a scene made of blocks illuminated in such a way that the surfaces have different intensities. If you look closely at the upper right you'll see that there's a block of nines, indicating a high intensity portion, and immediately to the left of it a block of zeros where there is low intensity. You probably can't see much structure in that at the moment but it will emerge.

FIGURE 2.12   An array of numbers representing a simulated image

```
lib greypic;
;;; LOADING LIB greypic
display();

0 0 0 0 0 0 0 0 0 0 0 0 0 0 0 0 0 0 0 0 0 0 0 0 0 0 0 0 0 0 0 0 0 0 0 0
0 0 0 0 0 0 0 0 0 0 9 9 9 9 9 0 0 0 0 0 0 0 0 0 0 0 0 0 0 0 0 0 0 0 0 0
0 0 0 0 0 0 0 0 0 9 9 9 9 9 3 0 0 0 0 0 0 0 0 0 0 0 0 0 0 0 0 0 0 0 0 0
0 0 0 0 0 0 0 0 9 9 9 9 9 3 0 0 0 0 0 0 0 0 9 9 9 9 9 9 9 9 9 0 0 0 0 0
0 0 0 0 0 0 0 0 5 5 5 5 5 3 0 0 0 0 0 0 0 0 9 9 9 9 9 9 9 9 3 0 0 0 0 0
0 0 0 0 0 0 0 9 5 5 5 5 5 3 9 9 9 0 0 0 0 9 9 9 9 9 9 9 9 3 3 0 0 0 0 0
0 0 0 0 0 0 9 9 5 5 5 5 5 3 9 9 9 3 0 0 0 9 9 9 9 9 9 9 9 3 3 3 0 0 0 0 0
0 0 0 0 0 9 9 9 5 5 5 5 5 9 9 9 3 3 0 0 9 9 9 9 9 9 9 9 3 3 3 3 0 0 0 0 0
0 0 0 0 9 9 9 9 9 9 9 9 9 9 3 3 3 0 0 5 5 5 5 5 5 5 5 3 3 3 3 0 0 0 0 0
0 0 0 9 9 9 9 9 9 9 9 9 9 3 3 3 3 0 0 5 5 5 5 5 5 5 5 3 3 3 3 0 0 0 0 0
0 0 9 9 9 9 9 9 9 9 9 9 3 3 3 3 9 9 9 9 9 9 9 9 5 5 5 3 3 3 3 0 0 0 0 0
0 0 5 5 5 5 5 5 5 5 5 3 3 3 3 9 9 9 9 9 9 9 9 3 5 5 5 5 3 3 3 3 0 0 0 0 0
0 0 5 5 5 5 5 5 5 5 5 3 3 3 9 9 9 9 9 9 9 3 3 5 5 5 5 3 3 3 0 0 0 0 0
0 0 5 5 5 5 5 5 5 5 5 3 3 9 9 9 9 9 9 9 3 3 3 5 5 5 5 3 3 0 0 0 0 0
0 0 5 5 5 5 5 5 5 5 5 3 3 5 5 5 5 5 5 5 3 3 3 5 5 5 5 5 3 0 0 0 0 0
0 0 5 5 5 5 5 5 5 5 5 3 3 5 5 5 5 5 5 5 3 3 3 5 5 5 5 5 0 0 0 0 0
0 0 5 5 5 5 5 5 5 5 5 3 3 5 5 5 5 5 5 5 3 3 0 0 0 0 0 0 0 0 0
0 0 5 5 5 5 5 5 5 5 5 3 3 5 5 5 5 5 5 5 3 3 0 0 0 0 0 0 0 0 0
0 0 5 5 5 5 5 5 5 5 5 3 3 5 5 5 5 5 5 5 3 0 0 0 0 0 0 0 0 0 0
0 0 5 5 5 5 5 5 5 5 5 3 0 5 5 5 5 5 5 5 0 0 0 0 0 0 0 0 0 0 0
0 0 5 5 5 5 5 5 5 5 5 0 0 0 0 0 0 0 0 0 0 0 0 0 0 0 0 0 0 0 0
0 0 0 0 0 0 0 0 0 0 0 0 0 0 0 0 0 0 0 0 0 0 0 0 0 0 0 0 0 0 0 0
```

I can interactively type in commands to create or display such images and the output will come into the editor file, with the result that it's not lost if I want to go back and look at it. I can then give an interactive command to run a library program, such as 'findedges' (see Figure 2.13), which will run and tell me that it's processing the picture looking for vertical edges; that's to say, it's looking for where there's a high contrast step as you go in a horizontal direction across the image. It tells me what mask it's using, and then it prints out its result. At any time I can interrupt and change something, make it use a different mask, redefine one of the procedures, and see what difference it makes. I get (Figure 2.14) a new array of numbers, and where there was previously a contrast step between the region of nines to the region of zeros, we now have just a thin row of nines in the top right-hand corner.

Another module will then run through that, looking for places where there is a low number, a

FIGURE 2.13   Running the library program 'findedges'

```
findedges();

** processing picture
        looking for vertical edges

Using mask
** [[1  -1]]
```

FIGURE 2.14   Result of running 'findedges'

```
RESULT OF CONVOLUTION:
000000000000000000000000000000000000000
000000000900009000000000000000000000000
000000009000063000000000000000000000000
000000090000060300000000900000000900
000000050000020300000009000000006300
000009400002060090009000000060300
000090400002600630090000000600300
000090040000400603090000000600003 00
000900000000060030500000000200300 0
009000000000060003050000000200003 00
090000000000600006000000400020003 00
050000000000020006000000620002000300
050000000000020060000006020002003000
050000000000206000000600200020300 00
050000000000020200000020020002300000
050000000000020200000020020005000000
050000000000020200000020030000000000
050000000000020200000020300000000000
050000000000020200000023000000000000
050000000000235000000500000000000000
050000000000500000000000000000000000
000000000000000000000000000000000000000
```

high number and a low number, to find where the edge points are. It gives a report on what it's doing (Figure 2.15); it's finding peaks using in this case a different mask, and thresholding, and so on. When it's done that it gives me a graphical display (Figure 2.16) of the places where it found a contrast step going horizontally across. These are essentially an approximation to vertical edges, but of course it will find diagonal ones as well — I have chosen a very simple algorithm just to illustrate the sorts of thing one can do.

   You can do the same looking for horizontal edges, and it finds some of those and again finds the diagonal ones (see Figure 2.17). You can then ask it to superimpose them and print the result (Figure 2.18). As you see, it has found some of the diagonal edges twice (in fact, nearly all of them), and a more intelligent program would use information about where those edges came from to merge them.

   Now I can have that picture analyzed. First of all, a command is typed to clear the database (Figure 2.19). Then I can run the library procedure 'findlines', which will automatically be compiled and started running. When it's finished, which may take a few seconds or a few

FIGURE 2.15   Finding the peaks

```
FINDING  PEAKS  IN  PICTURE:
   . . . . . . . . .
Using mask:** [[1 0 1]]
   . . . . . . . . .
THRESHOLDING picture with value: 2
   . . . . . . . . .
THRESHOLDING done
```

FIGURE 2.16   Graphical display: 1

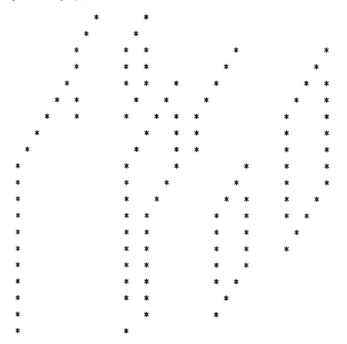

minutes depending on the size of picture and other things, I can ask it to print out the current state of the database. I've actually left out parts of it (in Figure 2.19), but you can see that there's a collection of descriptions of lines giving an indication of their slope (whether sloping up to the right or to the left or vertical or horizontal), and for each line its start location and end location. So we are beginning to mix up numerical and non-numerical descriptions here.

I can then call another procedure (called 'findjuncs') which knows rules for discovering different kinds of junctions between lines (Figure 2.20). When it's finished, I can say, 'For each item in the database which starts with junc (for junction) print it out and print a new line.' Then you see printed out for each junction: what type it is (it may be an end, an L junction where two ends meet, an arrow junction, a T junction, and so on), the coordinates of the junction, and which other junctions it's connected to.

This is a richer description, which it is quite hard to take in. So I can ask the computer to give me a graphical description (see Figure 2.21). The procedure 'paintpicture' creates a two-dimensional array in which it puts special character codes to indicate slopes of lines, and letters to say what junctions it has found. It tells me where it thinks it's found horizontal, vertical and diagonal lines, and shows a 't' for T junctions and 'e' for ends, and so on. It hasn't really seen all the structure that you or I would see but that would require further analysis. A logic programming style might be useful, at least for exploring alternatives.

FIGURE 2.17   Graphical display: 2

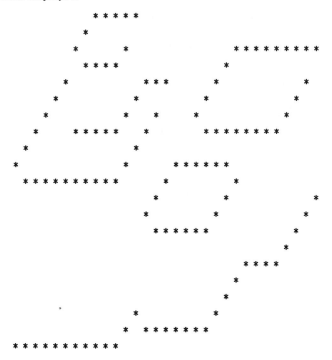

FIGURE 2.18   Graphical display: 3

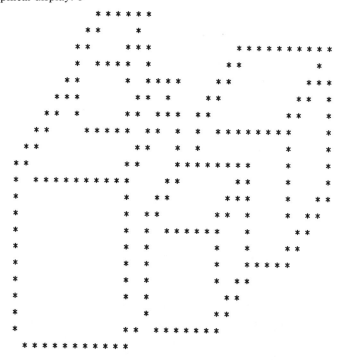

I've tried to give you a feel for the kind of mixture of computing that you can do, and the kind of way you can interact with your program. The commands I type in would go into an editor file and would be available for me to use later. On one of the more advanced

FIGURE 2.19   Finding the lines

```
          [] -> database;
          findlines();

          database ==>
          ** [[line rht [29 6] [33 10]]
             [line rht [28 6] [33 11]]
                  . . . . . . . . . . .
             [line lft [18 15] [17 16]]
             [line lft [17 16] [16 17]]
                  . . . . . . . . . . .
             [line vrt [33 10] [33 11]]
             [line vrt [33 11] [33 17]]
                  . . . . . . . . . . .
             [line hrz [10 21] [11 21]]
             [line hrz [11 21] [15 21]]
```

FIGURE 2.20   Finding the junctions

```
     findjuncs();

     foreach [junc == ] do
         pr(it); pr(newline);
     endforeach;

     [junc end [13 1] [3 1]]
     [junc end [13 18] [12 18]]
          . . . . . . . . . . .
     [junc ell [15 21] [11 21] [12 18]]
     [junc ell [18 17] [16 17] [17 16]]
          . . . . . . . . . . .
     [junc arw [25 12] [20 12] [22 9] [25 11]]
     [junc tee [26 6] [25 6] [25 5] [28 6]]
          . . . . . . . . . . .
     [junc crs [8 18] [11 21] [8 19] [2 12] [8 17]]
          . . . . . . . . . . .
```

environments, I could have graphical output coming on to one window on a screen and printed output on another, and so on.

CONCLUSION

We might ask, after all that: why aren't artificial intelligence languages perfect? Well, there are some problems; for the moment they do need rather powerful, expensive machines. But prices are falling and the one thing we needn't worry about is whether there will be enough computer power or memory, at least in the next few years, although, at the moment, it is not a very cheap process to get into this field.

Also, they don't yet have enough compile-time checking, as I've already mentioned, and not enough compile-time optimization, although that's something people are working on. Sometimes the systems could help you more than they do. One of the problems with AI

FIGURE 2.21   A graphical description

```
          [] -> database;   findlines();
          findjuncs();   paintpicture();

          display();
                    e---l
                 *     *!
                lt--l  !                1-------a
                  c    !  t            /        / !
                 /!    !  lc-a        /        /  !
                / !    !* c!         /        /   !
               /  1---l  / t    a-------f    !
              /        / !  !            !    !
             /        /  !  !            !    !
          a--------f      tt-t---a    !    !
          !        !       t     /!    !    1
          !        !      /     / !    !   /
          !        !    a-----f  !    ! /
          !        !    !       !  !    !/
          !        !    !       !  tt--a
          !        !    !       !  t
          !        !   t       ! /
          !        ! /!        !/
          !        !/ 1-----a
          1--------a
```

languages can be linking to existing software. In POPLOG we can link to almost anything in VMS or UNIX that is based on VMS or UNIX conventions, written in whatever language. Some of the LISP systems also enable you to link things in other languages. For instance, with one version of LISP (FRANZLISP on UNIX), it's possible to link in other UNIX programs, written in C or whatever.

When you have lots of people working on a complex task, problems of configuration management and controlling the program development can be quite difficult. People have begun to develop tools (although it's not yet entirely clear what sorts of tool are good tools), and I think that when they're done using artificial intelligence tools, you'll get something better and more powerful than you could get with more primitive languages like PASCAL.

In general, AI systems need better support and documentation because there's not yet as much resource behind them as for the conventional languages. But that is increasing, as shown, for instance, by the Alvey directorate's decision to fund the POPLOG development in collaboration with System Designers Ltd. and Sussex University. Some of the American systems are getting quite a lot of money behind them, and therefore there will be better support and documentation in time. So I think some of these are temporary problems.

My conclusion then is that despite their imperfections, which I acknowledge exist, artificial intelligence languages, especially in an AI environment, are the best thing available right now for developing complex intelligent systems, although often you will have higher level tools built on top of them, which help you with specific tasks like building a particular sort of expert system, or a vision system, or a speech understanding system. But I think that they can also be useful, and this is not generally appreciated, for reducing the development costs of non-artificial intelligence programs. Even if in the end you have to rewrite your LISP or POP-11 program in PASCAL to run it on your micro, the time saved in developing the program, when the problem doesn't start off as a simple and clear one, may be far greater than the cost of switching ultimately to another language. But, of course, in the end we need to have that last step automated, and then you won't need to think in terms of primitive languages any more.

QUESTIONS

Q.   Do you feel that AI languages and environments have a relevance to the majority of young people learning computer programming, who are at the moment stuck with a language like BASIC?

A.   I think the people who are teaching BASIC are teaching what you needed to know in the past and what you might need to know for the next year or two. We would prefer to teach them to use AI environments and languages, and that means more powerful computing facilities than schools can afford at the moment, because that way they'll learn what computing can be. We are talking about people who maybe are going to be programmers or users of computing systems in five, ten or fifteen years' time. We shouldn't be teaching them about the past.

Q.   I have some expert knowledge which I wish to formalize. My shopping list includes LISP and PROLOG and suchlike but a colleague has already made a choice, and chosen FORTRAN. Now I see some aspect of fashion in these languages: two years ago it was LISP, last year PROLOG, next year POPLOG, and of course the Japanese are working on PROLOG but it's a different sort of PROLOG. Could you give me your opinion as to whether these languages could form a tool that I can use, because I am not an AI programmer.

A.   That's a question that has many embedded questions. Yes, to some extent these things are a matter of fashion. The reason we decided in POPLOG to have the three different languages is not because we think it really is necessary to have all three, but because we thought that it's not going to be possible to convert everybody to use one language and because there's a lot of software development that's gone on in one language which one doesn't want to have to translate into another. So we provided a system whereby you can link things in. Also, some languages, as I was trying to indicate, have features which make them more suitable for certain purposes. PROLOG is suitable for certain kinds of things and I think it can be clumsy for others, whereas POP or LISP, which are regarded as more or less on a par, are useful for others. One reason why I would encourage someone in industry to look at POP rather than LISP, apart from personal prejudice, is that our experience has shown that when we have visitors from industry who come to talk to us about LISP and we show them what you can do in LISP in our system, and we then show them POP, which they haven't heard of before, they have an instant reaction which says, 'Oh, I can understand that a lot more easily.' I think that even though that may be because they haven't had the right kind of education in the mystique of LISP, which would have prepared them for this and therefore it is not an essential difference, just that historical fact may mean that for many people POP is the best choice, rather than LISP. Even though far more people at the moment are using LISP, there are actually people in the States and other countries who are beginning to use the POPLOG system using POP rather than LISP for some of their work. I think, depending on your problem, you might well benefit from one of these languages. There are some problems where there's a whole bunch of library routines available in FORTRAN, and you would have to do a lot of work to start from scratch in a LISP or POP or PROLOG environment to make them available. There are other problems where you'd be starting with a much more powerful set of tools that are suited to your problem if you switch to an AI language. But you haven't told me what your problem is and I am therefore going to hedge on that one.

Q. I noticed you said computers could be used as an intelligence amplifier. I would like a little more on that if possible.

A. Well, 'intelligence' I define, and this is not yet a widely accepted definition, as productive laziness. There are many ways in which we can be lazy; that is to say, we can save ourselves time and effort. One of them is by making lots of results of previous work available; another way is asking someone else to do the work. In general, I think that if you've got something like an AI environment you can share some of the load between your brain and the computer — the bookkeeping, the remembering of things. For instance, in a POPLOG system there are over 800 help files on POP-11 alone, with more on PROLOG, etc. And even though I was one of the people who helped to develop the POPLOG system, there are things I just cannot remember. So I treat the help file system as an extension of my memory and the same is true of other users. You do get into other problems, of course, for you have to be able to find your way around such a complex system, and for that we need yet more intelligent front ends to make the intelligence amplifier a more effective amplifier. But I think the evidence is pointing in the direction of these systems enabling people to solve, much more rapidly than before, much more difficult problems.

FURTHER READING

Barrett, R., Ramsay, A. and Sloman, A. (1985) *POP-11: A Practical Language for AI*, Ellis Horwood and Wiley, Chichester
Clocksin, W.F. and Mellish, C.S. (1981) *Programming in Prolog*, Springer, Berlin
Kowalski, R. (1979) *Logic for Problem Solving*, North Holland, Amsterdam
O'Shea, T. and Eisenstadt, M. (Eds.) (1984) *Artificial Intelligence: Tools, Techniques and Applications*, Harper & Row, New York
Wilensky, R. (1984) *LISPcraft*, W.W. Norton, New York
Winston, P.H. and Horn, B.K.P. (1981) *LISP*, Addison-Wesley, Reading, Mass.

3
AN EXPERT SYSTEM FOR MEDICAL DIAGNOSIS
ALAN BUNDY

UNIVERSITY OF EDINBURGH

Expert systems have received a lot of attention in the press recently. You may have read accounts of the sorts of thing they can do: diagnose illnesses, assess the mineral prospects of a geological site, configure a computer system. What I want to do is to explain a little bit about how such systems work inside — to look behind the scenes — and also to tell you what it's like to run such a program.

The example that I've chosen to use throughout is from medical diagnosis. It is a program called MYCIN and the job of this program is to diagnose a blood infection and to recommend treatment. Treatment is usually some kind of antibiotic, of which there are a large variety. The name MYCIN comes from a common ending of many antibiotics, like Streptomycin.

There is a problem whenever anyone explains an expert system, because these systems are meant to work in fairly narrow, esoteric areas of knowledge where there are only a small number of experts in the world who possess that knowledge. It is inevitable that I have to mention some of those pieces of knowledge in explaining the system to you. But *don't panic*: it's not necessary to understand the technical details of this knowledge; for instance, I don't understand it. All you have to do is to use the examples just to get a picture of how these systems are working.

WHAT MYCIN DOES

What MYCIN does is carry out a consultation with a user (who might be a general practitioner or a hospital doctor) who does not possess a detailed technical knowledge of this area. MYCIN has to decide whether the patient has a significant infection. If so, MYCIN has to determine the likely identity of the offending organism, what kind of drugs are useful for treating this organism, and, given that the particular patient may not be able to take some of these drugs, or they may not be appropriate given the state of his illness, which particular course of drugs to recommend for this illness.

As well as being a good example to illustrate how expert systems work, this is quite a well motivated area to work on, because it's well known that a lot of antibiotics are prescribed in general practice and in hospitals, often by people who don't have detailed knowledge of exactly what drugs should be prescribed for different illnesses and so on, and it is not always done very well. What such a program as this can do is to give your general practitioner access to the kind of expertise that is possessed by only a few rare consultants in this area, and to make that information cheaply available to the person on the 'coal-face', as it were.

DESIGN CRITERIA

So, when we come to design a program like MYCIN, what are the design criteria? What sorts of thing must we take into account? The advice that the system gives us must be accurate, the system must be pleasant to use, and it must explain its advice. Let me say why these criteria are important. First of all, nobody is going to use a system unless its advice is reasonably accurate. We want to get the same sort of order of magnitude of accuracy as you would get from a consultant. Also the system has got to be able to keep up with the latest information, for it's no good if in ten years' time it's completely out of date. We must be able to input new information as it becomes available. This argues for a modular organization of the program so that we can put in a new piece of knowledge without really disrupting or having to change all the old bits of knowledge.

Secondly, the system has got to be pleasant to use. It's no good if the system requires precise typing with no spelling mistakes, for instance, or if the system requires some complex computer language to use it. It's not going to be usable by a general practitioner unless it is pleasant and easy for them to use.

Thirdly, the system has got to be able to explain its advice, because it is not possible for a computer program to take legal responsibility for its advice. The ultimate responsibility for the decision which is made on a particular patient belongs to the GP or the hospital doctor — whoever is actually using the system. So, if they're going to take this legal responsibility, they have to understand how the system came to the decision it did, so that they can appreciate it and regard it as their decision and take responsibility for it. More than that, even if they did not have the legal responsibility, most people in that position would want to have the advice explained to them (so that they could understand the reasons for it) and not just use some sort of black box. That argues for an organization of the program in which the way the knowledge is stored in the program is intelligible to the user. They must both somehow share the same sort of language. I don't mean they must both speak English; I mean that the sorts of steps the program makes must be something like the kinds of steps that the physician or the consultant himself would make.

MYCIN OVERVIEW

An overview of the organization of MYCIN (Figure 3.1) goes some way to show how MYCIN meets these design criteria. We have three computer programs (boxes 2, 5 and 6). Box 2 is the *consultation system*, which actually conducts the consultation and gives the advice. Box 5 is an *explanation system*, which explains that advice to the user, a doctor for example. Box 6 is a *rule acquisition system*, which is able to accept new information. There are also three kinds of data that the program requires. Obviously the consultation system has to have available data about a particular patient, and that is entered by the user, the doctor. And then the consultation system uses decision rules actually to make the decision during the consultation.

Then we come to the explanation system. The explanation system is going to explain what went on in the consultation, so it has to have access to a record of the current consultation, the questions that were asked, the decisions that were made, and so on. It has also to have access to the decision rules which were actually used during the consultation.

FIGURE 3.1   MYCIN overview

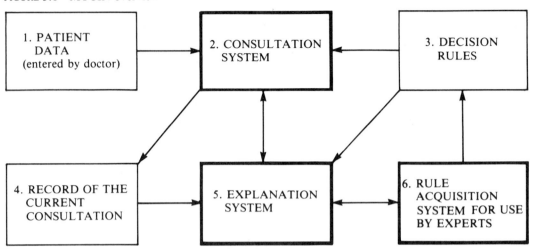

Lastly, the rule acquisition system has to be able to take from the expert, in this case it would be a consultant, new rules which have recently been discovered about the diagnosis of blood diseases, and incorporate them in the corpus of decision rules. The idea is to have a set of rules which represents the knowledge about diagnosing, so that one can easily add new rules, or change existing ones, and so get different behaviour from the consultation system.

USING MYCIN

Let me explain what it's like actually to use a system like this. Figure 3.2 gives the beginning of a sample dialogue with the MYCIN system. Now any system of this kind requires you to start by inputting some fairly mundane information in order to identify the particular patient and the general characteristics of that patient. This example is a made-up one — Jeremiah Sample is not a real patient's name! In this Figure the things typed by the user of the system are given with a double asterisk in front of them and in capital letters, and everything else is typed by the computer system. You can see in fact that the user has to type very little, usually just one-word or one-number answers to the various questions that he is asked. He is asked first for the name of the patient, then the sex, then the age. Then the consultation goes on to get to grips much

FIGURE 3.2   Sample dialogue with the MYCIN system

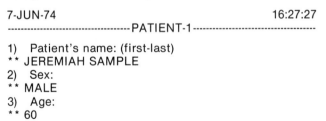

more with the actual data about the particular illness which the patient is suffering from. The main clinical evidence that comes in this area is from cultures, which are developed in a laboratory. The cultures are made by taking samples from various parts of the patient's body. In each culture there may be a number of organisms. Obviously, the program has to keep a record of these during the consultation.

So, looking at Figure 3.3, the program first asks for the first culture, which it's going to call Culture-1, logically enough. It asks 'Where was this culture taken from?', and you notice here that the user (remember the user types in things preceded by **) answers 'Blodd'. Now this is unlikely to be the site of the culture — of course, it's a spelling mistake. But the program is quite robust about that sort of thing, and types back at the user 'Blood'. In other words, it has recognized the spelling mistake, and has decided to interpret what the user typed as the word Blood. At this stage the user could say, 'No, it wasn't that I meant, it was Body', or something.

FIGURE 3.3 MYCIN dialogue continued

I will refer to the most recent positive culture for which you desire therapeutic advice as ---CULTURE-1---

4)   From what site was the specimen for CULTURE-1 taken?
** BLODD
     BLOOD
5)   How many days ago was this blood culture (CULTURE-1) obtained?
** 2

I will refer to the first offending organism from this blood culture (CULTURE-1) as:
---ORGANISM-1---
6)   Enter the identity (genus) of ORGANISM-1:
** UNKNOWN
7)   Staining characteristics of ORGANISM-1 (gram):
** ?
         WHAT IS THE STAIN OF ORGANISM-1?
         Expected responses are:
         ACIDFAST GRAMPOS GRAMNEG
         Enter HELP for list of user options
** GRAMNEG
8)   Is ORGANISM-1 a rod or coccus (etc.):
** ROD

.... (and so on)

But in fact 'Blood' was what the user meant to type, and so MYCIN goes on to the next question. 'How many days ago was this culture taken?' Presumably MYCIN wants to know how developed the culture is likely to be.

Then MYCIN starts asking some questions about this particular culture. It wants to know what organisms were discovered within the culture, and it calls the first organism 'Organism-1'. So it asks, optimistically, 'What's the identity of this organism?' Of course, if the user knows then there would be little point having this session, but it's always worth asking even the most obvious question! But, of course, the physician doesn't know the answer so he is able to type 'UNKNOWN' at this point. MYCIN now goes into more detail to try to figure out what that organism actually is. Apparently, one of the pieces of evidence one can use to find out about organisms in cultures is to ask about their staining characteristics (whatever *they* are). So, the program asks for the staining characteristics of Organism-1. Instead of answering the question, the user types a question mark. What this means is, 'What sort of answer were you expecting from this question?' As the Figure shows, MYCIN then types to the user a more elaborate form of the question, with some expected answers ('Acid Fast', 'Gram pos', meaning Gram positive, 'Gram neg', meaning Gram negative), and how to get even more information if the user should require it. But that's enough for the user in this case, and he is able to figure out that it's Gram negative that he should answer. This is an example to show you the friendliness of the system, how you can ask for more help in actually answering the questions.

Next, something very similar, with the program asking whether the organism is a ROD or a COCCUS (which is something to do with the shape). The answer is ROD. The dialogue goes on much in this vein, but I'm not going to bore you with the details. Suffice it to say that the user is asked about other organisms and other cultures and so on until the program is satisfied that it has got everything that it wants.

Then it says what it believes to be the identity of the offending organisms in this case (Figure 3.4). There is a short list of five organisms in order of likelihood according to the program.

FIGURE 3.4   MYCIN's identification of the offending organism(s)

My therapy recommendation will be based on the following possible identities of the organism(s) that seem to be significant
(item 1)   The identity of ORGANISM-1 may be PSEUDOMONAS
(item 2)   The identity of ORGANISM-1 may be KLEBSIELLA
(item 3)   The identity of ORGANISM-1 may be ENTEROBACTER
(item 4)   The identity of ORGANISM-1 may be E. COLI
(item 5)   The identity of ORGANISM-1 may be PROTEUS (Subtype unknown)

That is not the end of its task, however, for MYCIN is supposed to recommend antibiotics. But before it can recommend any antibiotics it has to know a little bit more about the patient. So the question session continues (Figure 3.5) to find out, for instance, how seriously ill the patient is, because the more seriously ill the more drastic the treatment MYCIN would recommend. MYCIN also wants to know if the patient is allergic to any of the drugs that might

FIGURE 3.5   Further dialogue

48)   On a scale of 0 to 4, where higher numbers indicate increasing severity how would you rate Jeremiah Sample (PATIENT-1)'s degree of sickness?
** 4

49)   Does Jeremiah Sample (PATIENT-1) have a clinically significant allergic reaction to any antimicrobial agent?
** NO

be recommended. In this case, the answer is no. When these questions have been answered the program then gives a preferred therapy recommendation (Figure 3.6). In this treatment MYCIN recommends two drugs, GENTAMICIN and CARBENICILLIN, with some notes about the amount of dosage, and what to do if it doesn't seem to be working, what kind of drastic things might go wrong, and so on. These two drugs are to cover for all five of these possible organisms. One of the advantages of this system is that it tries to recommend as few drugs as

FIGURE 3.6   MYCIN's recommendations

(rec 1) My preferred therapy recommendation is as follows:
In order to cover for Items (1) (2) (3) (4) (5):
Give the following in combination:
    1.   GENTAMICIN
      Dose: 1.7 MG/KG Q8H-IV or IM
      Comments: MODIFY DOSE IN RENAL FAILURE
    2.   CARBENICILLIN
      Dose: 25 MG/KG Q2H-IV
      Comments: MODIFY DOSE IN RENAL FAILURE

Do you wish to see the next choice?

possible to cover all the possible organisms that might be there, rather than (as doctors sometimes do) recommend a drug for each organism, which will end up perhaps giving the patient more antibiotics than he really needs. If necessary, the program is willing to give a second choice and a third choice about possible therapies if the doctor is unhappy about the first one.

So now we've made a diagnosis and we've a suggestion about possible treatment. But that's not the end of the matter, because remember that we said that it was very important that this program explains its advice, and that is what the consultation goes on to.

Figure 3.7 gives some examples of the kinds of question the user might want to ask. He might want to know not just what the organisms are that MYCIN diagnosed, but how certain MYCIN is about them. So, in the question about the final decision regarding the identity of Organism-1,

FIGURE 3.7   The user can interrogate MYCIN

** WHAT IS THE FINAL DECISION REGARDING THE IDENTITY OF ORGANISM-1?

The identity of ORGANISM-1 is Pseudomonas (.357) Klebsiella (.177) Enterobacter (.166) E.Coli (.137) Proteus (.118) Serratia (.042)

** WHAT MADE YOU THINK ORGANISM-1 MIGHT BE PROTEUS?

I used Rule 163 to conclude that the identity of ORGANISM-1 is Proteus. This gave a cumulative c.f. of .277. The last question asked before the conclusion was made was 26.

I used Rule 084 .... (and so on)

MYCIN gives not just a list of the offending organisms, but also some numbers, .357, .177, and so on. These numbers are what the authors of MYCIN call 'certainty factors'. These are numbers between 1 and -1, where 1 means 'I'm absolutely certain that something is the case', and -1 means 'I'm absolutely certain that something is not the case', and 0 means 'I've got evidence equally balanced both ways'. So, you can see that all of these organisms actually have quite low values, with the highest one being .357.

But the user can also ask, 'How did you come to this conclusion?' — 'What made you think that it could be Proteus?', for instance (see Figure 3.7). Then the program responds that it used Rule 163 to conclude that Organism-1 might be Proteus. It tells you what accumulated score it had got at that point, and also at what point of the dialogue, namely when it was asking question 26, that it actually came to this conclusion. It will also tell you about other rules, so this explanation could get quite long. The user can find out what these rules are if he wants to. (I'll give you an example of such a rule shortly.)

So, we've seen an overview of the program, how the various pieces are put together, and we've seen what it's like to run a session using MYCIN.

THE MYCIN RULE BASE

Now I'd like to go behind the scenes a little more, and explain the underlying mechanisms of MYCIN. You have seen in the dialogue that MYCIN refers to the existence of various rules which had helped it to come to its diagnosis and we saw in the overview that there was a place where such rules were stored. So, the next question is 'What would such a rule be like?'

Figure 3.8 is an example of one of the rules used by MYCIN (it's called Rule 047 for internal use). It consists of a number of hypotheses, 1, 2, 3, 4 and 5, and a conclusion after the 'THEN'. This is a kind of logical inference: if the five hypotheses are true, then the conclusion follows

FIGURE 3.8   An example of a MYCIN rule

RULE 047

IF: 1)   THE SITE OF THE CULTURE IS BLOOD, AND
       2)   THE IDENTITY OF THE ORGANISM IS NOT KNOWN WITH CERTAINTY,
            AND
       3)   THE STAIN OF THE ORGANISM IS GRAMNEG, AND
       4)   THE MORPHOLOGY OF THE ORGANISM IS ROD, AND
       5)   THE PATIENT HAS BEEN SERIOUSLY BURNED

THEN: THERE IS WEAKLY SUGGESTIVE EVIDENCE (.4) THAT THE IDENTITY OF
            THE ORGANISM IS PSEUDOMONAS.

from them. So, as an example of the kinds of hypothesis, here we've got (1) that the site of the particular culture we're interested in is the blood, (2) we don't know the organism at the moment, (3) that the stain of the organism is gram negative, (4) the morphology, that is the shape of the organism, is a rod, and (5) the patient has been seriously burned. Then, if these things are true, there is 'weakly suggestive evidence', we're told, that the identity of the organism is pseudomonas. After the 'weakly suggestive evidence', there is a 0.4, which is one of those certainty factors that I mentioned. It shows us how sure we are about this particular rule, and in this case in fact we're not very sure, because 0.4 is in the bottom half of the numbers from zero to 1. So, there is some evidence, but not very strong evidence, 'weakly suggestive evidence', as it says.

So how are these rules used? I think it's easiest to see how they're used if we look at the topmost rule that's available to MYCIN. (I'll explain in a minute what it means to be the topmost rule.) Rule 092 (shown in Figure 3.9) is the topmost rule. This rule really defines the overall task of MYCIN. It says (1) if there is an organism that requires therapy, and (2) we've considered any other organism which might require therapy, then what we should do is the following: we should compile a list of possible therapies and then we should determine the best of those therapies for the particular patient. Otherwise, if these conditions don't hold then we can conclude that the patient requires no therapy at all.

There's another rule which is used by MYCIN (Rule 090 in Figure 3.10): if a significant organism has been identified, then that organism requires therapy. Don't worry about the actual details of the rule, but just recognize that this sentence, 'that organism requires therapy', which is the 'THEN' part of the second rule, Rule 090, is the same as one of the hypotheses of Rule 092. That's the key observation.

MYCIN starts with Rule 092 and tries to establish the conclusion, so that it can actually make a list of possible therapies, and so on. It tries to establish that conclusion by establishing the hypotheses. The way that it establishes a hypothesis is to find another rule whose conclusion matches this hypothesis. So, to satisfy hypothesis 1 of Rule 092 it can use Rule 090. Then it has another problem, to establish that a significant organism has been identified. For that it will use another rule (see Figure 3.10).

So now, if MYCIN's task is to establish that a significant organism has been identified, it can use Rule 044, whose conclusion is, 'there is evidence that a significant organism has been identified'. So you see how these rules fit one on top of the other, in a sort of tower of rules. A hypothesis of one rule matches to the conclusion of another, a hypothesis of which, in turn, matches the conclusion of another, and so on. Does this chain ever stop? Yes it does, because some of the hypotheses can be established by asking the user of the system. Some of them refer, for instance, to laboratory data. For example, we can ask the doctor if the site of the culture is normally sterile (the first hypothesis in Rule 044). If MYCIN wants to know how many cultures were actually taken, it can ask the doctor that too. So, this chain bottoms out by asking the user.

FIGURE 3.9   The topmost rule

RULE 092

IF: 1)   AN ORGANISM REQUIRES THERAPY, AND   `TREAT FOR`

2)   CONSIDERATION HAS BEEN GIVEN TO   `COVER FOR`
THE POSSIBLE EXISTENCE OF
ADDITIONAL ORGANISMS REQUIRING
THERAPY

THEN: DO THE FOLLOWING
1)   COMPILE THE LIST OF POSSIBLE
THERAPIES
2)   DETERMINE THE BEST THERAPY   `REGIMEN`
RECOMMENDATION FROM THE COMPILED
LIST

OTHERWISE: INDICATE THAT THE PATIENT DOES NOT
REQUIRE THERAPY

FIGURE 3.10   Other MYCIN rules

RULE 090

IF: A SIGNIFICANT ORGANISM HAS BEEN   `SIGNIFICANCE`
IDENTIFIED

THEN: THAT ORGANISM REQUIRES THERAPY   `TREAT FOR`

RULE 044

IF: 1)   THE SITE OF CULTURE IS NORMALLY STERILE,   `SITE`
AND

2)   THE NUMBER OF CULTURES IS GREATER THAN   `NUMCULS`
1, AND

3)   THE NUMBER OF CULTURES CONTAINING THE   `NUMPOS`
ORGANISM IS GREATER THAN 1

THEN: THERE IS EVIDENCE THAT A SIGNIFICANT   `SIGNIFICANCE`
ORGANISM HAS BEEN IDENTIFIED

Against the rules in these two Figures (Figures 3.9 and 3.10) I've attached little labels (SIGNIFICANCE, TREATFOR, SITE, etc.) as abbreviations for the various hypotheses and conclusions. I now want to show how all these rules are chained together (Figure 3.11).

There is rather a lot of detail here, but it should give you a feel for the overall structure. This

FIGURE 3.11   The overall structure of MYCIN's rules

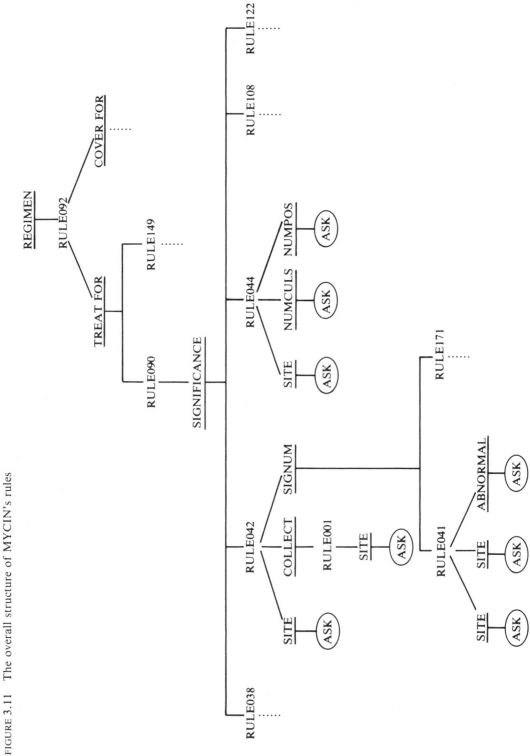

kind of organization is called a tree. Labelled on this tree we have various hypotheses or conclusions (and they can be both, of course) and rules. Rule 092, called the topmost rule, because it's at the top of this tree, has above it the word 'REGIMEN', which is the label that I put on the conclusion of that rule (Figure 3.9). The 'TREATFOR' and 'COVERFOR' are the hypotheses that were attached to that rule. Then 'TREATFOR', for instance, is the conclusion of Rule 090, and, as it happens, also Rule 149, which we didn't see before. When we look at the hypothesis of Rule 090, which I've abbreviated as 'SIGNIFICANCE', we find that in fact there are lots of ways of establishing that hypothesis, because it happens to be the conclusion of Rules 038, 042, 044, 108, 122. Rule 044, in fact, was the one we looked at.

This process of chaining, fitting the rules together in this way, goes on until at the bottom, there are things labelled 'ASK'. These are questions that we can ask the user. So the MYCIN program develops this tree, by starting off at the top with the topmost rule and then gradually unpacking it by coupling rules together, and then asking questions of the physician, and then backing up and asking other questions, and so on, gradually building up the whole tree. It actually builds a slightly different tree for different cases, because sometimes the doctor will answer the questions and give such a low certainty factor that it is clear that it's not worth exploring that branch further. So different parts of this tree are developed in different cases.

On top of this process of hanging the rules together we also have to cope with the certainty factors, the numbers that we attached to the different hypotheses and conclusions of the rules. These certainty factors are assigned to the actual rules; as we saw, one of the rules had a .4 attached to it, indicating weakly suggestive evidence. It is also possible to attach certainty factors to the facts. For example, if a laboratory technician looks down the microscope, and is not quite sure whether something is gram negative or not, but is perhaps .8 sure, then that .8 can be attached to that fact. Then that .8 will find its way into the reasoning process, and affect how certain MYCIN is of the different diagnoses.

So these numerical certainty factors come in at the bottom of the tree, and they have to be inherited up the tree to the top so that the certainty factors can be attached to the final conclusions.

Let's just see how that inheriting process works. Figure 3.12 is a part of the tree from the bottom. The three labels, SITE 1, SITE 2 and ABNORMAL, are questions that MYCIN might actually ask of the user of the system. Let's say that when the user is asked question SITE 1, which is about the site of one of the cultures, he attaches to it a numerical value of .7. That represents how sure he is about that particular piece of information. He might also attach numerical values to the other two, SITE 2 and ABNORMAL, say .8 and .6, respectively.

FIGURE 3.12 The use of certainty factors

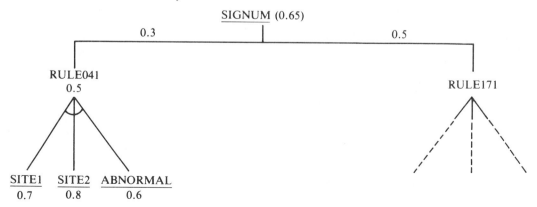

Now, these three numbers are all certainty factors associated with the hypotheses of Rule 041. Of course, the rule doesn't hold unless all three hypotheses are true. So what MYCIN actually does is regard the overall contribution of these three as being the minimum of the numeric values. So MYCIN regards .6 as being the weakest link in the chain at this point, and the .6 is inherited up the tree. But, of course, the rule itself has a numeric value attached to it, in this case .5, which means that MYCIN is half sure about this rule being true, and that has to affect its conclusion as well. In this case, MYCIN takes the .6 and .5 and multiplies them together to give an overall value of .3, which is inherited up to the SIGNUM hypothesis that MYCIN is trying to establish.

Another rule (Rule 171) is also contributing to SIGNUM. Let's say that that contributes a value of .5. So we've now got two contributions, and either of these rules on their own would be enough to establish SIGNUM. MYCIN could simply add those two contributions together. However, there is a possibility that the facts which are justifying those two rules in some way overlap, in which case MYCIN might do a certain amount of counting twice, if it just added them. So MYCIN actually multiplies them together and subtracts the product (.15) from the sum (.8) giving .65 as the value that is inherited up. Then this process is repeated. The .65 will be inherited on up the tree, until eventually MYCIN gets to some overall certainty factor for the particular conclusion that it is drawing in this case.

That gives you some idea of the reasoning mechanism used by MYCIN — how it puts together the rules in a dynamic way to deal with each particular case, and how it uses the certainty factors to establish how sure it is of its conclusions. That's the basic system, as it were, but the system has now to be made acceptable to the doctor, so that the doctor is prepared to use it.

MAKING MYCIN ACCEPTABLE TO DOCTORS

There are various ways in which the system can be made more palatable to the doctor. Here are three ways in which that could be done: (i) we can have a spelling corrector, (ii) the program can converse in English, and (iii) it can explain its advice. We saw an example of the spelling corrector when I went through the session with MYCIN. We saw that the doctor typed in 'BLODD' and the program corrected that to 'BLOOD'. That's vital, of course, because some of the information that the doctor/user is typing in to this program consists of rather long, rather nasty, latin names, and it would be very easy to type those wrongly. It would be very tedious if you had to keep retyping them until you got them right. It's quite easy for MYCIN to cope with that, because the range of possible answers it's expecting, for any particular question, is quite narrow. If MYCIN asks 'Where were these cultures drawn from?' then there are actually only a few possible answers, and it's easy to compare those answers with the one given to see which was the one that was intended.

You will also see that during that session the conversation between the program and the user appeared to be in English. The questions were all in English to the user, but also some of the questions the user asked back of the program were also in English. Well, that was rather more apparent than real. In fact, the general problem of providing an all-purpose natural language 'front-end' to a computer program is very hard, and it's not yet within our capability to be able to converse with the computer on any topic whatsoever. But if you can narrow the domain in which you are going to speak it is possible to do something. If we can narrow the topic of conversation, as we can in MYCIN, to just this consultation, and the kinds of things you might ask and be asked in the consultation, and if we can narrow the range of possible grammatical structures, which we can, then it becomes a tractable problem. The narrow range in which one can converse in MYCIN was called 'doctorese' by the authors of MYCIN. You can imagine making similar artificial languages in other narrow areas of expertise. So we can have something that passes for an English conversation then, provided we are prepared to limit ourselves in this way.

Last of all, I explained before that it was very important that the program be able to explain what it had done, and to explain the advice it had given. One of the things that makes that possible is the organization of the program into modular rules, where each of those rules seems to capture some small piece of knowledge about the diagnosis task. Then MYCIN can explain what has happened by showing how those rules were chained together in a particular case to draw the conclusion that the user is asking about. Actually, it can be rather verbose, and people are currently studying ways to make the explaining of the advice even more accessible to people. But it is possible with a program of this kind at least to give some understandable account of what's going on without getting embedded in the actual programming language — without giving Fortran, or Pascal, or whatever to the user.

So, that's the MYCIN system, an overview of what it is like to use it and how it works. What is it all going to mean? What sort of impact are systems like this going to have on society?

IMPACT ON SOCIETY

I've talked about MYCIN because this is one of the classic expert systems. MYCIN, in fact, has never found its way into the ward on a regular basis. It has been used on an experimental basis, but it is not in general use. But systems like it are. Another system built using the same techniques as MYCIN, called PUFF, which dealt with pulmonary heart disorders, is in regular use now on real wards. I mentioned that there are systems for assessing the mineral prospects of a geological site. There's a program called PROSPECTOR which does that, based on very similar technology to the MYCIN system, and that is in use. It is reputed to have saved some people a million dollars, by reassessing the mineral prospects of a site and suggesting that the best place to mine for molybdenum was where the geologists had decided to put the slag heap. And this was confirmed by subsequent drilling. There is a system that configures VAX systems for the Digital Equipment Corporation which is now in everyday use. So these systems are actually earning money. So we're going to see more of these systems in use increasingly over the next few years. And they are relatively cheap technology, in the sense that once one has put in the manpower to develop the system it's very easy to multiply them — you only need to copy them on to yet another floppy disk or tape. So we can expect to see a very widespread use of such systems over the next few years.

What effect is it going to have? Well, one of the things that you can see from the case of MYCIN is that we might expect a better quality of service in some areas. Whereas in the past expert knowledge in particular narrow areas of medicine was only in the hands of a few consultants, who were very expensive to hire, that kind of advice might soon be available to the general practitioner via a terminal on his or her desk. So we might come to expect a higher quality of service from doctors — and from other people, for we don't need to stick to medical diagnosis. I think we are currently getting a better quality of service from DEC salesmen when they sell us VAXs. And that service will be much cheaper than it previously was.

The exercise of building these programs is itself valuable. That is, without them going into production and actually being used in computers, the task of extracting the rules from an expert in such a form that they can be put into a computer can itself be a valuable exercise, because the knowledge then becomes much more explicit. Knowledge which was previously in the head of a consultant of blood infections has now been unpacked into explicit rules. Very often these experts start off by thinking that the task can't be done, that they are not able to output this formal representation of their knowledge, and then are surprised when they discover they can. It helps them to clarify their own ideas about just what their knowledge is.

Because the knowledge is more explicit, it can lead to an extension of knowledge. Once you have got it down on paper you can think about what is wrong with it, and in particular your colleagues can think about what is wrong with it. Two colleagues who have radically different views about a matter may now have a formal account of their difference. Whereas previously they didn't talk to one another, they may now have students who compare their rules and come up with some knowledge which is actually superior to either of theirs individually.

It may lead to better teaching as well. Previously, such knowledge could only be gained by being an apprentice at the elbow of the master, following him around and watching him solve various cases, and, gradually, by a process of osmosis, picking up the expertise that that expert had. Now that the knowledge is written down explicitly it's possible for a student to go to that knowledge base and read it. There are reported cases of this happening, not with MYCIN as far as I know, but with some other expert systems. Students have gone to these rule bases and have used them as a source of knowledge.

So that is an indication of some of the likely impacts of these expert systems. We're currently in a position where we're just beginning to discover the range of possible applications of these systems. We don't have a very good idea of what the ultimate limitations of the system will be. It's very difficult to predict, but it does seem to be quite an exciting prospect.

What's it going to mean for people? How are people going to react to the products of artificial intelligence? Are they going to be intimidated and worried about software which appears to imbed some intelligence, or are they going to be very happy about the improved level of service that they get? Or will it be both? It's very difficult to know. What is clear, however, is that the destructiveness of that reaction will be proportional to the degree of ignorance that people have about the technology. If people have fears about this technology, we want them at least to be well-placed fears, and not to be based on misconceptions. So I think that it is very important to explain to people what these systems can do, how they work, what their capabilities are, so that we do not have these misconceptions.

QUESTIONS

Q. Is it easy for the doctor to adjust the certainties on a temporary basis, for example during an epidemic?

A. Yes, it should be. Of course, the certainties attached to the actual facts are provided dynamically in the case of each patient, so that is easy to adjust. The certainties attached to each rule can be adjusted by using the rule acquisition system, and bringing up each rule you want to adjust and then making the adjustment. So it would be quite easy to do that.

Q. Can I ask how much effort it took to build MYCIN and how much with present-day technology it would take to build it a second time with the knowledge in building the system that has been acquired?

A. The original MYCIN was a Ph.D. thesis. I don't know the exact number of man-hours or whatever, but we can think in terms of years. Obviously of the order of three or four years. After the MYCIN system was built the medical knowledge was stripped out of it, to form a system called essential MYCIN or E-MYCIN for short. That was cleaned up into what is called an expert system 'shell', which is a system for doing the basic kinds of inference, handling the uncertainties and handling the explanation system, but without any particular rules in it. Armed with that system, the PUFF system for pulmonary heart disease was developed in 50 hours of consultation with the expert and 10 man-weeks of work. Now PUFF was actually a good deal smaller than the MYCIN system, but I think it gives an order of magnitude figure. In other words, of the order of a few months to develop that system; perhaps, for a more complex system, a year or something like that. There can be a decrease, an order of magnitude decrease perhaps, in the amount of development time once that basic mechanism is in place. Now, not all expert systems lend themselves very readily to that kind of shell. Some systems can be built just by adding a few rules in that way to an existing shell. Some require a more intimate knowledge of the shell and modification of the shell and of course they take much longer, and require more expertise to do.

Q. One thing that worries me with expert systems as they stand at the moment is that the user will be very untrusting of it, particularly in a medical situation where incorrect diagnosis for whatever reason, whether it's personal incorrect diagnosis or computerized incorrect diagnosis, could obviously lead to very serious consequences for the patients themselves. I think that one point that maybe I missed or which wasn't stressed sufficiently was that expert systems should be regarded perhaps as a guide only, and not as a solution, but simply as a guide to enable the practitioner in the medical situation (in this case) to go to other sources of information for confirmation of the diagnosis presented mechanically, as it were.

A. I agree absolutely with what you say, and I think that expert systems lend themselves particularly well to that approach. I think I did say that obviously the doctor has to take the ultimate legal responsibility. One of the things that makes that possible is the fact that the system can explain its output. Now in fact we've had automatic decision aids for medicine for quite a while before the age of expert systems. Decision aids based on Bayesian probability, where you would just take the probabilities of the kinds of symptoms for various kinds of disease, and then do a massive statistical calculation to come up with a diagnosis. Now those systems have not proved very successful in clinical use. I think one of the reasons is that they work as a huge black box — you put the data in and you get an answer out — and there is no way to know what went on inside. I think expert systems, for the first time, offer you a view of what goes on inside. I think the existing systems are inadequate in that respect, and we can work to improve them, but it does give you for the first time the possibility that you can know on what basis the program took a decision and therefore form a rational opinion yourself as to whether you are willing to accept it or not. Certainly, you can then go away and make other tests in order to follow that up and make other confirmations.

Q. I wonder whether in the MYCIN case there is that instruction, as it were, at the beginning of the program, that says, 'Don't use this as a definitive solution, merely use it as a guide and such and such sources are available to further the investigation.'

A. Yes, I think that it's a good point and obviously from the dialogue that I showed you MYCIN doesn't currently do that. I think, had it entered normal clinical use, it might well have done, if only for the fact that the authors of the system would want to protect themselves against litigation.

Q. Can you give any indication of the computing facilities needed to build and to use expert systems, say in terms of programming languages, processing power, size of main memory, that kind of thing?

A. It seems to vary a lot, and there seem to be two views on this on either side of the Atlantic. The systems that have been built in the States, like the MYCIN system, were built on very powerful processors, typically DEC 20s with many megabytes of memory, and a large number of rules. One of the things which seems to take up the capacity is a very elaborate explanation system, and an interface for the consultation, the explanation, and rule acquisition, and so on. In this country, a number of people have built some very small and cheap shells, which basically just do the inference part of it, and those run on home micros. Some people do claim to have used such systems to have input rules and to be satisfied with the results. I would not want to say any more than that.

Q. Do you have any views on programming languages? Do you do it in COBOL or BASIC or what?

A. Yes, well, that's a very good question. There is a range of artificial intelligence programming languages, of which LISP and PROLOG are perhaps the two most famous. I think such languages are particularly suitable for this kind of symbolic reasoning. Of course, because expert system shells are available, one can now get these shells off the shelf and just have to input the rules. Sometimes those shells are built in PASCAL or FORTRAN or whatever. So that is quite suitable for building these quite simple expert systems, where you are just inputting rules, but if you want to get to grips with the thing and actually modify the shell itself, I think you have to be working in a language like LISP or PROLOG.

Q. How do you go about calibrating the thing in the first place? How do you assign these certainty factors?

A. In the case of the rules, the certainty factors are assigned by the consultant, the expert who is originally asked. When he provides the rule, you say, 'Well, how sure are you of this rule?' He may reluctantly then offer some opinion. You then refine it over time. Having developed some of these rules on a few cases, you then go and program the rules, run them on some more cases and come back with the resulting consultations, and show them to the expert. He then says, 'That's rubbish, I would never come up with that decision.' You then query him further until you get to the point where you can pin down the mistake. It may be in the rule, it may be missing a hypothesis or something, or it may be in the certainty factor that he has attached — it may be too large or too small, and you modify it in that way. But all the information of that kind has to come from the expert himself.

Q. Can you see any resistance from the medical expert on this, because, if this works, he is handing over all his knowledge for common knowledge, isn't he?

A. From the consultant or the general practitioner?

Q. Well, from both.

A. I think the consultant, hopefully, will not be made unemployed by this. What it will do is free him from the more routine tasks, and allow him to devote his attention to the more difficult tasks. If you look at those rules you will notice that they are in fact very shallow. They don't really sum up any kind of underlying model of how people work or how the illness might actually have been caused, and so on. They are just very shallow, empirical rules connecting cause and effect, and those rules seem to be successful in a wide range of cases, perhaps 70 or 80 per cent of cases, the more simple cases. But as soon as any kind of complication arises — you might be suffering from several organisms, and the symptoms may be reacting in nasty, unpredictable ways — that kind of MYCIN system won't work. Those are the cases where the consultant will have to be called in. For him, of course, that is a more interesting case. I think there are sufficient of those cases around that we needn't have any redundancy among consultants. They will have a more interesting job to do. Now, in the case of the general practitioner, there is obviously some resistance there, I think — more resistance probably than from the patient. The patients on the whole seem to be quite enthusiastic about such things. What can one do? All one can do is make the system more friendly, make the explanation better, and so on.

FURTHER READING

For an overview of expert systems:
Feigenbaum, E.A. (1979) *Themes and case studies of knowledge engineering.* In Michie, D. (Ed.) (1979) Expert Systems in the Microelectronic Age, Edinburgh University Press, Edinburgh

For a general text on expert systems:
Hayes-Roth, F., Waterman, D.A. and Lenat, D.B. (Eds.) (1983) *Building Expert Systems*, Addison Wesley, Reading, Mass.

For a more detailed account of MYCIN:
Shortliffe, E.H. (1976) *Computer-based medical consultation: MYCIN*, Elsevier, New York

4
DEALING WITH UNCERTAINTY
JOHN FOX
IMPERIAL CANCER RESEARCH FUND
LABORATORIES, LONDON

Early artificial intelligence research into theorem proving and problem solving, and more recent work on such subjects as automatic planning and automatic design techniques, showed that there are important aspects of intelligence which can be modelled by purely logical reasoning. Logic, of course, requires that the reasoning mechanisms and the data they manipulate should be completely reliable. But with the generalization of AI work to practical problems outside the laboratory (such as medical diagnosis, geological sample analysis, equipment fault-finding, and so on) purely logical techniques are no longer always appropriate.

Let me give a couple of examples. Suppose that we have to make a decision between various options, as, for example, management have to when trying to choose between several possible technical designs for a product or when choosing between possible company policies. In making that decision, we may have to consider many sources of information or evidence. But our information sources in the real world — our measuring instruments, say, or even our beliefs — are often unreliable.

Secondly, many decisions require some sort of prediction or forecasting. What we decide to do will depend perhaps on what the weather is likely to be tomorrow or on whether a particular component is likely to fail. Predictions of this kind can be based on a theoretical model or on a statistical database of previous cases, or a combination of both. But models and previous experience are not, of course, always certain predictors of future events.

Medical decision making is a good example to illustrate uncertain reasoning in expert systems, since it is typical of complex decision making involving many types of uncertainty. Doctors, for example, have to make many decisions, among which might be these: What's wrong with my patient? How can I go about finding out? What treatment should I use once I know? Will it work? and so on.

I am going to discuss how people, as well as expert systems, deal with uncertainty. One thing I will emphasize is that expert system designers were not the first people to realize that uncertainty is an important problem, nor the first to try to develop techniques to help people make decisions. For many years, researchers in statistics and in psychology have tried to understand how people cope with uncertainty, what mistakes they make, and so on. Over that period, we seem to have seen something of a change of attitude about how good people are at dealing with uncertainty. A 'pessimistic' school of thought seems to have grown up, which doubts people's abilities to make decisions in uncertain situations. 'Optimists', of course, believe otherwise. This debate between the pessimists and the optimists is very relevant to the design of expert systems.

THE PESSIMIST'S VIEW

The pessimists start off with a number of observations which are, to some extent, straightforward and uncontroversial, although people do differ about their interpretation. The

FIGURE 4.1   The case for pessimism

THE CASE FOR PESSIMISM

Ignorance
Coping under pressure
Bias
Superficiality

case for pessimism — that is, that people cannot deal in a rational way with problems involving uncertainty — falls into four main categories:

1.   People are often ignorant when called upon to make decisions. They may be ignorant of particular facts or circumstances which may be relevant to the problem, either due to lack of experience, lack of education, or just the lack of availability of relevant material.

2.   People may have to make decisions quickly or under pressure, for example in life-threatening situations, as in the medical case. Of course, people often cope less well under pressure than in quieter surroundings.

3.   Human decision making is biased or in some way inadequate as compared with a 'correct' mathematical or formal, logical model. Research work on biases has shown that people do not take into account many of the mathematical factors which statisticians or probability theorists would argue should be taken into account, such as variance and sample size.

4.   People tend to be very influenced by the superficial characteristics of a problem. For example, if people in an experimental situation are asked to make decisions about (a) saving lives or (b) numbers of people being put at risk or killed in an accident, say, then, even though the two problems are structurally identical, the superficial form (that is, whether one talks about saving lives or people dying) can produce quite different decisions.

The pessimist's solution (Figure 4.2) is to say that since we cannot have an enormous amount of respect for people's ability to deal with uncertainty we should formulate a correct, accurate,

FIGURE 4.2   The pessimists' solution

THE PESSIMISTS' SOLUTION

Rely upon the correct mathematical model, not human judgement, when there are significant amounts of uncertainty.

mathematical model for the particular decisions we are trying to make and use that in preference to human judgement when there is a lot of uncertainty involved.

Let me illustrate how that might be put to work with a medical example. Figure 4.3 is a simple

FIGURE 4.3   Medical example of the structure of the pessimists' solution

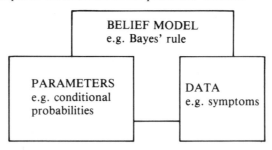

structure, representing a computer program, which can be used to help a doctor make decisions, perhaps about a diagnosis or a treatment. One of the boxes, the DATA box, represents the data that are available about a particular patient, the symptoms, some laboratory tests, and so on. Then there'll be some sort of mathematical model (such as Bayes' rule or various other techniques) of how to revise belief in the light of evidence (in possible diagnoses, say) which is used to interpret that data. Finally, the model is informed by a set of parameters, which might be a set of conditional probabilities describing how often particular symptoms occur with particular diseases. So, the *belief model* uses the *parameters* to interpret the *data*.

We can illustrate this decision-making process visually with a graph (Figure 4.4). This shows a simplified case of medical diagnosis in which we imagine somebody is trying to make a decision between whether a person has liver cancer or hepatitis, another kind of liver disease.

FIGURE 4.4   Graphical illustration of the decision-making process

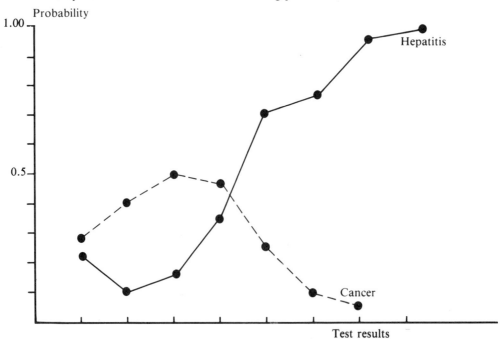

On the vertical axis is the probability and on the horizontal axis we have a number of test results obtained as time goes on. The dotted line represents the probability of cancer, the solid line represents the probability of hepatitis. As more tests are done more information is acquired, and gradually the probabilities of the two alternatives change. At the end of the series of tests we have a clear distinction between cancer and hepatitis: in this case, the decision is hepatitis.

That summarizes the pessimistic approach, which says that we must use a correct, formal, mathematical model of how to make decisions involving uncertain information. The mathematics provides us with good ways of accumulating evidence and combining information to make a final decision.

THE OPTIMIST'S VIEW

The optimistic school takes a rather different view of human decision making: see Figure 4.5.

FIGURE 4.5   The optimistic school

THE OPTIMISTIC SCHOOL

People can be educated, trained under stress, and debiased so they deal with uncertainty more effectively.

People are being judged against an arbitrary theory — they cope well with novel, constantly changing situations which the mathematical models do not address.

This suggests, first of all, that many of the problems that people apparently have are really matters of education or training, and that some of their weaknesses are due to unfamiliarity with the situation or can be corrected by training in decision-making techniques. But a more radical claim of the optimists is that, while the probabilistic view of decision making may be an important approach, it really doesn't take into account the fact that people deal with a far wider range of decisions involving uncertainty than the available mathematical methods can cope with. For instance, we deal with problems which are constantly changing, the alternatives available to us are never fixed, and we have to be constantly rethinking our position. So the optimists feel that the pessimists have been over-influenced by their own models when thinking about decision making, and have been led to ignore other kinds of decision making to which those models don't apply.

In many ways, expert systems fall in this second camp, or, at least, much of the philosophy of expert systems does, for we may be interested in trying to use computers to emulate the ability of human experts to make decisions under uncertainty. We are implicitly assuming that the methods people use are worth copying. Those methods (in the artificial intelligence view of things) involve knowledge.

Figure 4.6 is an extremely simplified diagram of an expert system. We have three boxes, as in our previous mathematical system, but two of the boxes are labelled differently. Instead of having a belief model or mathematical model for manipulating probability, we have some sort of inference, often logical deduction. This inference mechanism is informed not by

FIGURE 4.6   Simplified diagram of an expert system

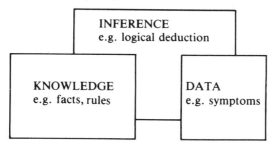

mathematical parameters, not by numbers like conditional probabilities, but knowledge in a rather everyday sense: knowledge about particular diseases, the rules of thumb that an expert doctor might use, and so on. So in this case we make *inferences* using *knowledge* to interpret the *data* about a particular patient.

Figure 4.7 illustrates a logical approach to dealing with uncertainty. There is a very simple rule, which we could write in a language like PROLOG or many other production rule languages: if P is a patient, and D is a disease, and P has S, where S is a symptom of the disease D, then D is a possible diagnosis for P. With this very general rule, and particular bodies of facts, we can start to make simple inferences about particular patients. Given the fact that spots is a symptom of measles, and data about a particular imaginary patient called Annie Boddie, who unfortunately has spots, then we can conclude, by the general rule, that measles is a possible diagnosis for Annie Boddie.

FIGURE 4.7   A logical approach to dealing with uncertainty

RULE

    If: P is_a patient
    and: D is_a disease
    and: P has S
    and: S is_a_symptom_of D
    Then: D possible_diagnosis_for P

FACT

    spots is_a_symptom_of measles

DATA

    'Annie Boddie' is_a patient
    'Annie Boddie' has spots

CONCLUDE

    measles
        possible_diagnosis_for
        'Annie Boddie'

Now, what I've done is present two extremes. Statistical models have clearly shown themselves to be effective, and often cost-effective, for helping to make medical diagnoses or various industrial or commercial decisions. But the view of the optimists — and I think the view of people in AI — is that those statistical models only apply to a limited range of problems involving uncertainty. We may well wish to look at other types of problem, where people are expert and statistics are not enough. Unfortunately, however, logic in the form that I've just illustrated is also not enough, because in many situations it may not be that a particular person with measles has spots — it's always assumed in medicine that nothing can ever be relied upon. So the question I will address in the next section is how some of the well-known expert systems have learned lessons of logic *and* of statistics and have put them together in a way that allows them to achieve high performance on complex tasks. I will then try to draw some general conclusions.

REASONING WITH UNCERTAINTY IN EXPERT SYSTEMS

The place to start is with MYCIN, an expert system published some ten years ago now, which has inspired so much of the modern work on expert systems. MYCIN was originally designed for diagnosing bacterial infections and helping to choose appropriate antibiotics for treatments. Its knowledge of the medical problem concerned is largely in the form of rules, although other forms of knowledge representation are used as well. I will concentrate on the rules.

In Figure 4.8 we have a rule that is about blood and the characteristics of an organism that may be infecting the patient. We have the familiar condition part of the rule, the 'If' clauses, 1, 2, 3, 'the site of the culture is blood', 'the organism was able to grow aerobically', and so on.

FIGURE 4.8   Example of a rule in an expert system

MYCIN

RULE027

    If: 1)   The site of the culture is blood, and
           2)   The organism was able to grow aerobically, and
           3)   The organism was able to grow anaerobically

    Then: There is evidence that the aerobicity of the organism is
                facultative (.8)
                or anaerobic (.2)

When these conditions are true the rule allows the system to conclude something about the organism. But the important thing to see is that the conclusions are not merely asserted logically but are also qualified with what are called certainty factors. Every time the rule is used, the levels of certainty in each of the hypotheses that the rule refers to are changed using these factors. These factors are acquired from the domain expert when building the knowledge base. The expert makes an assessment of the strength of the association between the hypotheses and the conditions which lead to it. So, in MYCIN, we see a fairly straightforward combination of logic and simple statistics.

PROSPECTOR is another early expert system, although not a medical one in this case. It was designed to predict likely sites of deposits of oil or of minerals. In many ways it is quite similar to MYCIN, but one way in which it differs is that it doesn't just calculate the strength of a conclusion using the rules' certainty factors but also takes account of the reliability of data as well. The way that PROSPECTOR does this is illustrated in Figure 4.9. At the top we have a body of rules (in PROSPECTOR, this consists of several hundred rules) of which I have distinguished one, Rule-45. The rules examine a semantic network of material about the problem being considered. The semantic network contains information about particular geological samples and their particular interpretations, such as the sort of crystalline structure found. Underneath the box labelled 'Antecedent', which is the condition of the rules, is an assertion or pattern 'Barite overlying sulfides'. If PROSPECTOR has built up this description of the current terrain then the antecedent of Rule-45 is true. The overall truth will be calculated from the truth of the individual elements in the semantic network which is stored numerically. Without going into detail, the techniques used for this calculation are from fuzzy logic.

But it's not simply the strength or the believability of the evidence that is taken into account: the rules themselves, just like in MYCIN, have associated likelihood ratios, or strengths. These are used to modify yet again the level of belief in the conclusion on the right-hand side of Rule-45, the 'Consequent', which is that there are ore deposits. So we have a number of bits of information, about rocks and their physical relationships to each other, we have belief in those fragments of information, and an overall belief in the statement which is a combination of the belief in the fragments. Then the rule itself has a certain reliability or certainty associated with it.

MYCIN and PROSPECTOR are probably the two most famous early expert systems, but since they have appeared a variety of other techniques have been reported. The next example is

FIGURE 4.9   Rules in the PROSPECTOR expert system

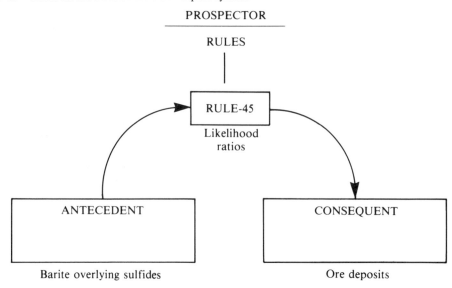

taken from a system called CASNET. CASNET was originally designed for diagnosing glaucoma, an eye disease. It uses a variety of different types of knowledge focusing on a causal understanding of disease processes. There are three main types of knowledge that are available to this system (Figure 4.10). At the bottom level is what you might call clinical knowledge, information about the observations that are made on a patient, such as whether the patient has had any pain, whether the eyes are red, and various technical tests such as tonometry and perimetry. This information draws attention to pathophysiological states, or physiological knowledge; that is, knowledge about what causes what. In Figure 4.11 I've distinguished, for example, high intraocular pressure (high pressure inside the eye) which is known to cause a reduction in the visual field of the patient. From the pathophysiological states (Figure 4.10) lines flow to the final kind of knowledge, which you might think of as textbook knowledge or medical terminology.

The important level is the middle one, because it is in this part of the knowledge base that CASNET represents information about the patient, and conclusions like elevated intraocular pressure. It examines its physiological knowledge and finds that there are facts that allow it to conclude that if there is elevated intraocular pressure then this may lead to visual field loss. But, as usual, it's not a logical conclusion, for you can't always rely upon that being true. So as we've seen before, a numerical value is associated with this causal relationship. Once again we see the use of a combination of mathematical and logical techniques.

In the next example, called INTERNIST, the scene begins to shift a little. INTERNIST is an extremely large system, developed in Pittsburgh by Harry Pople, who is a computer scientist, and Jack Myers, who is a doctor. INTERNIST can diagnose something in the order of 600 different conditions in medicine. But a particular emphasis there, perhaps a stronger emphasis than in other expert systems, has been on actually emulating or simulating the expertise of Dr Myers, an eminent diagnostician. It's not simply a matter of engineering the best technique but of explicitly attempting to copy certain aspects of Dr Myers' decision making, and indeed the decision making of other doctors. A particular characteristic of that decision making, which is quite distinct from the traditional view that has been taken in the statistical world, in the decision analysis world as it's called, is that the problem of decision making is a highly dynamic one. Remember the point that the optimists make, that people are actually rather good at

FIGURE 4.10   An example from CASNET

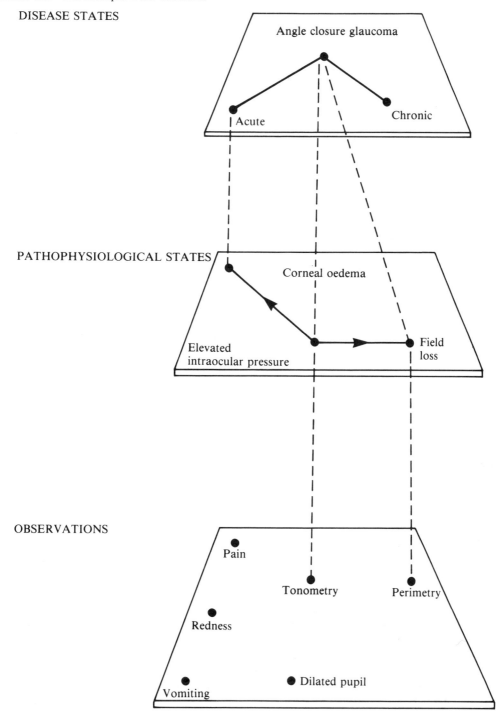

DISEASE STATES

Angle closure glaucoma

Acute

Chronic

PATHOPHYSIOLOGICAL STATES

Corneal oedema

Elevated
intraocular pressure

Field
loss

OBSERVATIONS

Pain

Tonometry

Perimetry

Redness

Vomiting

Dilated pupil

FIGURE 4.11   Detail from CASNET

EXPERT

Emphasizes causal facts:

ELEVATED   VISUAL
INTRAOCULAR ⟶ FIELD
PRESSURE   (.6)   LOSS

making decisions in changing situations. This is a characteristic of INTERNIST which is very important: as information is acquired, the form of the problem, never mind the solution, becomes clearer.

Figure 4.12 shows that the sort of knowledge that's available to INTERNIST is a network once again, containing causal and taxonomic (or textbook) knowledge, just as we've seen before. But the fragments of the network are linked in more complicated ways. Imagine that our patient has been observed to have jaundice. That fact might suggest to a doctor, and would suggest to INTERNIST, an abnormality called hyperbilirubinaemia. As the figure shows this comes in different forms, conjugated and unconjugated. So from the fact of knowing there is jaundice present, we can conclude possible hyperbilirubinaemia. From this we see two links going away to the right saying it's important to 'find out about' liver involvement. This will help sort out whether the hyperbilirubinaemia is unconjugated, via the 'caused-by' link. At any point in this network it's possible to suggest the questions that might be asked or tests that might be carried out to try to narrow down on the final diagnosis.

Now, if we look at the way that inference is done in INTERNIST it's actually very simple (Figure 4.13). On the left we have the 'noticing and evoking mechanism', which simply means that if the system notices there's something like jaundice (or spots or a temperature or what-have-you) this immediately evokes or suggests possible diagnoses, and as more and more information about the patient comes in, the set of *possible diagnoses* is built up over time. Similarly, on the right, once we know that there are particular diagnoses then we would expect certain sorts of symptoms to be associated with them. So, to take a rather trivial example, if I suspect there's measles or there's mumps, I'm probably going to expect a temperature, and might go looking for that.

As always, those bits of information, the 'presenting symptoms' as they're called, and the other information that is collected about a particular patient, do not lead to logically determined conclusions about the diagnosis. INTERNIST associates simple numerical scores, We and Wm, with those conclusions. So, in INTERNIST, although we still see some use of numbers, there's more of an emphasis on emulating the style of decision making, using terms like 'suggests', 'find out about', 'caused by', and so on, giving a fairly rich type of inference, that reflects Dr Myers' own style of thinking.

As my final example I'm going to describe a system called PSYCO, which I developed a few years ago. Its name indicates that it was developed in detail as a model of human decision making (even more so than INTERNIST). It's also an acronym for Production SYstem COmpiler. PSYCO is a smaller system than any of the others that I've mentioned. Its main purpose was to examine the power of human decision making, explicitly simulating doctors. PSYCO was applied to the diagnosis of dyspepsia or indigestion (Figure 4.14). Imagine a patient comes to his or her doctor, complaining of indigestion. This might suggest in the doctor's mind any one of a number of organic conditions: gastric cancer, peptic ulcer, gall stones, a number of other possibilities, and also (more likely) non-organic conditions. Peptic ulcer itself is broken down into gastric ulcer and duodenal ulcer.

Now PSYCO, as I say, was not only designed, taking a lot of psychological literature into account, to simulate human thinking, but also goes further than the other systems I've mentioned in moving away from a statistical, quantitative or numerical view of uncertainty. We

FIGURE 4.12 Part of the network of knowledge available to INTERNIST

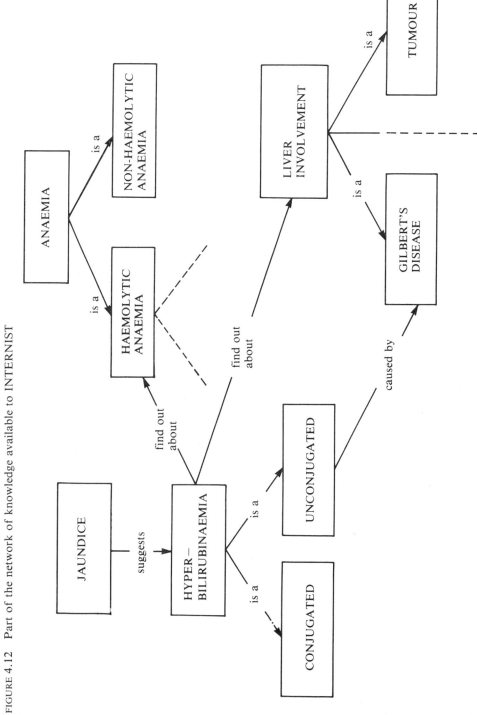

FIGURE 4.13   Inference in INTERNIST

INTERNIST

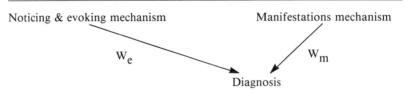

Noticing & evoking mechanism   Manifestations mechanism

W_e W_m

Diagnosis

FIGURE 4.14   PSYCO applied to the diagnosis of dyspepsia

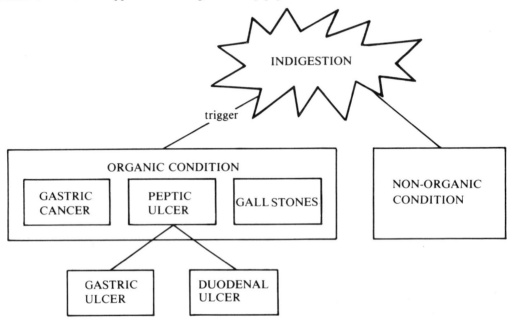

INDIGESTION

trigger

ORGANIC CONDITION

GASTRIC CANCER   PEPTIC ULCER   GALL STONES

NON-ORGANIC CONDITION

GASTRIC ULCER   DUODENAL ULCER

can see this illustrated with three example rules from the indigestion system (Figure 4.15). The first one simply says 'if the patient's age is elderly' and 'the weight has fallen recently' then

FIGURE 4.15   Three example rules from PSYCO

PSYCO

"Covert" representation

If: age elderly
  and: weight down

Then: possible cancer

If: pain severe
  and: site ruq
Then: probable gallstones

If: probable peptic_ulcer
  and: pain delayed_after_meals
Then: probable duodenal_ulcer

there is a 'possibility of cancer'. (I hope you won't get too alarmed, this is a somewhat simplified presentation!) Also, if the 'pain is severe' and the 'site of that pain is in the right upper quadrant', then there is 'probable gall stones'. And, if there is 'probable peptic ulcer' but 'the pain does not come on immediately after you've had a meal, maybe twenty minutes after', then there is a 'probable duodenal ulcer'.

These rules are terribly simple and the only reference to uncertainty is these 'nominal labels' or 'covert terms', as I've called them: possible, probable, suggested and so on. In fact, PSYCO was only able to 'count on its fingers', i.e. count up the pros and cons for the various alternative diagnoses. But even though it had no ability to make precise calculations in the way that statistical techniques can, it nevertheless proved surprisingly effective in limited situations. It was in fact able to achieve roughly the same level of diagnosis as a conventional statistical or mathematical diagnosis system. The main reason for this was its ability to express complicated patterns of data about the patient. So the power of rules is surprisingly great, even though we may make relatively little use of numbers.

REVIEW

At the beginning I drew a distinction between the pessimistic view of how good people are at making decisions under uncertainty, leading to arguments for the careful, scientific use of mathematical and quantitative techniques, and the optimistic view, which draws attention to the extraordinary flexibility of knowledgeable and experienced human decision makers. Perhaps the moral you should draw is that there is a reasonable case for saying that expert system designers might look not simply to using statistical methods, though, of course, they must when those are appropriate, but also look at the ways that people deal with uncertainty and simulate those techniques. I hope you could see as I went from MYCIN and the early systems through INTERNIST and the final small system for indigestion, that there is an increasing emphasis on the simulation of how people solve problems and a decreasing emphasis on the use of precise quantities. This is where we are at the moment, but I think there's actually still quite a long way we can go.

Now, I want to draw attention to just how rich our vocabulary and our ideas about uncertainty are. We've only just begun to explore them, particularly by emphasizing abstract techniques for representing uncertainty. Let us look at a few examples (Figure 4.16). At the top is a simple one. Somebody might say 'it is possible that John has cancer'. That's rather like one of those 'suggests' ideas in the earlier examples. Or we might say, and mean something very different, 'it is possible that Aunt Agatha will come again this weekend'. Here, we're not really saying there's a probability, or attaching some sort of estimate of our certainty that this will happen, but perhaps we're saying that she came last weekend and that things are pretty much the same as they were then. There's an implicit reference to prior knowledge. If some person communicates the fact to somebody else that 'it is possible that the United States will invade Grenada shortly', then that's not a statement of probability. There aren't any other examples on which you can estimate the probability. It is perhaps a reference to the fact that you've been informed by American sources that that is one of the options that's being considered.

So, we have a great deal of knowledge and many ways of expressing knowledge about uncertainty. In fact, we go even further than this, for we use it in a very pragmatic way. Take the next case (Figure 4.16): 'It is unlikely that John has cancer', to which a doctor might add 'but it is possible'. We might interpret this as cautious reassurance to a relative. We use the terms of uncertainty in more complicated ways. Consider 'it is conceivable that there will be a strike in sector 44 in the North Sea'. This could almost be a warning: if this contingency should arise then somebody will need to mobilize a lot of activity and resources to deal with that strike. And finally, 'it is inconceivable that anyone would start a war in Europe', by which we really

FIGURE 4.16   The meaning of uncertainty

THE MEANING OF UNCERTAINTY

It is possible that
John has cancer

It is possible that
Aunt Agatha will come
again this weekend

It is possible that
the United States will
invade Grenada shortly

It is unlikely that
John has cancer but
it is possible

It is conceivable that
there will be a strike
in sector 44

It is inconceivable that
anyone would start a
war in Europe

mean that when judging certainty or uncertainty we must also take into account the costs and risks associated with particular events.

But the main thing I want to illustrate with those somewhat lighthearted examples is that our concepts of uncertainty are really very, very rich. We have traditionally just treated uncertainty as a mathematical concept, which has meant that all of those different ideas that we have on certainty and uncertainty are collapsed onto a single mathematical idea, that of probability or belief or confidence, whatever we wish to call it. Artificial intelligence systems are slowly beginning to break down that single monolithic concept into some more specific ideas of possibility, probability, conceivability, and so on.

I will now summarize the relationships between the various attempts to deal with uncertainty in the systems I've discussed. Statistical methods, of course, are extremely well established. They've been around for 20 to 25 years — actually, they've been around a great deal longer, but they've been explicitly, consciously applied to many decision-making problems over that sort of period. The methods have been primarily used for hypothesis testing; that is, for choosing between a fixed set of alternatives, rather than for hypothesis formation. As we saw in the INTERNIST system, and in PSYCO to a lesser extent, the uncertainty associated with hypothesis formation is something that we must deal with if we're going to deal with the range of problems that are found in medicine, say. Numerical methods, of course, are confined to concepts which are measurable, where you can actually attach numbers to them, which is by no means always the case. If there is simply no number to be found then you must find some other non-numerical method for reasoning about the uncertainty. In general, one can say that the expert systems that are around today plump for precision in the ways that they calculate uncertainty using numerical methods, but in the future they will probably go for more richness, with more dimensions of meaning than numbers alone can represent.

Finally, I will summarize the three main approaches to representing uncertainty in expert systems as I see them at the moment. The first is simply to combine logical and numerical methods, but to keep them rather separate in the computation by the program. That is easily the best established approach. The second is what I call 'covert', or perhaps a better term might be 'nominal', ways of dealing with uncertainty, in which we use terms like possible, probable, conceivable and so on, but only in a very limited way. What *you* mean by those terms is by no means fully captured in the expert system's knowledge base. Thirdly, I believe we will increasingly see (reflecting the kinds of examples I've discussed) an emphasis on linguistic or propositional ways of dealing with uncertainty, in which the emphasis is on *describing* the uncertainty rather than simply *measuring* it. This is an area in which we've not made very much progress, but which holds out promise for the future.

At the beginning I said that techniques to deal with uncertainty are not always required in artificial intelligence programs. Indeed, one might note that a survey of practical industrial applications in the UK suggests that many designers have completely ignored the problem for a number of successful applications. But it must be said, I think, that most of these systems are small and the applications that they worked with have probably been chosen to avoid the sorts of ambiguity and uncertainty which are characteristic of complex fields like medicine. Furthermore, the capabilities that are needed for, shall we say, everyday reasoning, for interpreting the spoken word or the visual image, are known to involve high degrees of ambiguity, and as our skill and confidence grows in this field we shall be drawn towards increasingly demanding expert systems applications. For the moment, conventional mathematical techniques for dealing with uncertainty are valuable (and available), but the future will probably demand entirely new techniques for coping with uncertainty, and some of these may use ideas which are gained from a careful study of our own thinking and our own decision making.

QUESTIONS

Q. You seem to be suggesting that all these uncertainties, or statistical measurements, are already available. Is there any work going on in the area of systems which would learn the probabilities applicable to certain rules?

A. Learning, in the sense of building up a body of experience that can estimate probabilities, likelihoods or certainties, is something that AI people have, of course, looked at, but not only them. People working in many areas of statistical decision making have also been aware of the potential in that area. Yes, I think that's a very important way by which expert systems might gradually improve their performance, by accumulating knowledge and gradually estimating those critical, quantitative parameters associated with certainty. But if you talked to AI people and used the word 'learning' to refer just to estimating parameters they would feel that that is trivializing the idea of learning. Learning is an extremely complex process that involves the acquisition of new concepts, not just refining old ones, with very subtle structural changes in our beliefs and our thinking. That sort of process is what many people are working on and, where uncertainty is involved, I don't think the quantitative approach, which loses many of the underlying dimensions of the uncertainty, will be adequate. We'll need much more emphasis on this propositional side so that the system can learn and acquire new skills in a rational and reliable way.

Q. How should you evaluate an expert system? Should you compare it with a simple number-crunching mathematical model and choose whichever performs best?

A. The evaluation of expert systems is a thorny issue, just as is the evaluation of any kind of decision-making system. It should be said first that very few people ever evaluate, and that is a great pity because we desperately need at this stage of the subject a lot of careful measurement of performance. One of my criteria for choosing the examples I gave is that they have all been reasonably professionally evaluated, so that we can have some idea of just how good they are at medical diagnosis or whatever it is they are working on. In most cases the evaluation is simply done by comparing the performance of the system with the judgement of a human expert or in some cases a panel of experts — which is not entirely satisfactory because it may of course be the case that human experts aren't right and are not the proper 'gold standard', as the jargon has it. Ideally, of course, we would have some sort of objective measure of performance. One of the few studies that I know of where that's been done was in the work I did on digestion. Here we had a database of patients from Leeds Infirmary where the patients' final diagnoses were known, and so we actually had a gold standard that was as close to the correct diagnosis as medicine can get. That was an objective evaluation and it's that kind of evaluation that I think we would all emphasize as the important one, although, of course, in practice it's not always possible because the final diagnosis may not be known.

Q.   It's been shown that when we try to quantify verbal expressions the range of values assigned to the same words and the same contexts is very wide. How do you reconcile that problem?

A.   I'm not suggesting that we use language simply as a cover for numbers; that is, that when we say something is 'probable' we really mean 'somewhere between .5 and .6'. What I'm talking about is actually trying to understand the intentions, the concepts, the ideas behind the term. Even if we do that, your point still remains: people don't always use terms in exactly the same way — the concepts behind them aren't always the same, they vary from individual to individual, from medical school to medical school, from authority to authority. I'm not suggesting we should simply take one person as the authoritative definer of terms, but we should use terms which are acceptable to people but essentially represent a consensus. That's been done many times in every field. People establish a consensus within a professional discipline about how terms are going to be used. I simply extend the idea and say let's be clear about the terminology and the meaning and the definitions of terms in the area of uncertainty.

Q.   Isn't there a problem of how to choose the model on which the inferences are going to be made? In INTERNIST, for example, we had a particular doctor and his methods were studied. Now, why *that* doctor? In other words, what is going to be *the* model to choose from in any given area in an expert system?

A.   A lot of people have suggested that at some point in the future we would like to be able to combine the best features of all these different people. Some people are good at certain sorts of problem solving, perhaps involving imagery, others are good at other sorts of problem solving: maybe we could combine all those skills and indeed knowledge from different people in different areas. But at the moment the expert system's state-of-the-art is such that we don't know how to do that in any disciplined or reliable way.

Q.   One of the things that experts often seem to be very good at is making decisions that aren't necessarily the best possible decisions but are good enough for the purpose in hand. They often seem to be able to do this extremely quickly, under what seem to be adverse conditions, often with a lot of the necessary information missing. I would guess that GPs give reasonable treatment to patients far more often than they correctly diagnose what's wrong with them. Could you comment on that?

A.   Well, I'm no GP and I don't speak for the medical profession. I think it's probably true that an experienced GP has a number of rather high-level strategies, which might be like fail-safe strategies, which he follows to minimize the risk to the patient, for example. After all, the usual statistic is that he has an average six minutes per patient. With so much pressure on you, you've got to have some very general strategy that might not be ideal but which minimizes the risk perhaps for the majority of patients. So the GP might estimate that a particular skin condition is nothing to worry about and say 'Here's some cream — if it doesn't clear up in a couple of weeks, come back.' The system will catch the patient again, if necessary, and then he may be referred to a specialist. That sort of decision making is very tantalizing. There's a lot to be learned from these general strategies that skilled GPs follow. In the past, in expert systems work, we've perhaps pursued the specialist too much and concentrated on the high-grade, specialized doctor who's a whizz in some field, and rather assumed that general practice is an inferior form of this sort of higher level thinking. I don't think this is true. Decision making in those general situations is very different and very interesting, and, in the long run, if expert systems in medicine are going to be helpful to GPs they have got to emulate that kind of decision making as well.

Q. Can you envisage programs on your home computer replacing GPs for things like diagnosing indigestion or measles?

A. There is a big difference between what is technically conceivable (not possible at the moment, but conceivable) and what would be considered by society to be desirable. I think the medical profession would be extremely nervous about that kind of system, not simply for reasons of monopoly, but because one would have no control over how well it was used. This is already a problem — we don't know how big a problem — with medical textbooks: people read such books and imagine they have all sorts of conditions which really they have insufficient training to make a judgement on. I think the dangers are rather obvious in switching from space invaders to an indigestion adviser or a heart disease adviser.

FURTHER READING

Cohen, P. (1985) *Heuristic Reasoning about Uncertainty: an Artificial Intelligence Approach*, Pitman, Boston

Duda, R.O., Hart, P.E., Nilsson, N.J. and Sutherland, G.L. (1978) *Semantic network representations in rule-based inference systems*. In D.A. Waterman and F.R. Hayes-Roth (Eds.) (1978) Pattern-Directed Inference Systems, Academic Press, New York

Fox, J., Barber, D.C. and Bardhan, K.D. (1980) Alternatives to Bayes? A quantitative comparison with rule-based diagnostic inference, *Methods of Information in Medicine*, Vol.19, No.4, pp 210–215

Fox, J. (1985) *Knowledge, decision making and uncertainty*. In W. Gale and D. Pregibon (Eds.) (1985) Proceedings of Workshop on AI and Statistics, Bell Laboratories, Wiley, New York

Hacking, I. (1975) *The Emergence of Probability*, Cambridge University Press, Cambridge

Shortliffe, E.H. (1976) *Computer Based Medical Consultations: MYCIN*, American Elsevier, New York

Spiegelhalter, D.J. and Knill-Jones, R.P. (1984) Statistical and knowledge-based approaches to clinical decision-support systems, with an application to gastroenterology, *J. Royal Statist. Soc. (A)*, Vol.147, No.1, pp 35–77

Weiss, S.M., Kulikowski, C.A., Amarel, S. and Safir, A. (1978) A model-based method for computer-aided medical decision making, *Artificial Intelligence*, Vol.11, pp 145–172

5

AN INTRODUCTION TO PRODUCTION SYSTEMS
RICHARD M. YOUNG
APPLIED PSYCHOLOGY UNIT, CAMBRIDGE

One thing that is frequently mentioned in connection with expert systems is that they are based upon the techniques known as rule-based programming. These techniques include the use of production systems. I'd like to explain what production systems are, and how they work. I'll also try to explain what's meant by the term 'production system architectures', which is rather an odd term. Then I'll move on and draw a distinction between what I'll call 'condition-driven processing' and 'consequent-driven reasoning'. The third point I'd like to cover is 'conflict resolution', which is what you have to do if more than one rule in a production system is applicable.

What is a production system? Let's start with a single production rule. A production rule is a rule that is written like this:

Rule: condition(s) $\longrightarrow$ action(s).

It has an arrow in the middle, and to the left of the arrow, on what is called the left-hand side or the condition side, there's one or more conditions which may or may not be true at a given time. On the right-hand side there are a number of actions. The meaning of the rule is really quite simple: whenever the condition on the left-hand side is true we do what is called 'firing the rule', which means that the system obeys whatever the actions are that are on the right-hand side.

A production system is simply a collection of these rules. In Figure 5.1 I've shown just three of them, but normally there would be many more. The way that the whole system operates is that it first looks to see which rule has its condition side true. It then fires that rule — in other words it carries out the action that's on the right-hand side. Normally that action will change

FIGURE 5.1   A production system as a set of rules

Rule: condition(s) $\longrightarrow$ action(s)

Rule 1: condition$_1$ $\longrightarrow$ action$_1$
Rule 2: condition$_2$ $\longrightarrow$ action$_2$
Rule 3: condition$_3$ $\longrightarrow$ action$_3$

the world or the environment in some way, which means that next time around, if you ask which rule has its condition satisfied, perhaps it will be another rule, and then this rule would fire, and so on and on it goes.

AN ILLUSTRATION

Now to try to make these points a little bit more concrete, I'd like to give you a simple example of a production system. This is to do a box stacking task. Let me tell you how this came about. I was recently visiting a friend of mine, and he was in the middle of moving house. He'd collected together in his office a large number of cardboard boxes, all of different shapes and sizes. In fact I was amazed, because his office was just full of them, and I was trying to help him move these all out from his office to the car to get them home. We thought that in order not to have to go backwards and forwards from the office to the car too many times, we'd pack as many of the boxes inside each other as possible.

I've a simple version of that task in Figure 5.2. The idea is to get them all neatly nested inside each other. Now, if we have a task like this, there are some things that are obviously sensible to

FIGURE 5.2   A simple box stacking task

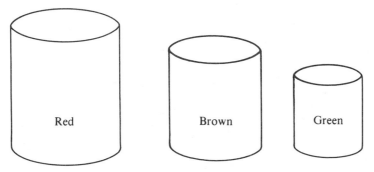

try to do. For example, since we're trying to put boxes inside other boxes, one thing we can think about doing is to pick up two of them (provided there are at least two that we can see) and put the smaller one inside the larger. So I can start writing a production system to do that (Figure 5.3).

FIGURE 5.3   Production system for the box stacking task

        Rule 1: At least two BOXes ⟶ use leftmost two: put smaller in larger
        Rule 2: Only one BOX ⟶ stop

My first rule says that, provided that there are at least two boxes, then we'll use the leftmost two (that's just for the sake of being definite) and we'll put the smaller one inside the larger. Another point that's obvious is that if we have just one large box that's visible, with all the rest inside, then of course we would have finished the task. So Rule 2 is another obvious rule that we can write. Rule 2 says that if we can only see one big box, then we should stop because we've finished. (I'm using 'BOX' to mean that you can see one box, but there may be others inside it; if I write a small 'box' that just means one single box.)

Those rules work properly for some configurations. If I start with that shown in Figure 5.4, then, using the leftmost two, I can put the green one inside the brown one, then the brown one inside the red and that works fine.

FIGURE 5.4　One possible configuration for the boxes

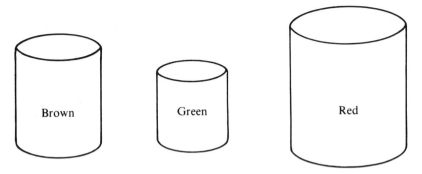

But they don't always work. If I start with a different arrangement (Figure 5.5), then, using the leftmost two, put the green one inside the red one, then the brown one inside the red one, but it doesn't go because the green one is blocking it. That's not covered by either of the rules we've

FIGURE 5.5　Another possible configuration for the boxes

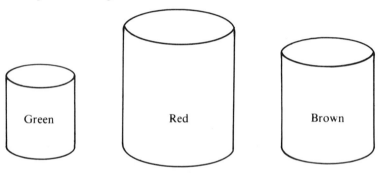

got so far. So obviously I need another rule to cope with this particular situation. So Rule 3 (Figure 5.6) says that if a box doesn't go in we take that box out and the small one inside that's blocking it (that is, stopping it going down as it should do), and we move them both over to the left. The effect of this rule is essentially to give the other rules another chance to have a go. And indeed, using these three rules on the opening arrangement (Figure 5.5), they'll do it properly in this case.

FIGURE 5.6　Adding an extra rule

Rule 1: At least two BOXes ——→ use leftmost two: put smaller in larger
Rule 2: Only one BOX ——→ stop
Rule 3: BOX won't go in ——→ put it and smallest box blocking it at the left.

I'd like now to go through the same task again but to try to give you more of a feel for what it's like actually to have the production system working and the rules firing off one by one. I'll be using a slightly more complicated task, in that I've got an extra box this time (Figure 5.7(a)).

Rule 1 fires, we use the leftmost two boxes and we put the smaller one inside the larger (Figure 5.7(b)).

Rule 1 fires again, again using the leftmost two boxes, putting the smaller inside the larger. But it doesn't go (Figure 5.7(c)).

Rule 3 fires and it says to put that box and the one that's blocking it over to the left (Figure 5.7(d)).

FIGURE 5.7 The production system in action

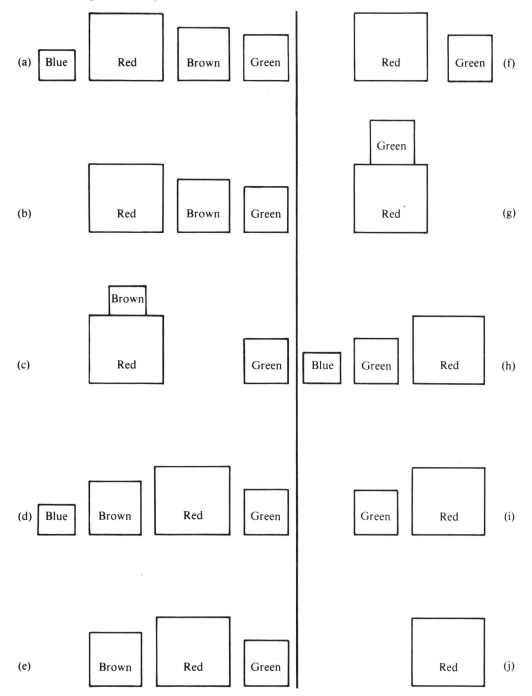

Rule 1, using the leftmost two boxes, puts the smaller into the larger (Figure 5.7(e)).
Rule 1 again, the leftmost two boxes, puts the smaller inside the larger (Figure 5.7(f)).
Rule 1 puts the smaller inside the larger. But it doesn't go (Figure 5.7(g)).
So Rule 3 fires and we put that box and the small one that's blocking it over on the left (Figure 5.7(h)).

Rule 1 again, using the leftmost two boxes puts the smaller inside the larger (Figure 5.7(i)).
Rule 1, using the two boxes there, puts the smaller inside the larger (Figure 5.7(j)).
Now Rule 2 fires and we stop.

Well, we can see that that system works satisfactorily with the configuration we had, but if we have a slightly different configuration to start with (Figure 5.7(k)) then things get a little bit more complicated.

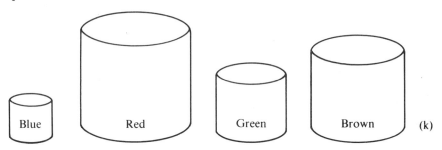

As you can check for yourself, the rules work eventually, but they take an awfully long time doing so. Where there is clearly a predictable difficulty we might as well use any knowledge we have to add rules to speed up the process. If we've got the very small box and the very big box next together on the left, and we begin by putting the smallest in the biggest, that's a bad thing to do because we're going to have to take it out again straightaway. So what we can do with the production system is to encode that little bit of knowledge, that little help, as a hint. We add a fourth rule:

Rule 4: RED and BLUE boxes leftmost and at least one other
$\Longrightarrow$ move third BOX to the left.

It says if you've got the smallest and the biggest box together on the left, don't put one inside the other; instead, take one of the other boxes and move it to the left. Then at least you've got a better starting position, and a chance of getting through to the end more quickly.

I'd like to draw a few lessons from that demonstration. First, notice that the order in which the rules fire is not the same as the order in which they are written down. We don't just simply fire Rule 1, and then Rule 2, then Rule 3, then Rule 4. The firing of the rules is determined by when their left-hand sides become true.

The next point is that, as was shown by the demonstration, the rules have a kind of independence. Each rule can independently and separately decide when it is that it ought to fire.

There's another sense in which the rules are independent, which is that when you consider them one by one they are each in their own right sensible things to do as part of getting the task done. I'm drawing a contrast here with what one might do in ordinary programming, where you think of a method you're using as a whole and a part of it typically only makes sense in relation to that whole. By contrast, if we look at the four box stacking rules one by one: Rule 1 says take two boxes and put the smaller inside the bigger one, which is clearly a sensible thing to do, given what the task is; Rule 2 stays stop when there is only one left, which is simply what we mean by having succeeded with the task; as we also saw, you have to have something to cope with the situation that can arise when one box doesn't go into another, and the sensible thing to do is pull those boxes out and have another go (Rule 3); and Rule 4 gives us independently a sensible kind of hint. (In fact, Rule 4 is redundant with the other rules, but it speeds things up if you have a heuristic like that to help you on your way.) So that's another sense in which the rules are independent.

The third way in which they are independent is that, as we've seen, when necessary it is possible to modify the behaviour of the system by simply adding rules one at a time, perhaps when you realize that some case has arisen that you hadn't previously thought about.

PRODUCTION SYSTEM ARCHITECTURES

I'd like now to go over the same ground again, but a little more systematically and discuss what's called the 'production system architecture', which is a grandiose way of saying how it all fits together.

It is the case that almost all expert systems that I know of conform to something like the overall architecture shown in Figure 5.8. We have a *rule memory*, which is the memory that stores the rules in the form that we've just been looking at. Then, in addition, there's what I call a *working memory*, which is a dynamic memory whose contents change during the course of the problem solving. What's held in there is the information that's specific to that particular problem. Now in principle that may be enough but, typically, expert systems also have a database of more permanent knowledge, the *fact memory*. In the fact memory shown there is some information about plastic gnomes. In a slightly more serious application there may be background information about the permitted dosage levels of particular drugs, if it's a medical application.

FIGURE 5.8   Production system architecture

FACT MEMORY

Item no: 302
Type: Gnome
Style: Plastic

WORKING MEMORY

GOAL = Decorate garden
CASH available = £250

Rule 1: GOAL .... ⟶ CASH ....
Rule 2: TYPE .... ⟶ ....
Rule 3: ...&...   ⟶ ....

RULE MEMORY

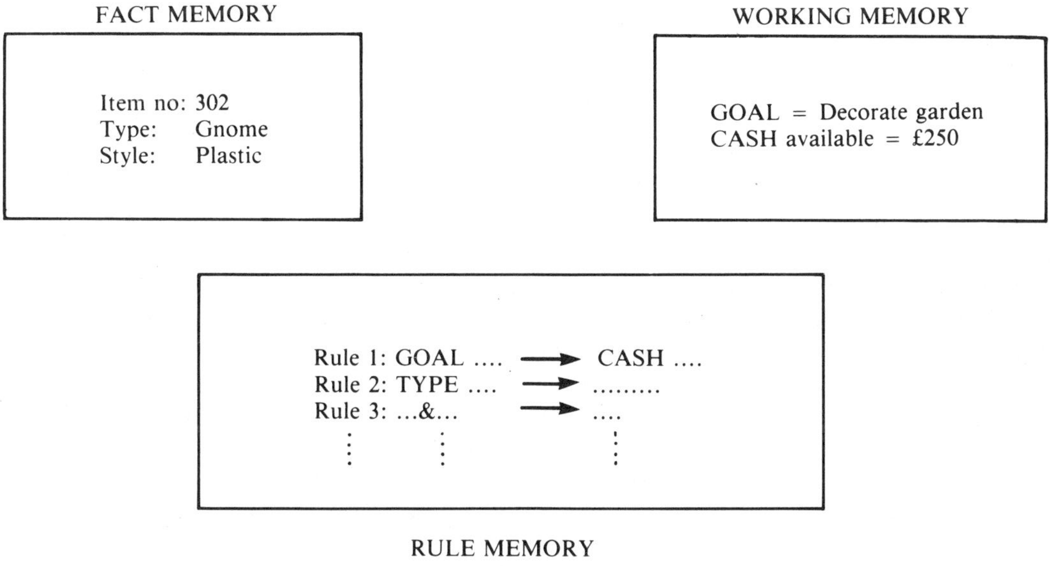

What's meant by a condition being satisfied is that the things written on the left can somehow match onto information in the fact memory or the working memory. So in the first rule (in Figure 5.8) it's specified that the goal is something or other, and this may well match something that's up in the working memory where it says that the goal is to decorate your garden. In the second rule in the rule memory it specifies that there's a certain type of object that might match information in the fact memory where it says that your type is a plastic gnome. So what's meant by a left-hand side being satisfied is that there exists information in the memories which matches onto those conditions.

On the right-hand sides of the rules there are two possibilities. The more straightforward one is that there may be further information there which is to be deposited in the working memory as you go along. Perhaps when Rule 1 fires it asserts some new information, perhaps about the cash you've got available, which then gets written into the working memory and is available to trigger further rules. Sometimes the right-hand sides of rules, though, also cause external behaviour to happen. There may be actions like printing something out on your VDU screen, or perhaps even moving a robot arm. So it's from the right-hand sides that you get the behaviour.

What happens when the production system executes is that we go through a series of cycles. The cycle begins with testing to see which rule has its condition satisfied, by trying the rules against the memory. When we find which rule, we fire the rule; in other words, we do whatever it says on the right-hand side. When we fire the rule we may deposit some new information into the working memory. That of course changes the memory, so we can then go round again to ask which rule is applicable and fire it in its turn. That cycle is often called the 'recognize-act cycle', because sorting out the conditions is 'recognizing' which rule is the right one to fire, and having recognized what to do, you then 'act' it, and then you recycle.

I'd like to try drawing a distinction now between two things which otherwise get a little bit confusing. This is the distinction between *condition-driven processing* and *consequent-driven reasoning*. Figure 5.9 shows two schematics of a production rule, where I've deliberately used a different notation in the different cases. In the first case I'm focusing very much upon actual behaviour. I've written the left-hand side as a condition, and when it's true you take some action. But for the second case I've used a logical notation, where instead of an arrow I have a logical inference symbol. We think of this rule not as doing behaviour, but as carrying out logical inference. In other words, given some facts, which are your antecedent facts, you can

FIGURE 5.9   A production rule using two different notations

$$\text{condition} \implies \text{action}$$
$$\text{(behaviour)}$$

$$\text{antecedent} \supset \text{consequent}$$
$$\text{(inference)}$$

infer from them that some consequent is true. Typically this is used, as it were, going the wrong way round from right to left; where, given some desired consequent that we would like to be true, we come back and we ask whether the antecedents are true.

In the case of condition-driven processing, which I've really been assuming up to this point, there are two flavours to a right-hand side, whether it produces actual behaviour like moving a robot arm, or whether it just deposits new information in the memory. The way that we were going through before, we were deriving this behaviour from the conditions. Some configuration arose in the memories that meant that some rule had its condition satisfied, which meant that we took some action.

I'd like to give a comparable example now which goes the other way round, in which we are going to be doing inference, driven from the consequent side. So we're doing consequent-driven reasoning.

I've again changed the notation deliberately to make it look more like ordinary logic. So in Figure 5.10 we have a memory full of facts, such that there is somebody called Margaret who's a human, there's someone called Mark who's a human, and that Mark is the son of Margaret. We also have a number of rules: the first rule says that anyone who is human is also mortal. The second rule says that somebody who has poor judgement will make mistakes. The third rule says that somebody who is mortal eats food. And the fourth rule says that somebody who's mortal makes mistakes. Of course, as ever, in practice you would expect to have many more rules than that.

FIGURE 5.10   Consequent-driven reasoning

FACTS

Human (Margaret)
Human (Mark)
Son-of (Mark, Margaret)

RULES

Rule 1: Human (x) ⊃ Mortal (x)
Rule 2: Poor-judgement (x) ⊃ Makes-mistakes (x)
Rule 3: Mortal (x) ⊃ Eats-food (x)
Rule 4: Mortal (x) ⊃ Makes-mistakes (x)

Now let's look at an example of how this system operates, and remember that this time we're not going to be driven from the conditions to the right-hand side but instead we are going to focus on the right-hand sides, on the consequents. Suppose our goal is to conclude that Mark makes mistakes (see Figure 5.11). Now what we do with a consequent-driven system is firstly to look through our fact memory, and if we don't find there what we want then we look down the right-hand sides, the consequents, of the logical rules to see whether there is any rule there that looks like it gives a conclusion of the kind we're interested in. Is there a rule that would

FIGURE 5.11   The system in operation

conclude something like Mark makes mistakes? Yes, Rule 2. But Rule 2 could only fire if in fact we could show that Mark has poor judgement. Now that does not actually get us anywhere because we don't know that Mark has poor judgement: it's not in the fact memory, and there is no rule which has that conclusion on its right-hand side. But, if we try again, we notice that there's another rule, Rule 4, which also concludes that somebody makes mistakes. So another possibility is to think that Mark makes mistakes if Mark is mortal. So can we show that Mark is mortal? Once again we don't know that that's the case from the facts, but there is a very handy rule, Rule 1, which will conclude that somebody is mortal, if we know that that person is human. If we can imagine Rule 1 firing (if we could show that that person was human) then we would be home and dry. Indeed, we do know that Mark is human because we are told that in the fact memory.

So, by working backwards, we are able to show that our goal is true, by using the rules as it were from the right-hand side back to the left-hand side. That run-through of how such a system works is actually very similar to the way that so-called logic programming languages work. If you were to look at a trace of a PROLOG program running it would produce a tree very much in the same style as that shown in Figure 5.11.

THREE EXAMPLES

I'd like to go on to show the way one fleshes out this framework to be more like a real expert system.

I'm going to use real examples, but these are somewhat old ones. The reason for this is that I want to use them as examples to illustrate as clearly as possible the points I'm making. In fact, I suspect that what I'm saying about the systems is not always 100 per cent true, but I think you can take it as 95 per cent true.

For each of the examples, I'm going to discuss them under four headings. I'm first of all going to ask, 'When you're at the beginning of the cycle, which of the rules are relevant?' So our first heading is *relevance*. There's then the question of 'How do you know which rules are true?', or, in other words, 'How do the left-hand sides become satisfied?' That's the issue of *evaluation*. (Evaluation here doesn't mean how good the expert system is.) I will then deal with the question of 'Which one or ones do we fire?' and, in particular, if there is more than one applicable and we only want one, 'How do we choose which one?'. That comes under the heading of *conflict resolution*. And, finally, there's the question of 'What will we then have to do?' I'll take that under the heading of *action*. I'll look at three systems now, one by one.

MYCIN

The first one is MYCIN, which advises on the diagnosis of bacteriological infections. I'll assume that you've actually heard about this program before: I just want to show how it maps onto our framework.

MYCIN is a much-quoted example of a consequent-driven system. In other words, unlike the boxes that we were dealing with before, we don't get driven by asking 'Which rule has its condition satisfied?' — we ask instead, 'What is the conclusion that we would like to draw?' and, given that, 'Are there any rules around which look like they would draw that conclusion if it were the case that they could be fired?' The rules that are relevant, therefore, are all those rules whose consequents match our current goal. When we're trying to conclude that this person has a certain disease, or perhaps that he doesn't have that disease, we look for all the rules that mention the disease in their conclusion. Those are the rules we think of as being relevant.

How do we evaluate the rules? Well, as always, of course, we have to check whether the left-hand sides are true. With condition-driven rules, like the boxes, when you come to fire the rule you only do that if you already know that the conditions are satisfied. With the consequent-driven rules, however, having chosen the rule that you'd like to fire, you then have to face the question of 'Are its left-hand side conditions in fact true?' So taking up a particular relevant rule leads us to ask questions about whether the left-hand side is satisfied.

Finally, with MYCIN we come on to conflict resolution, i.e. with what happens if there is more than one rule in the system which is true. The answer is that, more or less (this is where the 95 per cent comes in), you fire all of them. MYCIN has ways of combining the conclusions of different rules. For example, if there are two independent rules, both of which lead to the same conclusion, they both fire. Then MYCIN somehow strengthens that conclusion, because there are two independent arguments that lead to it. MYCIN has this notion of how strongly it believes in some particular hypothesis, so you can always strengthen it.

RITA

The next example is the system called RITA, which was an intelligent agent to help you at your terminal, particularly if you were trying to use computers remotely. Everytime I try logging on to a network, I have to log on to four different computer systems in succession. They all have the same general kind of feel to them, but the details are different. And when I try to come out of them, I have to say 'quit' for one of them, and 'control E' for another one, and 'logout' for another one, and it gets very confusing. So it would be very nice to have a little agent sitting inside my desktop micro who knew about the logging on process, and how to find out if I've got any mail, etc., and that's what RITA was intended to do.

The main characteristic of interest is that it used what's called explicit rule ordering. In other words, the rules were written in a particular order, and, unlike the examples I've been describing so far, that order mattered. The interpreter tested each rule in turn, to see whether its conditions were satisfied. If it found a rule whose conditions were satisfied then it fired it. So mapping that on to our framework, it says that, in principle, all the rules are potentially relevant at any one time. Now there's a question mark on that because if you've got a very large rule set, for efficiency reasons you may break it up into sub-procedures which are all relevant to particular goals. But certainly in principle all the rules are potentially relevant.

The evaluation, of course, is just to test the left-hand sides to see whether they are true. We have a condition-driven system again.

The conflict resolution, as we've just seen, is that the system fires the first rule in the linear ordering which it finds is true. A simple interpeter like that has some advantages and some disadvantages. One of the advantages is that it makes for an interpreter which you can hack together in BASIC in an hour or two. But of course it doesn't mean that it's a very efficient interpreter. Another advantage is that, because of its simplicity, it's quite easy (provided you've got a small number of rules) to hand simulate them. In other words, it's easy to look at the rules and see how they are going to behave.

But there are some disadvantages in using the written order as an important part of the system. Essentially, you start to lose all the advantages you've gained by using production systems in the first place. In particular, you start losing the independence of the rules, which was something I stressed very much earlier on. When you have a new rule, for example, you now have the issue of 'where do I put it?', which was not a question that arose before, because it didn't make any difference. Now, of course, it makes a difference whether a new rule goes near the top before some other rules, or further down nearer the end, in which case there may be some other rules that are fired before you ever get to it.

Equally, when you're writing a new rule, or even one of the original rules, you've got to be very aware of what the other rules are that are going to be in the system, or that are already in the system. Similarly, if you are doing anything like rewriting the system, or perhaps doing some automatic learning on it, you may have to consider reordering the rules, which is a very messy procedure and gets you into all the difficulties of automatic programming, which we'd tried to avoid by keeping the rules independent. So there are definite disadvantages to having explicit rule ordering.

OPS

The third example is a production system interpreter called OPS, and in particular OPS5. This has become very well known because it was used for a system originally called R1 that was written by John McDermott for Digital Equipment Corporation to configure VAXs.

It's again a condition-driven production system, so we're driving from the left-hand side conditions. All rules are potentially relevant, and so at any one time any rule whose condition is satisfied might fire. There is a very efficient network into which the rules get compiled so that the system can run very fast.

The evaluation involves, as ever, asking whether the left-hand sides are satisfied. The network in which it's implemented gives you an efficient way of finding rapidly which are the rules whose conditions are satisfied. But then there may be more than one such rule, so what we do then is to move into conflict resolution and say, 'How do we choose the one rule to fire?'

When we're going through at this point in the cycle and asking about which rules have their left-hand sides true, all those rules together are called the *conflict set*, because they are the rules that potentially conflict with each other. What OPS does with the conflict set will depend on how many rules there are in it (Figure 5.12). The first two conditions are fairly obvious. If the conflict set has size zero, in other words there are no rules that are true, then there is nothing the production system can do, so you stop. Equally obviously, if there is only one rule which is true then of course that's the rule you choose to fire. More interesting is when there's more than one rule in the conflict set, when you really need to apply conflict resolution. The conflict resolution gets carried out by asking a series of questions about these rules.

FIGURE 5.12   The conflict set

Instantiations of all satisfied rules ⟶ conflict set

If $|CS| = 0$ stop
If $|CS| = 1$ fire that one
If $|CS| > 1$ then ...

The first principle is *refractoriness*, which means that the system never fires the same rule more than once matched to a particular set of data. This is a very useful property to have. Typically, what happens is that some situation arises in a production system, some rule becomes true and fires, and, unless you do something about it, such as undoing one of the things that made the rule true, that rule will still be satisfied after it has fired so it has always got the potential for firing again. So, with most production systems, there's a tendency to have infinite loops of the same rule firing over and over again. Having refractoriness with the production system architecture takes care of that for you: you don't have to do any special housekeeping in order to prevent it happening.

Another principle is called *recency*. This means that rules which are matched by data that's recently come into the working memory take precedence over the rules that only match on data that's been around for a longer time. In fact, I pulled a fast one on you earlier on when we were doing the boxes, because there we relied quite heavily upon this principle of recency, even though I didn't mention it. You will remember that one of the rules there said that if there are more than two boxes then you take the leftmost two and put the smaller one inside the larger one. Well of course that rule is always true as long as there are at least two boxes around. So it should be always saying, 'I'm the one to fire.' But we had another rule that said that when a box won't go in then there's something else you may do. Because that has only just now become true, by the recency ordering, that's the rule that would take priority over the other rule that deals with two boxes. So we were in fact using this principle earlier on.

A third thing that OPS does in conflict resolution is give priority to what are called *special case rules*. Imagine having two rules, both of which are true but one of which is more specific than the other one; for example, it may have more conditions, or it may specify more particular conditions instead of just having variables that will match anything. We had such a rule, the fourth rule, which was a much more special rule than the more general ones because rather than just asking 'Have you got any two boxes at the end?', it asked, 'Have you got the particular two which are the very largest one and the very smallest one?' This principle says that if a special rule is true than it's the one to give priority to.

The effect of all these in conjunction is normally to come out with just one rule, which is the one that is fired. This multi-step conflict resolution is very important in governing the behaviour of an interpreter like OPS. It's responsible, for example, for focusing attention. In other words, you've got some task going along and there are various things you might do, but at any one time you are trying to do something particular, you're trying to solve a sub-problem of the overall problem. If we are working on a sub-problem, or we've just got some new information about it, and if there's some rule around which is looking out for that new information, then because of recency that's the one that will fire, even though there may also be some other rules around that could fire given what's known so far. But it's the new information that determines what fires, so the effect, particularly of recency, is to keep you focused on the current sub-problem.

But, equally, recency also gives you a sensitivity to new data. Imagine you've got something like a real-time system where there is information coming in independently of the processing you're doing. Maybe suddenly a fire alarm rings and that becomes information in the memory. Then because that's recent information it guarantees that any rule around that will respond to that is the one that takes control next. So this multi-step conflict resolution is an important factor in getting sensible behaviour out of the production system.

There are just two more points I'd like to touch upon briefly to do with properties of production systems. One is that so far I've been talking as if things were always black and white, that either a condition side of a rule matches, or else it doesn't. Now this is certainly true with RITA and OPS and similar production system interpreters, but there are also production systems around which have a notion of graded matching or partial matching. In other words, rather than saying, 'Does this item exist in the working memory so that we can match it?', we can say, 'How well does the left-hand side of this rule match on working memory?' Maybe it matches, but not particularly well, whereas some other rule has conditions which are more solidly satisfied. If you have a system like that, then there is an obvious conflict resolution method, which is that you choose the rule whose left-hand side is best satisfied. This idea of having a partial match also comes up a little bit in a system like MYCIN, where you do get this notion that a conclusion is not necessarily black or white, but can be held with a degree of confidence. But I should point out that in MYCIN the confidence factors, although they say how confident the system is in a particular answer, tend not to influence what happens very much, because in MYCIN you do everything you can anyway.

The final point I'd like to talk about as a property of production systems is to come back to something I mentioned earlier, which is their interesting flexibility of control. There's an implicit contrast here with more ordinary programming languages, such as FORTRAN and COBOL, and also with LISP. Whereas normally the program itself specifies the order in which things are to happen, with a production system it has much more of the flavour that the order is determined by the data, the situation, or the circumstances in which it finds itself.

Let me give you one illustration of this that you may have noticed earlier on with the boxes. With this task there are essentially two quite different ways of setting about it. One is to start with the biggest box, then take the next biggest one and put that inside it, and then the next biggest one, and so on. Alternatively, you start from the other end, by putting the smallest one into the next smallest one, picking up both, and then putting them inside the next smallest, and so on. So you can, as it were, start with the biggest one or start with the smallest one. If you can imagine a program written in PASCAL to do the task you would definitely plump for one or other of those techniques. Now the rules I gave, which are in fact a general purpose sorting algorithm (although they didn't look like a standard one), don't care which way they do it. They'll do it either way, depending on the circumstances. They may start from the smallest one or they may start from the biggest one, or, as we saw happen, they might put a couple of small ones together and a couple of big ones together and then put the small ones inside the big ones. The actual behaviour in terms of which method is used depends very much upon the particular configuration that we have.

CONCLUSION

Let me summarize what I've said about production systems and production system architectures. People sometimes ask, and it's an obvious thing to ask, given that I've laid out these examples of three different production system architectures (and of course there are many more, some of them available on the market), 'What kind of architecture is most appropriate for what kind of task?' The first answer to this is that we can't really say, for we just don't have enough experience and enough understanding to be able to say beforehand that for this sort of task in your application you should go off and use a backward driven interpreter, or whatever.

But there are a number of things that it makes sense to bear in mind about the relevant properties of the different kinds of architectures. We've seen that a production system driven by the left-hand side conditions to the right-hand side actions tends to have this flavour of producing actual behaviour. Whereas the consequent-driven system, reasoning from the right-hand side back to the left-hand side, has much more of this flavour of reasoning, trying to figure something out.

Similarly, the condition-driven engine tends to feel like one that runs repeatedly through a series of very simple cycles one after another, the recognize-act cycle. Whereas the backward reasoning system tends to start from its final goal and generate a complete and perhaps quite large tree of possibilities, which then needs exploring. With a system like that the behaviour often comes out as a side effect. For example, you start asking questions of the user about the patient he's trying to diagnose, as a side effect of trying to establish which rules have their left-hand side satisfied.

Now, bearing in mind that contrast, I do have a definite suggestion to make. If you've got a 'problem' to solve, which is essentially a reasoning task, then perhaps the consequent-driven system is an appropriate kind of architecture to use. Whereas if your task is one that involves real behaviour, perhaps controlling a robot in real time, or processing signals as they come in, then the condition-driven processing feels like it's much more the right thing to do.

Finally, let me summarize what we've said about the different issues mentioned at the beginning. On production systems, we've seen that the system is just a collection of rules, and that the architecture essentially specifies how it is that those rules get executed and obeyed. We've seen the distinction between condition-driven processing and consequent-driven reasoning. And for the conflict resolution techniques we've seen that although they can be very simple they can also be quite complex, and that the method used for doing conflict resolution can be an important consideration in getting sensible behaviour out of your production system.

QUESTIONS

Q.   Your final effort with the tin cans when, in effect, you measured them and took the largest and put the next smallest in it and so on was a much more efficient way of approaching the problem than the one we started with, where we had to go through several roundabouts in order to arrive at a solution. Is there a sense in which efficiency is an important issue here? I expected that some of your discussion on conflict resolution would actually mention the word efficiency. Does that make sense?

A.   Yes, it makes perfect sense, but I'd question your assumption. There is certainly a method for doing this task where, as you say, one can start with the smallest and then the next smallest, and so on. But if you simply say that, you're hiding a lot away, because you then have to ask, 'What does it actually take to find which one is the smallest?' Now, if we've just got four cans in front of us, we can look at it and see. But if you expand that out it essentially becomes the whole task again, and so if you were to write rules for that you'd see they were the same rules (or equivalent rules) to the ones we had. As for the second part of your question, I would certainly say that conflict resolution techniques make a lot of difference to the efficiency and that, for example, the focus of attention you get by using recent data to determine what you do is an important contributing factor.

Q.   The point about partially matching something worries me. Is it possible in some of these production systems to take it one step further and develop systems that actually have the intelligence to change the rules themselves? I'm thinking in particular of a doctor's diagnostic system where he's checking particular symptoms of a particular patient — not all the symptoms match the rules but a few do, and so we have actually a change in our system or our facts about that disease.

A.   There are two separate points in that question. One of them concerns the relation between having intelligence and doing partial matching. Talking about having real intelligence in an artificial intelligence situation is a contentious thing to do and I wouldn't want to get into deep water, but certainly we have the benefit of an 'official line' on that. The official line is that the intelligence is in the knowledge, and what we're buying by using production systems is a useful encoding of the knowledge into rules. If you want to have a system that behaves intelligently, then structuring it in the form of a production system is, so the argument goes, a good way to set about it.

You also touched on the question of learning — in other words, can we write a production system that learns as it goes along? Now, this is an active research area and you're quite right that there is a connection between learning and using rule-based systems, because of properties such as the independence of rules; that is, the fact that you can state a rule meaningfully without having to worry about what other rules there are and where it fits in. It's a very nice medium in which automatic learning can apply. If you look at the learning systems around, almost all of them do their learning on a rule basis. So there is a connection in terms of techniques, but we've got a long way to go. At the moment, we're not in a position to emulate a doctor's learning even though we can write systems that do a little bit of what the doctor does once he has learned.

Q.   You mentioned the programming languages BASIC, PASCAL and PROLOG. Are there any packages that you would recommend me to take away to get some idea of what this sort of system can do for me?

A.   Yes, there are some 'expert system shells'. A shell is an expert system without any rules inside it — it's all the trappings and the interpreter. That means that rather than having to start from scratch and write your own interpreter, you can buy one and then start typing some rules in. You get a little expert system that you can play with very quickly that way. I won't say any more about it, and I certainly won't make any recommendations.

Q. With a set of production rules is there any chance that there could be inconsistencies?

A. Absolutely. I said nothing about the correctness of the information that goes into the rules, and so there's nothing as far as the architecture goes that stops you putting in plain nonsense or things that are contradictory. Again, there's research which worries about this as a real problem — the difficulty arises even with databases, let alone intelligent rule-based systems. There are techniques that people work on which worry about how you keep the rule base consistent, how you detect any inconsistencies that arise, and how you keep track of how the conclusions that you've reached depend upon assumptions that you've made in the rule base in order to know what to undo when something else turns out wrong. So it's a very real issue, and certainly nothing I've said about the architectures can guarantee that you won't get contradictions or just be plain wrong — that depends on the information you put in.

FURTHER READING

There is, unfortunately, no good general introduction to production systems, whether for expert systems or otherwise. A collection of relevant papers, though beginning to get a little dated is:
Waterman, D.A. and Hayes-Roth, F. (Eds.) (1978) *Pattern-Directed Inference Systems*, Academic Press, New York

For a slightly different application of production systems, see:
Young, R.M. (1980) *Production systems for modelling human cognition.* In D. Michie (Ed.) (1980) Expert Systems in the Micro-Electronic Age, Edinburgh University Press, Edinburgh

For the three particular systems referred to in the text, see:
Shortliffe, E.H. (1976) *Computer Based Medical Consultations: MYCIN*, American Elsevier, New York
Waterman, D.A. (1978) *Exemplary programming in RITA.* In Waterman, D.A. and Hayes-Roth, F. (see above)
McDermott, J. (1982) R1: a rule-based configurer of computer systems, *Artificial Intelligence*, Vol.19, pp 39–88

For more about conflict resolution strategy, see:
McDermott, J. and Forgy, C. (1978) *Production system conflict resolution strategies.* In Waterman, D.A. and Hayes-Roth, F. (see above)

6

LOGIC PROGRAMMING IN ARTIFICIAL INTELLIGENCE AND SOFTWARE ENGINEERING

ROBERT KOWALSKI

IMPERIAL COLLEGE, LONDON

I would like to look at the role of logic programming in Artificial Intelligence and Software Engineering, and in particular at its potential application to the systems analysis stage of software development. I shall argue that logic programming allows us to execute systems analysis; and in some cases the execution is efficient enough to avoid the need for separate specifications and programs altogether. I would like to look at the British Nationality Act as a particular example, which is closely related to data processing — the execution of rules and regulations whether they have legal binding authority or not. I would like to mention some of the other interrelationships between Software Engineering and AI. And finally I shall discuss some of the human implications of the technology.

THE FIFTH GENERATION

The Japanese have identified the importance of Artificial Intelligence applications (Figure 6.1). They have identified logic programming as the underlying software technology; and they have identified new kinds of computer architectures. Certainly their new applications can be understood by the person on the street; and the electronics engineer can understand the computer architectures. But until the Japanese drew attention to the logic programming software, most computer scientists had either rejected it or knew nothing about it.

The conventional computer scientist's view of computing is conventional not only with respect to the applications and the hardware, but also with respect to software methodology: conventional number-crunching, scientific and commercial applications, executed on computers that run sequentially, have to be told every step, and cannot make any decisions for themselves. And how do we bridge the gap between the conventional application and the conventional computer? By using conventional software engineering techniques (Figure 6.2).

Feigenbaum and McCorduck in their book on the Fifth Generation emphasize a very

FIGURE 6.1   The underlying components of artificial intelligence applications

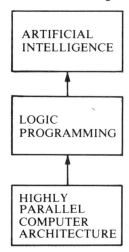

FIGURE 6.2   The conventional view of computing

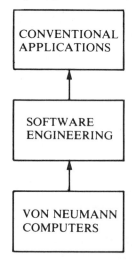

valuable, focal part of the Fifth Generation, its novel expert systems applications. They play down the new computer architectures and the logic programming software. I do not want to argue here that PROLOG is better than LISP or that PROLOG is suitable for all applications today. I would argue, however, that the new technology associated with logic programming supports not only new applications but old applications as well (Figure 6.3).

Thus I would argue that we must distinguish between technologies and applications. The new software technologies, of which logic programming is the most representative, not only enable new applications in areas such as expert systems and natural language processing, but also facilitate the implementation of old applications as well. They support a variety of software development methodologies, not only old ways of programming but also new ways of developing programs.

So what is this new technology? The new technology is characterized by the fact that it allows knowledge to be represented explicitly, disentangled from the way it is used to solve problems. The computer uses its knowledge to solve problems by reasoning deductively in a manner which simulates human reasoning, and which is congenial therefore to human thinking and to human–machine interaction. This means that compared with conventional software the new software helps us better to see the knowledge and therefore better to understand it. This means that we can develop knowledge in an incremental fashion, because it's not tangled together with the manner in which it is used. And it is easier to modify, if we've made a mistake or if the knowledge changes, as it does very frequently in applications such as the formalization of legislation.

FIGURE 6.3   New technology can support old applications

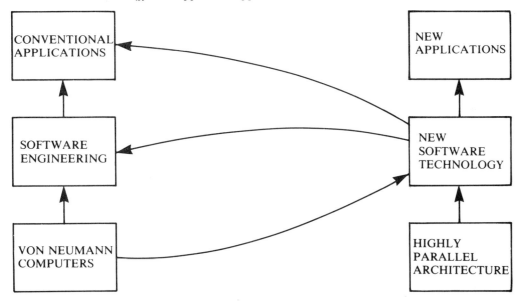

THE NEW TECHNOLOGY IN THE SOFTWARE DEVELOPMENT LIFE CYCLE

Let's look at the place of the new software technology in the conventional software development life cycle, as pictured for example by DeMarco (Figure 6.4).

I want to draw particular attention to the bottom path of the diagram, which is concerned with software. We start with the user requirement, namely the problem the user has or thinks he has. We analyze the requirement, construct a functional specification of a computer-based solution to the problem, and then design a software system which we eventually implement as a program in a well-structured top-down manner.

The *data flow diagram*, which describes the software development life cycle, is itself a convenient tool for systems analysts to interact with users in the analysis stage of the software development life cycle. It's a language which systems analysts have developed to communicate better with people. But data flow diagrams can also be interpreted as an alternative, graphical syntax for rule-based programming. Take for example the rule in Figure 6.5, which expresses that company x is a potential customer for product y if x has some work of type z and product y is suitable for z. A systems analyst would express this in terms of processes and data flow between processes, and picture these graphically in the form of a data flow diagram, as in Figure 6.5.

I would like to argue that the data flow diagram differs only in syntax from the logic-based language which has been chosen for the software basis of the Japanese Fifth Generation

FIGURE 6.4   Software development life cycle (from DeMarco, 1978)

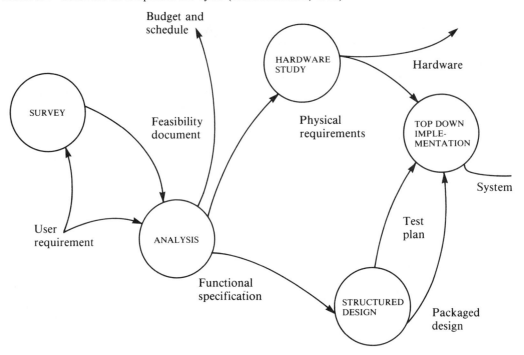

project. It is equivalent in semantics to a language of conclusion-condition rules:

x is a potential customer for product y
    if   x has work of type z
    and y is suitable for z.

The title of the diagram explains the purpose for which the processes in the diagram are to be used. In this particular example the purpose is to find products to sell to customers. This constitutes the *conclusion* of the rule, namely that some product y is suitable for the potential customer x. The processes, which are represented inside the diagram and drawn within circles, constitute the *conditions* that have to be satisfied for the conclusion of the rule to hold. The first process finds some type of work z which the customer has. The second finds a product y which is suitable for z.

FIGURE 6.5   x is a potential customer for system y

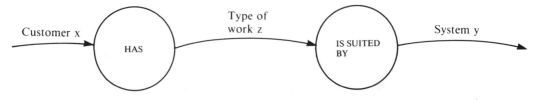

This example shows that logic-based programming is not necessarily programming, or even formal specification. In this example, logic-based programming is an *executable analysis* of the user requirement. Therefore it can assist the conventional software development life cycle at the earliest possible stage. The user requirement can be analyzed and executed before we construct a functional specification, design, or program. We can execute the analysis to test whether it conforms to the user's view of the requirement; and therefore we can eliminate misunderstandings at the earliest possible stage, before they give rise to further misunderstandings.

How is it that we can execute such rules? It is probably the main idea behind logic programming that the application of backward reasoning to conclusion-condition rules turns them into procedures. If we know, for example, the potential customer x as in the data flow diagram and we want to find something to sell him, then the procedure we obtain by using the rule backwards in a targetted, goal-directed fashion reduces the problem to two sub-problems: Find what kind of work the customer has and find something that is suitable for that work. That at least is one procedure. It is a procedure expressed in human terms, which reduces problems to sub-problems until eventually they need no further reduction. I can communicate such a procedure to a salesman who might know nothing about computers. Moreover, whether we use a computer or not, the two sub-problems can be solved sequentially by a single problem-solver or they can be solved in parallel, as they might be on a Fifth Generation Computer of the future.

But there is more to it than that; there is more than one procedure here. The data flow diagram has done disservice to the knowledge. It's not simply that we have a procedure which takes a customer and finds something to sell him. The same knowledge can be used to find customers for particular products: If we want to find a customer x for a given product y, find out what type of work the product can be used for and find some customer who has that kind of work. The knowledge can be used more flexibly than the systems analyst has seen and more flexibly than the user has required. What's wrong with conventional software engineering in this instance is that there is more knowledge hidden away in the user than simply his perception of the user requirement.

Structured systems analysis has its *strengths*; and the use of the new software technology to execute systems analysis adds to those strengths. Among its strengths are the fact that data flow diagrams themselves are a convenient, graphical language for communicating with users. They are sufficiently precise for the systems analyst to express what the user thinks he requires — so precise in fact that they can be translated automatically into rules which execute as procedures.

Data flow diagrams also provide a powerful tool for controlling scale and complexity. DeMarco's rule is that you limit the size of a data flow diagram to a single sheet of standard sized paper (A4 in the metric system). As soon as you need to go outside the sheet of paper you expand some process by means of a lower-level data flow diagram on another sheet of paper.

What are its *weaknesses*? Users don't know what they want; and often, when they do, they don't need what they want. So we have to determine what really is the case by starting from what users believe to be the case, using that as a clue to the knowledge that is locked inside. I believe that the declarative form in which knowledge can be expressed using logic programming technology gives us a way of liberating users from their mistaken perceptions of their problems and of using the knowledge they have for bigger and better purposes.

What are some of the solutions for the weaknesses of structured systems analysis proposed by such critics as James Martin? Perhaps the most popular is *rapid prototyping*. You prototype the solution to your problem as quickly and early as you can in the software life cycle. But how do you implement the prototype? In most cases, with a programming language, which was designed for the final stage of software development. The new logic-based software technology allows us to implement prototypes using languages designed for systems analysis, the first stage of software development after the preliminary feasibility study.

If you don't use a programming language you use fourth generation program generators. And what are they? In many cases they are simply generic, parameterized programs which can be tailored for a particular application by the user selecting a particular combination of answers to a predetermined menu of options. In other cases they are based upon the database approach. So let's look at databases.

Increasingly, the relational database approach is beginning to give way to the logic base approach, an approach which is very closely related to logic-based programming. This can be illustrated again by our rule relating potential customers to products. The rule can be regarded as a query generator. Given a problem of relating customers to products, it generates the query:

'find some type of work z for the customer x for which the product y is suitable'

In relational database terminology, the two conditions of the rule are joined together by the relational join operator. But this is not simply a query to a conventional relational database, where all knowledge is stored explicitly in the form of tables. Rather it is a query whose conditions are evaluated by other rules (or, equivalently, by other procedures). Thus rules behave as procedures which generate queries, and those queries are answered by applying other rules which generate queries in turn.

Thus logic-based software technology unifies executable systems analysis with databases containing rules as well as explicitly stored data. But what does this new software technology have to do with expert systems?

EXPERT SYSTEMS

The following example shows how well suited this new technology is to expert systems applications. This example comes from a logical reconstruction by Peter Hammond at Imperial College of an expert system originally implemented in the expert system shell EMYCIN by Peter Alvey at the Imperial Cancer Research Institute in London. The rule starts out in exactly the same way as the rule for selling products to customers, but this time we are concerned with treating patients. The rule expresses that a patient should take some treatment if the patient has a complaint which the treatment suppresses. But with a human patient we are more likely to care whether the cure is worse than the disease. In its final form, therefore, the rule has one conclusion and three conditions:

x should take y **if**   x has complaint z
                   and y suppresses z
                   and not y unsuitable for x.

Notice, in this example, another feature of declarative languages: how easy it is to modify knowledge when the knowledge is made explicit. Suppose our first formulation of the rule contained only the first two conditions and made the mistake, therefore, of treating humans the same as companies. If later we should decide the rule is too wide-sweeping, for whatever reason, we can restrict its application by adding extra conditions. Such changes can be understood and explained in declarative, human terms, without needing to consider their effect on the behaviour of a computer.

Notice too that we are only looking at a top-level rule, concerned with the goal of relating patients and treatments. We can unravel the conditions of the rule: what does it mean to say that y suppresses z, what does it mean to say that y is not unsuitable for x? We can unravel the conditions top-down in the same way that structured systems analysis unravels data flow diagrams. Here the negative condition

not y unsuitable for x

is assumed to hold if (and only if) the positive condition

y unsuitable for x

cannot be established. This treatment of negation is known as negation as failure.

y is unsuitable for x **if**   y aggravates u in x
                      and x has condition u

aspirin suppresses inflammation
aspirin suppresses pain
   etc.

aspirin aggravates peptic ulcer in x
lomotil aggravates impaired liver function in x
alcohol aggravates high blood pressure in x
                  if   x is over 40
                  and x is obese.

This example illustrates that we can use the new software technology both to implement new expert systems applications as well as to assist the computerization of the conventional software development life cycle. But we can do better. We can change the nature of computing itself and the nature of the software methodology which services it. We can make computers understand knowledge expressed in human terms and make them use that knowledge flexibly in different ways for different purposes. We can make them understand logic directly as their native language.

Such computers will solve problems in a manner which approximates human problem-solving and consequently will change the nature of *human–computer interaction*. If the computer needs to solve a problem, it can use its knowledge to reduce the problem to sub-problems or it can ask the user. Why should the computer know everything itself? It needs to do so only if the human reasons so differently from the computer that the two cannot naturally interact. But if the two work harmoniously within the same problem-solving paradigm, then the human can play an intimate part in the computer-based problem-solving process.

The computer can *explain* a conclusion by quoting the rules it has used to reach its conclusion. We can accept the explanation or reject it. We can use the explanation to reach a different conclusion. It's a common characteristic of human decision making that when we ask people for advice we want to hear their arguments in support of their conclusions. Having heard their arguments, we need to decide whether we agree with them or not, whether we accept the assumptions which justify their conclusions or not. This allows us to stay in control.

LEGISLATION AS A CRITICAL APPLICATION

Legislation is a particularly critical application, an application which illustrates that executable analysis can be sufficiently efficient that none of the later stages of conventional software development are required. On the other hand, legislation is by no means trivial. It requires complex knowledge representation and reasoning. It is more complex than such typical AI applications as understanding children's stories. So in one respect legislation is a harder domain to tackle. In another respect it is easier.

In AI we are inundated with problems of ambiguity. Researchers in natural language processing seem to welcome such ambiguity. In the case of legislation there may be ambiguities; but it is not, or should not be, the intention of the legislator to put them there. Legislation is an ideal domain for tackling hard problems of knowledge representation and problem solving without being sidetracked by potentially irrelevant issues.

The formalization of legislation also illustrates the incremental method of software development by *trial and error*. If we were writing programs when we represent the meaning of legislation by trial and error, then we would be bad programmers. Good programmers start with rigid, or at least formal, software specifications and then implement them correctly first time round. So a PROLOG programmer who is always correcting errors in his programs is a bad programmer. But for a person who is using PROLOG not as a programming language, not even as a formal specification language, but as a language for analyzing the knowledge that lies behind the user requirement, trial and error is unavoidable. Even mathematicians prove theorems and develop axiomatic theories by trial and error.

The formalization of rules and regulations is representative of a much wider class of applications. It is applicable whenever an organization uses rules to regulate its affairs, whether or not they have legal, binding authority.

What function do regulations serve? Having rules means not having to deal with each problem as it arises, as if no similar problem had arisen in the past. It means deciding what the general rules are, so that different customers are treated equally, applying the same criteria to one as we do to another.

Indeed, the whole concept of rule-based knowledge representation has important *human implications*. When we extract knowledge from experts in the form of rules, we see, often for the first time, what the rules really are. The process of eliciting knowledge from experts can be painful. It is difficult to know what the expert thinks and what he believes. But this is also true of normal people. It's hard for us to know what rules we use in solving day-to-day problems. If we could articulate them, then we could examine, criticize and improve them. Even if our first attempts at articulation were incorrect, we could improve them by trial and error. We could see them for what they are; we could challenge them; and we could see if they are fair, if they apply to one customer as well as to another, to ourselves as well as to others.

The formalization of rules and regulations also illustrates the potential of another application for expert systems technology, different from simply applying known expertise, and different from applying the law in individual cases. It illustrates how the trial and error process of formulating regulations can be used as a tool to develop and improve human expertise — where there is no expert within a given company, for regulating pension schemes, for example. One way to start is to propose some initial collection of rules. Instead of trying them out on people, try them out on the computer, in an interactive manner which is based on a common model of deductive problem solving which is shared by the human and the machine.

Let's look at one or two examples from the British Nationality Act and see to what extent they confirm the theory. The very first subsection of the Act is concerned with *acquisition by birth*:

A person born in the United Kingdom after commencement shall be a British citizen if at the time of birth his father or mother is:

(a) a British citizen; or ....

Notice how the word 'if' in the English text occurs almost exactly where it would occur in a rule-based logical representation.

The conclusion of this very first clause of the British Nationality Act is that a person is a British citizen. There are some logical conditions, however, tucked away inside the syntax of the conclusion. One condition is that the person be born in the United Kingdom and the other that he be born after the commencement of the Act, that is to say after the date on which the Act takes effect. The other conditions are explicitly written after the 'if'. Logic-based knowledge representation provides us with a very natural way of representing such knowledge:

x is a British citizen
>   **if**   x was born in the UK
>   **and** x was born on date y
>   **and** y is after commencement
>   **and** z is a parent of x
>   **and** z was a British citizen on date y.

My colleagues, Marek Sergot, Fariba Sadri, Frank Kriwaczek, Peter Hammond, and I have investigated the representation of the British Nationality Act in PROLOG. About 80 per cent of its approximately 70-odd pages have been written in PROLOG. We found the structure of the Act difficult to comprehend and so we tried using data flow diagrams to help. We soon came to the reluctant conclusion that data flow diagrams were inadequate, for two reasons. First, they required directions on the flow of data, which, as in the customer-products example, unnecessarily restricted the different ways the rule might be used. Second, it is not easy to represent the logical connections between different processes in such a diagram. In the end, we decided to use and-or graphs, a kind of data flow diagram in which logical connections between processes are made explicit, but data flow between processes is ignored.

The and-or graph helped to give us an overall view of the structure of the Act, but it gave us little help in deciding detailed knowledge representation issues. Moreover, it soon became clear that there was little alternative to trial and error refinement of the rules. The inadequacy of our first attempt to formalize subsection 1.1.a, in particular, did not come to light until we came to section 2.1.a, which is concerned with *acquisition by descent*:

A person born outside the United Kingdom after commencement shall be a British citizen if at the time of birth his father or mother —

>   (a) is a British citizen otherwise than by descent: or ...

Notice the disconcerting condition 'British citizen otherwise than by descent'. This shows that our earlier assumption that the conclusion of 1.1.a is that

'x is a British citizen'

was naive. Moreover, it also ignores the implicit assumption that x requires citizenship at the time of birth. Taking both of these omissions into account, we can revise our original formalization, obtaining the next approximation:

x acquires British citizenship by 1.1.a on date y
>   **if**   x was born in the UK
>   **and** x was born on date y
>   **and** y is after commencement
>   **and** z is a parent of x
>   **and** z is a British citizen
>   by w on date y.

Subsection 2.1.a can be represented similarly:

x acquires British citizenship by 2.1.a on date y
>   **if**   x was born outside UK
>   **and** x was born on date y
>   **and** y is after commencement

> **and** z is a parent of x
> **and** z is a British citizen by v on date y
> **and** v is **not** by descent.

However, in both of these rules there is a mismatch between the form in which citizenship is expressed in the conclusion and the form in which it is expressed in the condition. We need an additional rule, which is not explicitly stated in the Act, but which is taken for granted:

> x is a British citizen by w on date y
> **if**   x acquires British citizenship by w on date z
> **and** y is after z
> **and** x is alive on date y
> **and** x has not renounced British citizenship before date y
> **and** x has not been deprived of British citizenship before date y.

In other words, a person is a British citizen of a particular kind on a particular date if he/she acquired that citizenship on an earlier date, is alive, has not renounced it and has not been deprived of it.

The less obvious situation where a person who has died might be regarded as a British citizen after death is dealt with explicitly in subsection 48: A parent who is no longer alive at the time of birth of his child is regarded as being a British citizen at the time of birth, if he was a British citizen when he died.

These rules illustrate some of the top level of the British Nationality Act. The conditions which occur in these and other rules can be satisfied in a variety of ways.

Conditions can be *defined by rules*. For example, the condition

> 'z is settled in the UK on date y'

which is a condition of 1.1.b, is defined in subsections 50.2, 50.3 and 50.4; and its definition is naturally represented by means of rules.

Conditions can be *defined by data*. For example, the condition

> 'z is a British dependent territory'

is defined by a list of territories enumerated in schedule 6. Conceptually, for every territory there is an assertion, e.g.

> 'Gibraltar is a British dependent territory'

Each such assertion can be regarded as a trivial rule having one conclusion and no conditions.

Conditions can be *computed by programs*. For example,

> 'y is after commencement'

But any program is a procedure or collection of procedures which can be represented by rules which are used backwards to reduce problems to sub-problems.

Conditions can be solved by *querying the user*. For example,

> 'x was born on date y'

In general, any condition can be solved either by the computer or by the human user. The computer can recognize that it is unable to solve a given problem and can therefore automatically request a solution from the user.

Conditions can be solved by *querying an expert*. For example, the condition

'x is ordinarily resident in the UK on date y'

is not defined in the Act, but is decided by the Secretary of State. In the absence of the Secretary of State, the system would need to consult an expert — either a human expert or an expert system.

The rule-based formalization of the British Nationality Act by trial and error exemplifies the use of logic programming technology for an application which has both conventional and novel characteristics. On the one hand, if we restrict ourselves to problems of determining citizenship, it is not very different from a complicated data processing application. On the other hand, given appropriate inference machinery, the same representation can, at least in theory, be used to generate and test arbitrary logical consequences of the Act. In both cases we have short-circuited the conventional software development life cycle, completing it without leaving the systems analysis stage.

OTHER RELATIONSHIPS BETWEEN ARTIFICIAL INTELLIGENCE AND SOFTWARE ENGINEERING

So far I have concentrated attention on those applications of logic programming technology which revolutionize the software life cycle, which in many cases altogether do away with program implementation, and even system specification. There are of course other applications of AI technology to software engineering, and they are ones the software engineer might prefer to draw to our attention: intelligent tools which help to improve and preserve the conventional software engineering process; intelligent front-ends to otherwise inscrutable conventional computer programs; knowledge bases to support the conventional software process; expert systems which incorporate conventional software engineering expertise. Such applications of AI technology have their place, but they should not distract our attention from the longer term potential of AI to revolutionize software development completely.

There are other applications of logic programming to SE, which I have not talked about but which have great present value and future potential. The formal, computer-assisted derivation of programs from specifications, in particular, is an area which straddles the fields of artificial intelligence and software engineering. Formal derivation is needed if an executable system analysis does not perform efficiently enough to meet the user's performance targets. This was not the case, for the most part, with our formalization of the British Nationality Act, although even there we used program transformation techniques, by hand, to eliminate certain loops.

In many other cases, such as sorting files for example, executing an analysis of the user's problem isn't sufficient. We need to improve efficiency by restricting the class of problems to be solved and by identifying the specific knowledge which is required for solving problems in that class. This changes the systems analysis into an executable specification, still written in the same logic-based language. But now the specification has an appearance of formality and rigour. This appearance is only superficial, however, because syntactically there is no difference between the language of the formal specification and the language of the empirically derived systems analysis.

If the executable logic-based specification is still not sufficiently efficient, it can be transformed further into a more efficient program. If necessary, the program can be written in a conventional programming language. But given adequate software and hardware resources, it can also be transformed into a program expressed in the same logic-based language. Using the same language for all stages of the software development process greatly simplifies the problems of maintaining consistency between the different stages. Moreover, transformation and derivation techniques which are guaranteed to preserve correctness can be used to pass from one stage to the next. Such techniques have been developed within the community of declarative language researchers who live within the intersection of AI and SE.

I have talked about the applications of AI to SE. What are the applications of SE to AI? Certainly the software engineer has three major concerns, which do not always attract sufficient attention in AI:

correctness,
scale and
complexity.

I have already argued that many AI applications are better thought of as executable analyses or executable specifications rather than as conventional programs. To the extent that that is the case, such applications are as correct as any conventional systems analysis or specification. However, many AI applications go beyond analysis and specification in their concern with matters of efficiency. In such cases, the resulting programs are as much in need of validation and verification as any conventional program. The software engineer is right to criticize the AI programmer who uses AI techniques which do not have logical foundations, and are not amenable to rigorous verification.

This is an area in which logic-based approaches to knowledge representation and programming in AI have a distinct advantage over other approaches, such as those based on frames and object-oriented programming. Knowledge representations and programs expressed in logic are expressed in the same formalism as the software engineer uses for expressing formal specifications. Using the same logic-based language for both programs and specifications significantly simplifies the problems of proving program correctness.

What about scale and complexity? I wonder whether there is very much more to be said, other than to repeat DeMarco's advice about not using more than a single sheet of paper for a single data flow diagram (or the equivalent collection of rules, whether they represent an analysis, specification or program). It may be, however, that frames and object-oriented programming have some useful contributions to make here. If so, then I believe they would need to be integrated with logic-based approaches, probably along the lines suggested by Pat Hayes in his paper on the Logic of Frames.

HUMAN IMPLICATIONS

Finally, I would like to address some of the human implications of the new technology.

I don't believe that technology for technology's sake is a desirable end in itself. I believe that the technology of knowledge-based AI software is going to make life better on the average. But, unless we are aware of some of the potential dangers and take suitable precautions, there may be some spectacularly undesirable results.

It is all too easy to let computers take over and make decisions we ought to make for ourselves. We've done it before with humans, with professional advisors in particular. We let the doctor take responsibility for our health, and let the accountant run our financial affairs. The human expert can intimidate us by having greater knowledge and expertise. If humans can intimidate humans, then computers will be able to intimidate humans too; and they will do so, if we allow the enthusiastic technologist to have his way. The technologist will happily design computers to do more and more of our thinking for us.

I see real dangers: but on the average I see great potential benefits. The new computing technology has some obvious uses for implementing intelligent front-ends, not just for conventional software, but for any kind of unfriendly machinery — my oven, for example. I hate my oven. I don't know how to use it properly and it doesn't know how to help me to use it at all. The intermediary of something which is more machine-like than me and therefore more sympathetic to my oven than me, yet which understands the world more like I do than do computers today, can make the world of machinery more friendly and more understandable.

The new logic-based languages allow us to get rid of the 'take it or leave it' attitude of computers today. They make it possible for computers to explain their conclusions, and therefore easier for us to decide for ourselves whether to accept or reject their conclusions. Only when computer programs are expressed in logical, explicit form can we identify what assumptions they use, can we decide whether to accept their assumptions and therefore whether to accept their conclusions.

Such computers can also increase human knowledge and expertise. Computerized encyclopaedias are already beginning to give us ready access to the whole store of explicitly formulated human knowledge. Through the technique of knowledge elicitation, knowledge that is only known unconsciously can also be articulated and brought out into the open. In the same way that an expert system might give us a better understanding of a medical expert's previously unconscious knowledge and beliefs, knowledge elicitation can give us a better understanding not only of experts but also of common people.

Not only knowledge but also human reasoning can be enhanced. Once knowledge is made explicit, we can see more clearly what we believe. We can begin to see what others believe. We can begin to see the individual steps that explain and justify knowledge and belief. We can begin to think more rationally, because we can better understand ourselves and others. We can suspend our beliefs because we know what they are. We can temporarily assume another's beliefs because we can imagine what they might be; and we can reason with those assumptions to see where they might lead. I believe that, on the average, this kind of reasoning will result in a better world.

In summary, I believe that the mechanization of logic will make computing better, and is therefore the key to new generation computing. It is the link also between knowledge representation languages in artificial intelligence and systems analysis languages, program specification languages, and database languages in software engineering.

But in the end what matters is not computers, or software engineering, or artificial intelligence, but people. And, provided we take the right precautions, I believe the new technology will help us to be more human, to better understand ourselves, and to better understand others.

ACKNOWLEDGEMENT

This paper is a revised version of the author's 1984 SPL-insight award lecture. Earlier versions were published in *Future Generation Computing Systems*, Volume 1, Number 1, July 1984, and in *Datamation*, 1 November 1984.

FURTHER READING AND REFERENCES

Clark, K.L. and McCabe, F. (Eds.) (1983) *Micro-Prolog: Programming in Logic*, Prentice-Hall, London
Clocksin, W.F. and Mellish, C.S. (1981) *Programming in Prolog*, Springer, Berlin
DeMarco, T. (1978) *Structured Analysis and System Specification*, Yourdon, New York
Feigenbaum, E.A. and McCorduck, P. (1983) *The Fifth Generation*, Addison-Wesley, Reading, Mass.
Hammond, P. (1985) *Representation of DHSS regulations as a logic program*. In G. Mitra (Ed.) (1985) Computer Models for Decision Making: Mathematical Programming, Decision Analysis, Expert Systems, North-Holland, Amsterdam

Hammond, P. and Sergot, M.J. (1984) *APES Reference Manual*, Logic Based Systems, Richmond, Surrey

Hayes, P.J. (1979) *The Logic of Frames*. In D. Metzing (Ed.) (1979) Frame Conceptions and Text Understanding, Walter de Gruyter, Berlin, pp 46–61

Hogger, C.J. (1984) *Introduction to Logic Programming*, Academic Press, London

Kowalski, R.A. (1979) *Logic for Problem Solving*, Elsevier North-Holland, New York

Sergot, M.J., Sadri, F., Kowalski, R.A., Kriwaczek, F., Hammond, P. and Cory, H.T. (1984) *The British Nationality Act as a Logic Program*, Department of Computing, Imperial College, London

Martin, J. (1984) *An Information Systems Manifesto*, Prentice-Hall, Englewood Cliffs, New Jersey

Moto-oka, T. *et al.* (Eds.) (1982) *Fifth Generation Computer Systems*, North-Holland, Amsterdam

7

EXPERT SYSTEMS — SOME USER EXPERIENCE

STUART MORALEE

UNILEVER RESEARCH, BEBINGTON, MERSEYSIDE

(*Author's note*, added in January 1986: This chapter is based upon a lecture given in 1984. The focus of our work has changed since then, and now concentrates on building systems which assist knowledge communication. Our work and understanding has advanced considerably, and the general awareness in industry of the scope and limitations of expert systems technology has also advanced. However, whilst this chapter is dated in some aspects, much of it is still relevant today.)

INTRODUCTION

As the title indicates, what we are discussing is experience — experience of building and using expert systems, hopefully with profit. It is not my intention to deal with any theoretical or deep methodological issues. The objective is to indicate some of the issues that I believe you need to think about if you want to be successful in implementing and using expert systems. I will try to illustrate this with a range of applications which we've been working on at Unilever.

This paper can be summarized, with the tongue slightly in the cheek, by one sentence: 'How to succeed in making expert systems work for you.' I don't want you to take this too literally, but I think it's a sentence that usefully highlights two important points. Take the first half of the sentence: 'How to succeed.' I'll start by saying that it *is* possible to succeed. We can look at existing industries and companies and see that they have been successful in exploiting the technology. Digital Equipment Corporation have developed a series of expert systems to help them in processing orders and shipments for complex computer systems. Within the UK, at the University of Leeds, there is a system called LHASA (originally developed by Corey in the United States) which is concerned with planning organic chemical synthesis routes — this is an expert system that performs at the level of a Ph.D. in organic chemistry. Within my own laboratory in Unilever we have had some modest success with systems that have paid for themselves in financial terms. In one case the system paid for itself even before it had been completely developed.

So expert systems are not only of academic benefit; they can, have been, and are being used to industrial benefit. Now of course there is a corollary to this: that just as you can succeed, you can also fail. And I believe that unless you plan properly, and choose the right applications, then you have a good chance of failing. You do need to think carefully if you're going to be successful. I don't think it's necessary to think big: I don't think you need systems with fifteen hundred to two thousand rules. My own experience suggests that systems with one hundred to two hundred rules can perform useful functions.

The second part of the sentence, 'making expert systems work for you', is really what it's all about. As far as industry is concerned this is what matters; you have a problem and you want a solution. You aren't concerned about whether you're using the latest technology — you're concerned about whether it solves your problem. That's what I think any industry has to see expert systems for: as a tool complementary to conventional data processing to help you solve problems which perhaps you couldn't solve before, or which allow you to solve problems in a more efficient and more supportable way than you have so far been able to do.

I said that this paper will be concerned with experience, and it's important to give you a sense of the context in which this experience has been gained. It has been gained within an industrial research laboratory in Unilever, where we've been trying to use expert systems as aids to scientific research. We're not in the commercial marketplace developing packages to sell to people. We are looking at aids to scientific research and my comments must be flavoured by that environment.

IMPORTANT ISSUES FOR SUCCESSFUL USE OF EXPERT SYSTEMS

The first thing I'd like to do is look at some of the ingredients that I think are necessary if you're going to have any chance of being successful. There are many such items, but out of them I've picked three: you have got to create the right kind of culture; you have got to know what you want to achieve; and you have got to have the right mixture of tools. Let's look at these in turn.

CREATING THE CULTURE

Expert systems are no different from any other kind of new technology: the human needs are as important as the technical requirements. If you're going to have a successful application, that means getting the culture right, getting the environment right into which you're going to put this technology. Part of that is creating an awareness of what the methodology can do. You can do that through buying-in small commercial packages, developing demonstrator systems, perhaps even developing little useful systems, and by encouraging people around the organization to have a go and do it themselves.

You must also create trust. It's no good having a sophisticated expert system if, when a crisis happens, people say, 'We don't trust that' and find a solution elsewhere. You must have systems which are trusted, which people believe in, and which they will use for real problems.

The third aspect that I think is important in the culture is commitment — not just of the organization, but of the people involved in the application, both the end-users and the expert whose knowledge is being used. Your expert must be motivated, and there must be something for him in the development of the system. Our policy within Unilever Research has been to develop packages which we can give to chemists, physicists, biologists, etc. so that they can develop their own applications, and we provide them with the appropriate training on how to elicit knowledge, how to build and debug rule bases. There are a lot of problems still to be tackled, but we believe, and our experience supports this, that you can with some degree of success transfer the methodology for building systems out to the expert and end-user, so that he can build his own system.

I think any success we've had within Unilever in developing expert systems owes quite a lot to the very considerable effort we have put in to creating the right environment, e.g. through seminars and demonstration systems, and building small systems that may not yet be cost-effective, but show a useful benefit.

KNOWING WHAT YOU WANT TO ACHIEVE

The second ingredient for success is knowing what you want to achieve. Any expert system must meet a real organizational need. Therefore it must have facilities within it that allow that need to be met. You have to identify very carefully the facilities that the system must provide in order to meet your needs. So let's look at some of these facilities. These are not all-encompassing, but they indicate the range of facilities you could expect to get from an expert system.

Perhaps you want a specific problem solver: you have one problem that you want the system to answer and nothing else. Or maybe you want a more general adviser, to handle a variety of questions. Perhaps your motivation is to retain some key expertise, and the expert system provides a useful vehicle in which to do that. Perhaps you're concerned with having an intelligent front or back end to an existing algorithmic package. Perhaps you want to put very strong emphasis on allowing people to browse around the knowledge that you've elicited from the experts, so they can get a feel for the subject. Maybe you want to integrate the expert system into other software, such as conventional databases or graphics packages. Maybe you're concerned about very detailed explanations.

There are a wide variety of facilities that you can look for in expert systems, and you need to identify them, in order to be sure that you're getting a package that's going to meet the needs of your application.

THE RIGHT SET OF TOOLS

Having identified the kinds of feature that your expert system should have to meet your needs, you have got to go out and look for the software that will do that. Do you want a production system? Are frames more appropriate? Will a commercial, PROSPECTOR-like, expert system, an empty shell, meet your needs? How important is it to get a commercial database interfaced? You've got to look around for the tools that provide the facilities that meet the needs. An off-the-shelf package may suit you, or you may have to develop your own.

Here are two guidelines that I think one can offer. (And because we're concerned with expert systems, they're offered in rule form.)

(i)   If what you want to achieve is creating awareness then choose an application that suits the technology available to you. If you're getting started, I would strongly recommend you buy a commercial package. It may not meet all your needs, you may not be able to implement a real application, but your progress along the learning curve will be very rapid.

(ii)   If, however, you have a real need then clearly you've got to define that need, and you've then got to find the right technology for that application. That may mean developing special packages for yourself to meet your specific needs.

OVERVIEW OF APPLICATIONS

So far we've looked at some of the ingredients that I think are necessary if you're going to have a chance of success. I want now to discuss the types of system that we've developed within Unilever Research in order to illustrate the range of applications and the range of possibilities. Remember this is an industrial research laboratory, where a key capital asset of the laboratory is knowledge and understanding. The overriding objective we had in developing the applications was 'How can we use expert system techniques to make more efficient use of research knowledge?' This is the thinking that dominates our use and that makes us see potential in expert systems. We are not interested in de-skilling people — we are interested in making sure that our computer applications increase the professionalism of the end-user.

There are three areas that we are active in:

(a) Induction of rules from data,
(b) The display and communication of knowledge,
(c) Guided problem solving.

I want to discuss induction briefly and then spend more time on the display and communication of knowledge, and on guided problem solving.

USE OF MACHINE INDUCTION

Historically, a lot of the work on induction has been concerned with trying to extract rules from data, in order to put those rules into expert systems. Sometimes it may be difficult for the expert to articulate what he knows, but you may have a lot of data which you can explore and try to extract rules from. The major work in the field is by Michalski at Illinois and his classic example produces rules which diagnose diseases in soya bean plants.

We are interested in induction, but not for that reason. We are not interested in extracting rules from data to go into expert systems, but we do see potential in these inductive techniques for aiding scientists to get an understanding of structured data, in helping to generate hypotheses that might explain classifications.

There are two reasons that we're not so interested in induction as a means of getting rules into expert systems. First, we haven't come across the problem of elicitation. It is said that knowledge elicitation is the big barrier to developing expert systems. But if you talk to a lot of users in the UK, they all appear to have managed with quite a high degree of success. Now this may be because we are eliciting knowledge which is at the surface level, and we're not trying to get the underlying causal models out of the person. Unquestionably there will be some hard problems in getting knowledge from people, but our experience to date is that with commonsense methods and interviewing techniques, you can make a lot of progress in eliciting knowledge. So we haven't seen the need to really get involved in induction for extracting knowledge from people.

The other reason we are not so interested at the moment in induction as a means of getting rules is that we don't believe the techniques are robust enough yet. If you have any noise in your data, most of the techniques just come to a halt. If you put some data into an inductive algorithm and nothing comes out the end, what's that telling you? Does that tell you there's no information in your data, or does it tell you that you used the wrong algorithm to investigate that data? There is a lot of work that needs to be done in understanding the properties of the current algorithms and in developing new algorithms. I don't want to put you off induction — it is an interesting and potentially useful area, but it is not, I would submit, a technique which can be used routinely. It is something for the skilled person to use, almost as a research tool.

KNOWLEDGE COMMUNICATION AND PROBLEM-SOLVING SYSTEMS

Now let's turn to the other two areas, displaying and communicating knowledge and guided problem solving, where we're trying to help non-experts to use expert knowledge. I want to look at four examples of the work in these areas.

EXAMPLE 1: AN EMPTY EXPERT SYSTEM

We needed to have an empty expert system with which to build applications. We started by looking at the commercially available packages and in the end purchased one, and got some very useful experience with it. But it became clear quite quickly that we would not be able to implement a routine application using a commercial package, because the user interface that was provided with those packages (and I'm thinking back two or three years now) was very inadequate. It was all right for me as the knowledge engineer to put up with the poor interface, but the end-users would not accept it. It would just put them off and so the system would lack credibility.

The packages that were available dealt with uncertain inference along the lines of PROSPECTOR. Now I'm sure there are problems around where uncertain inference is important. But the customers who came to us with problems were not interested in uncertain inference — they were talking mainly about problems where they were dealing with certainty.

So we wrote our own package, paying particular attention to the needs that we have. There was no alternative, if we wanted to make any progress.

In many ways it's a fairly standard kind of package. It's backward chaining (so you start with your goal and you subdivide it until you get matches between the sub-goals and your database), prompted input from the user, and certain inference. It's written in LISP, which we used for really very pragmatic reasons: we had expertise in it, and we had a machine that had a good implementation of LISP. (We didn't have a machine that had a good implementation of PROLOG and we didn't have expertise in PROLOG.) There is another good reason for using LISP, of course: there is a lot of LISP software already written that you can pick up and use and build into your systems.

We have so far used the system to develop six applications. I wouldn't say any one is yet complete — in fact, I don't know if a complete expert system ever exists, for they're always ongoing. We have about two hundred rules in each system and they're in such diverse areas as analytical chemistry, microbiology and fault diagnosis on industrial plants. (Everybody seems to deal with fault diagnosis — it's the easy one!)

However, we had to incorporate certain features that we felt were important. We put in a spelling correction and lexical root facility. If people make spelling mistakes (and people do) they expect the system to accommodate them. There are still problems, for you can fool any spelling corrector, but most of the time it picks up and corrects the mistakes.

We were concerned with browsing. If you go to all the expense of eliciting an expert's knowledge and formalizing it and representing it in some way, to answer a specific problem, then why not look for other ways of using that knowledge and try to get something else back on your investment? It occurred to us that it would be useful to let people browse around the rules. I think our approach is very simple so far, in that we simply keyword all the technical terms within the rules and build an inverted file to index the rules. So you can say, for example, 'Show me all the rules that refer to copolymers', and you'll get a nice list of all the rules and the text that lies behind the rules about copolymers. This is a very simple approach to browsing but it seems to be useful and wanted.

We also provide a variety of explanations. We have people who are not too familiar with the technical terminology that's used in some of these systems, and so we need to be able to give an explanation of a technical term, such as 'sachet' and 'seal'.

We need to be able to get amplification of a rule. People may not understand the rule in the concise form that we present it to them, and so we need to give some supportive text that explains what the rule is all about and what is expected of the user.

We have to provide the classic explanation facility of just walking through the backward chaining process and showing what rules are fired to arrive at a conclusion. I think that's really very inadequate as an explanation — it's really telling you more about what the program is doing than about the underlying reasoning behind the answer, but it's the best that can really be done at the moment. We have sponsored some research into trying to provide deeper levels of explanations, so that you can drop down from the heuristic rules into a causal model underlying them. There is some progress but there's a long, long way to go before we will get really good explanations out of expert systems.

We provide an 'unsure' facility — remember we're dealing with certain inference, but sometimes people can't say 'yes' or 'no' and have to say, 'Well, look, I just don't know.' For some rules there is a natural default that you can build into the system if a person doesn't know: there's an answer that's sensible on statistical grounds. Otherwise we will allow the system to guess, and the dialogue progresses and eventually arrives at some conclusion:

The problem with your plant is x,y,z, but remember that we have arrived at this conclusion by assuming the following:...

So it allows the user to speculate a bit and work his way through, and then be reminded so that he can undo the process and work backwards to the point at which he speculated and try an alternative chain.

There are a number of areas that we need to develop further. We would be very interested in having a mixed initiative system, where the user could start by freely volunteering what he knows about the problem. The system would then look at that data and make some tentative hypotheses which it would present to the user. The system could then take control and go through a normal backward chaining process. We have natural language problems that we want to address. I've already mentioned we want deeper levels of explanation. That's an ongoing programme, for it will be quite a number of years before we get any satisfactory solution there.

EXAMPLE 2: A SPECTROSCOPIC SYSTEM

The second example is in the world of infrared spectroscopy. Some infrared spectrometers are fairly cheap analytical instruments costing £400 to £500. (They can cost £40 000 pounds, but you can buy cheap ones.) Infrared spectroscopy is a very powerful aid to the chemist in analyzing chemicals, and they are used quite widely by non-specialists in spectroscopy. These users have some understanding of infrared spectra but they are not specialists. We wanted to help these people. So we had two objectives in developing the system. First, to aid a non-specialist in interpreting spectra, and secondly, in so doing, to increase the level of understanding that the user has.

An infrared spectrometer tells you the functional groups that make up the chemicals. Functional groups you can think of as the building blocks of the molecules and each functional group has a characteristic pattern. So we wanted a system to look at the spectra, pick out these characteristic patterns and advise the chemist of the likely candidate functional groups. However, the chemist is interested not so much in functional groups but in chemicals. So we wanted a second level that would take the suggested functional groups and try to assemble them together to say, 'Right, these chemicals are likely to be there.'

Now to do that for all chemicals is an enormous problem, and one which it would not be economically viable for our laboratory to tackle. But we were able to identify a small sub-domain of chemicals that we were very interested in, and work within that sub-domain. By making that restriction we were able, within reasonable resources, to build a system that performs a useful function for these non-specialists. The system had to perform with both pure spectra and mixed spectra; it had to explain its reasoning; it also had to be portable; and, since these spectrometers may be in laboratories with no telecommunication link to a big machine, it had to run on a small machine. In fact our target machine was an eight-bit CPM micro running Micro-PROLOG.

The nature of the problem was such that it was sensible to volunteer everything the user knew right at the beginning. So the spectrum is described to the system to start with, and then it forward chains, to come up with a hypothesis, i.e. it's likely that (with certainty A) you've got functional group X, functional group Y, functional group Z.

We had a simple additive model for certainty handling. Our limited aim is not to say you definitely have functional groups X and Y, but that it's possible that you have these groups present. We're trying to help the user make an objective assessment of the data, and help him to think about the analysis.

The package was written in Micro-PROLOG in about $2\frac{1}{2}$ hours. (We didn't elicit the rules in $2\frac{1}{2}$ hours, that took a bit longer, quite a bit longer!) Putting a good interface on it took about another week's effort. So you can get somewhere quite quickly. It's not a sophisticated system, but it's a useful system.

The only way we could tackle this problem was by working on a narrow group of chemicals. That brings its own problems. Suppose a chemical is analyzed which is not in the rule base. The system cannot identify to the user the presence of this chemical, although it will identify constituent functional groups if they are defined in the rule base. Now that is a serious problem, and it's certainly one that we're addressing, but it's not a catastrophic problem. It doesn't prevent us using the system, because the final check of any spectroscopist is a very large file of reference spectra, and the purpose of our system is to suggest a small list of chemicals that are likely to be present. The chemist will then go and look at them in his reference files, and by so doing he will identify that there are a lot of peaks that haven't been accounted for. So he can trap the problem, but in the long term we have to handle it automatically. We have to recognize that there are chemicals that are outside the domain for which we have built the system.

EXAMPLE 3: A MANUFACTURING MODEL

Some people will say that this example is not an expert system: I would disagree with them, very strongly. This is an attempt to build a model of how a particular product performs during manufacture. We don't have an overall mathematical model to explain the whole process. We do have a lot of experience of the process, we do have some mathematical models of part of the process, and we have some heuristic rules, but we can't put together a complete formal model. We want the user to be able to come along and say, 'I want to make this product. This is what's in it. It should have the following properties. Can I make it? If I can't, why can't I?'

Within this problem we have a variety of knowledge types: we have algorithmic knowledge; we have some heuristic rules; we have a lot of experience which we tend to represent graphically, in this instance using triangular diagrams. Figure 7.1 shows how a property X varies as a function of three chemicals: if you have an equal amount of A, B and C you're in the middle of the diagram; if you have 100 per cent of chemical A then you are sitting at the apex labelled A of the triangle. The rule that we want to put into the system is 'if we know the ratio of A to B to C, then we want to compute and return the value of property X'.

We could fit an equation to that diagram, and then, when the rule fires, simply go and solve that equation and return the value. But that's not good enough, because in some instances there is a second property that we are concerned about at the same time, and this property has essential discontinuities. The shaded area in Figure 7.2 can be thought of, for example, as a region of high viscosity. If you're in an area of high viscosity your pumps may not be able to

FIGURE 7.1   Graphical representation of how a property X varies as a function of three chemicals

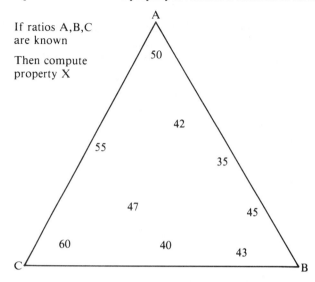

FIGURE 7.2   The inclusion of a second property with discontinuities

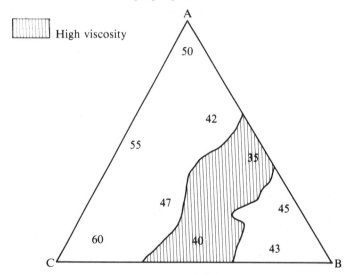

pump the product around. So you need to know if you're in or close to that area: you don't just want the value of property X, you want to know if it lies in or close to a bad area, because if it does then there are quality control issues to think about. We have elected to develop systems where we present this sort of information in graphical form to the user so he can see how the property varies, he can see where the discontinuities are, and he can absorb a lot more knowledge than if we had just fired that rule, solved an equation and returned a value. So we are dealing with quite a wide variety of knowledge types, and we want to deal with them in a variety of ways.

The system is concerned with solving a specific problem: 'Can we make this product in a factory? If we can't, what can we do to correct the problems?' The system must give understanding to the user as it's working through the analysis of any problems. It must identify the problems, describe the background of the problems, and suggest ways of overcoming them.

But, at the same time, if the system says, 'Look, you've got a problem, you can't do that', the user should be able to say, 'Never mind, let me speculate, and see where that leads me.' The user has to retain control of the system. If you're going to allow that facility, then when the user comes to the end of the program and he is given a summary of the problem he has worked through, he must be reminded of the assumptions he has made, and of the advice he's ignored. That is what we do in our systems.

We envisage such a system being used by people all over the world, and we want to get feedback on how the models we've used relate to the particular environment of those people. So at any point in the dialogue the user should be able to put a comment in. We need to track that comment and the context in which it was made, i.e. where in the program it was made and how the user had arrived at that point when he made it.

Browsing is also an important factor. We want to find other ways of using the knowledge we're building into these systems. We want people to be able to just browse through what we've encapsulated within the system in order to get an overview of what the issues are and what the problems are.

When we set out to design this system two years ago our state of knowledge was such that we didn't feel that we could do it using expert system technology. Expert systems are systems that allow you to get explanations, that are updatable, that allow you to get in and look at what knowledge is there, and that perform at the same level as human experts. However, we did not know how to use standard expert system tools to build the system. But we took the concept of an expert system, of it performing openly, of the reasoning being accessible to the user, and we went ahead and implemented it with traditional procedural tools. I make no apologies for referring to it here, for it undoubtedly has expert performance and the user undoubtedly has access to the knowledge in it. In those terms, within an industrial environment, it is fair to call it an expert system. Moreover, not only did we build it but it met the needs of the user. Not only did it do that, but it paid for itself. We would not have built it if we had not had involvement with expert systems first — it wouldn't have occurred to us that this was a useful way of tackling the problem. It has also brought us to the point, two years later, where we now feel competent to tackle this kind of problem using expert system techniques, at least in large part, if not entirely. So our level of understanding has been raised in the process. Building the system has clarified in our minds the kinds of tool that we're going to need to develop such systems.

EXAMPLE 4: DISPLAYING AND COMMUNICATING KNOWLEDGE

The final example is one we really haven't succeeded in doing very much with, and that is the idea of trying to display and communicate knowledge. The key asset, as I've already said, of any research laboratory is its knowledge, not its equipment. It's important to find ways of communicating that knowledge and keeping updatable, authoritative statements of what we know. Most organizations have some kind of paper reporting system, and I'm sure most organizations are well aware of the limitations of that sort of system. The real advances in knowledge that the author of a written report is trying to get across are often hidden.

We are looking to see whether there is anything in the expert systems domain that will help us to develop such knowledge communication systems. We are concerned with authoritative statements of knowledge, which should be updatable. The systems should be able to handle text, graphics and equations. They should link to videodisk technology. In many ways, this has similarities with computer-aided instruction systems. But I believe there is a very significant difference of emphasis, in that we are concerned with letting people browse around in whatever way they want. We are not interested in having a model of the user so that we can recognize when he's having trouble performing a task and then increase the level of instruction. We just want people to browse around, see what's new, get a feel for the subject, explore equations that are there.

We are limited in what we can do at the moment. But expert systems should be very relevant: they have an updatable body of knowledge — the rule base and database. We should be able to devise rules that will control the browsing and help guide people around the system. Expert systems are also concerned with giving explanations, which is part of what we would want in browsing.

We believe that this is a very important area — in fact, I would say that this was far more relevant to us than the classic diagnostic expert system. There is little work that we can find that's been done, although Marek Sergot and Peter Hammond in Imperial College are developing a PROLOG browser.

We have made some limited progress by developing pilot systems which are geared more than anything else to helping us clarify the definition of a browser: what are the functions it should perform, what kind of inference do you need, what kinds of knowledge representation are going to be appropriate? We hope in the next few months to be able to formalize this specification and to start trying to build something. It's an area that within the research community is very important. The life-blood of a research lab is how it communicates and uses its knowledge and a tool to help that is going to be very important. We believe expert systems are relevant to this problem.

SOME CONCLUSIONS FROM EXPERIENCE

I would emphasize that my conclusions are based on my experience within a particular research environment.

The first conclusion is that if you have a narrow view of the concept of an expert system and of the types of task to which expert systems can be applied then you are going to miss a lot of opportunities. Expert systems have a much wider use than just diagnostic tools.

From an industrial and commercial point of view, the needs of the problem must come before any question of the purity of the methodology. It's right and proper that within the academic environment people should be working on advancing understanding, on developing new methodologies, on tackling the hard problems; but in industry, when you have a real problem to solve by a certain date, you can't wait for the methodology to come.

In the long term, no doubt, all the research will result in a methodology that allows the strict definition of an expert system (if such a thing there is) to be fully realized. But in the short term you can do a lot with what is available now. Take what you can from the expert system domain, and what's missing take from conventional data processing. There is no point in re-inventing the wheel. If you can take some conventional data processing and bolt it onto an expert system axle, then fine. The thing may rumble a bit but in due course you can get the wheel balanced properly and you'll have a nice, smooth system with all the benefits of expert systems. The important thing to industry is to get on and solve your problem now. There are quite a few things from expert systems that you can take and use with benefit.

Lastly, if anybody is wanting to get started, he really shouldn't set his expectations too high. Don't try the difficult things: you can do simple things that are still useful. So get in there and start using them on real problems, but simple problems.

QUESTIONS

Q. What has been the opinion of the end-users to the expert systems that you've built? Have they found they're comfortable using them? Have they accepted them or do they react badly to them?

A. It's a mixture, but the bias is very definitely towards a favourable reaction. We have a number of systems that are being used routinely every day with no involvement from the knowledge engineering people at all. We have developed them, handed them over to the customers, and they get on and use them. There are some other systems which are less well received and I think that to some extent that is because we haven't paid enough attention to the style of the system to make it comfortable for that class of user. However good the system is in terms of producing the correct answer, if it hasn't got the right style, it is unlikely to be accepted.

Q. To what extent has it been important in your unit, developing expert systems, to have computer science training in your staff, and how do you balance that against the primarily scientific knowledge needed to create expert systems?

A. I'm very grateful for that question. We have nobody with a formal computer science background. I would almost suggest that a classic data processing background, which is not computer science necessarily, is actually a disadvantage. You need people who understand the end-user's needs, and to that end we tend to use people who are zoologists, physical chemists, physicists, etc. These are the people within our knowledge engineering team. We had one person only who had a formal training in knowledge engineering, a cognitive psychologist. But he alone would not be enough — you need this mix of expertise and background within the team. That's my experience. I don't know how general one could make that statement.

Q. You said that knowledge acquisition hadn't been much of a problem. Why?

A. I don't know. The process we've adopted is when we're developing an expert system we invite the candidate expert round and we show him a few expert systems. We show him how we develop and store the rules, we talk about decision trees, and then we say, 'Now you go away and write down what you know, in what ever form is most comfortable. Write us an essay, write some rules, write some decision trees, give us some diagrams.' We then take what he's provided us and put it into what we think is an appropriate rule form. Then we get him round and let him see the mistakes and omissions and then the iterative cycle starts. We've now started teaching people to do the whole thing themselves, and part of that training involves talking about rule structures. I don't know whether we've just chosen the right problems by coincidence, but the experts find it relatively straightforward to say what they know. I can only think of one who had difficulty, and his area of expertise was a very experiential one. There was no real hard theoretical background to it. He had acquired expertise over twenty-odd years and some of the decisions he was making were second nature. He had difficultly getting underneath his skin, if you like, to think how he reasoned about those decisions five or ten years ago. But he's the only one we've had real difficulty with. Also, our experts, I think all bar one, had no real exposure to computing prior to doing this. They tended to be late middle-aged, some getting near retirement, having done virtually no computing. That may help, I don't know.

Q. You said at the beginning that one of the most important things in tackling an expert system application was, to use your terms, 'to create the culture'. But it seemed to me that in some senses your culture was preformed for you, in that you're dealing with knowledge professionals accustomed to thinking in these kinds of ways, rather than with people who have no experience at all of thinking in this way.

A. Well, with that part of the culture, in that sense, yes, I think we are lucky. But you can still have chemists and physicists who don't want to know about computer technology, and you've got to create a culture which makes them sympathetic towards it. But I think you're quite right that these are people who are trained in thinking and reasoning and, once you've got their interest and support, that may make the work that much easier. But you've still got to let them see that this methodology is something that is useful to them and to make them want to use it. In that sense we had to create the culture.

Q. Did you find that the problems were mostly in writing the expert system itself, to perform the inference or whatever, or in putting the package around it that does the communication with the user?

A. The easiest thing was writing the inference mechanism. In a real-life system you need a bit more code; for example, hashing algorithms to get efficient access. But the real meat of the systems we've had to develop is the user interface, so that, for example, he can do on-line editing of rules. It's really the packaging that goes round the inference net that's the hard work.

Q. Given that you've done six or so expert systems, how fast do you feel you're moving up a learning curve? Is there a learning curve?

A. Oh, there is, yes. I think you can move up it quite quickly. Then I think there is a bit of a plateau, when you think you've learnt it all and you get a bit confident. Then suddenly you realize you don't, and you start learning again. But I think the second slope is much shallower than the first slope.

Q. Is that because the tasks you've attempted to do are roughly the same complexity?

A. That may be so, yes. It would certainly be a contributing factor. We have deliberately chosen tasks that we knew to be feasible. Our activities are concerned with solving real problems, and in that area we have to choose problems that we know it's feasible to do something with; but we have a second line of work within the group which is developing methodology, and there we are looking at some harder applications.

Q. You've chosen problems deliberately that come out to be a hundred or two hundred rules in most of them so far. You said you've chosen tasks that you knew ahead of time to be feasible. Can you give any advice to other people to try to guess whether a task is feasible or not?

A. I think your expert is a key element. You must have a feeling right at the beginning that you've an expert who is going to be not only willing but able to articulate what he knows. Another feature must be that there has got to be a real need that you're trying to meet. That's going to, in a sense, provide you with a subset of applications that you can choose from. Once you've got that subset then I think people will be a dominating influence. Cost will be another factor, if you feel it's going to be a very long elicitation process. If you feel that the representation and the inference mechanisms you're going to need will not fit naturally into an existing package, you're going to have the overhead of developing a package of your own or going out and obtaining one. Then that's going to be an expensive application and take some more time to do.

Q. You have shown a preference to allow the user to retain overall control of the system. How important is it for the system itself to have some measure of knowing the inconsistencies in the logic of the user?

A. Pass.

Q. How would the expert system itself detect the logic of the user and illustrate any inconsistencies to the user? Suppose that the expert system is supposed to help with a non-expert job. Suppose that the reasoning through which the user is trying to do the job is not consistent. Is the system capable of detecting it, and if so is the system capable of illustrating to the user where the deficiency lies?

A. In some situations, I think it can identify that the user's trying to do something not necessarily inconsistent but certainly likely to lead him to problems, and it would give advice to him. Now this is purely based on rules that we've built in. We say, 'In our experience, in this situation you should do this.' And we try to pick up the fact that the user is trying to do *that* and tell him, 'OK, *this* is what you should do.' But formal logic inconsistencies, no, I don't think we can pick them up.

Q. You mentioned a five-figure cost. Can you break it down a bit and also say how you think it might change in the future?

A. Well, yes, it would change quite considerably. The cost of one application, I'd say, was about £50 000, equally split across a knowledge engineer and one or more physical chemists. The majority of the work that came from the knowledge engineer was, I think, a cost that we're not going to have to bear in future applications. Instead of bearing 50 per cent of the cost there, we will have maybe 10 per cent because we've learnt a lot doing it. There is no way I think we will reduce the input that the expert has to put in. It's still going to be a hard job, doing the intellectual operation of thinking about what you know, representing it, debugging the system. We can get a few tools to help that, but we're not going to make significant in-roads into that. But I think the cost from the knowledge engineering side is going to be a lot smaller.

Q. To what extent do you think the success of your systems has been due to the adoption of expert system technology, and to what extent do you think it might have been simply because you've adopted the symbolic processing languages like LISP and PROLOG?

A. It's very difficult to separate the two, isn't it? I think that the reason why we've been successful is that we have kept the expert system concept in mind. The thing we're after is providing understanding and communicating knowledge. It's not the code that's the important thing to us. If we could do it just as well without using expert systems we'd be happy, but expert systems provide us with a lot of potential benefits, in updatability, explanation facilities, etc. The 'empty shell' concept allows you to recoup a lot of your investment in developing some software which is not so obvious in classical data processing.

FURTHER READING

Dietterich, T.G. and Michalski, R.S. (1981) Inductive learning of structural descriptions: evaluation criteria and comparative review of selected methods, *Artificial Intelligence*, Vol.16, pp 257–294

Duda, R.O., Gaschnig, J. and Hart, P.E. (1981) *Model design in the PROSPECTOR consultant program for mineral exploration*. In D. Michie (Ed.) (1981) Expert Systems in the Microelectronic Age, Edinburgh University Press, Edinburgh

Kraft, A. (1986) *Artificial intelligence: next generation solutions*. In this volume.

Winston, P. (1979) *Artificial Intelligence*, Addison-Wesley, Reading, Mass.

8

ARTIFICIAL INTELLIGENCE: NEXT GENERATION SOLUTIONS
ARNOLD KRAFT
DIGITAL EQUIPMENT CORPORATION, BOSTON

My aim is to give you a better feeling for some of the practical applications of expert systems and hopefully to enable you to draw some analogies to instances in your own work of how expert systems and artificial intelligence might apply. AI should not be thought of as a replacement vehicle but rather as something that you should add to your toolkit to help you solve problems.

Artificial intelligence, broadly speaking, has two purposes:

1. To better understand the nature of intelligence, which is really the concern of university research laboratories today, and
2. To make computers more useful, which is what I will be concentrating on.

There are several different views of AI. Professor Davis of MIT thinks of it as a new way to represent knowledge similar to the way people do. Dr Hassing of a government agency in the United States thinks that it is a good way to amplify intelligence; that is, to capture knowledge and put it to use. Dr Bob Balzer of the University of California at Los Angeles says that it allows you to delay commitments; that is, you are able to prototype what is going on rather than write out large specifications ahead of time. Lastly, Dennis O'Connor at Digital says that it allows you to solve problems that previously seemed intractable.

When we look at the applications at Digital we will see that many of them concern problems which bothered us deeply in the past, but which we had tried and failed to solve using conventional technology. Hopefully, this will be a way to illustrate how you can overcome some of your own problems.

AI is considered by some to be a new field in computer science. In fact, it had its beginnings in the late 1950s but is only now coming to the commercial stage. There is a hardware and a software division in AI. On the hardware side, vision and speech input/output are very relevant although I will not discuss them much here. On the software side there are natural language capabilities, search and knowledge representation, and expert systems, which are the most important for Digital.

WHY IS DIGITAL SUPPORTING EXPERT SYSTEMS?

First, we want to increase the quality of our products, for we want to be the preferred vendor to all of our customers. Secondly, we want to increase our productivity, which means we cannot continue to put too many people on a problem for it gets too inefficient. Thirdly, there are definite financial benefits. Almost all of our projects, with the exception of a few early prototypes, did pay for themselves. We went through a rigorous financial analysis to see whether the benefits outweighed the costs and the answer always came up yes, or we would not have continued. The problems we tackled were tough, as you will see, but needed to be solved. We captured the expert knowledge in a flexible way, which is an important point, for the world's technology is changing very very rapidly, and we have to be able to keep up with it and integrate it with current solutions.

WHY SHOULD ANY OF THIS MATTER TO YOU?

There are three reasons:

1. You may need solutions to previously intractable problems.
2. Expert system solutions to your business problems may have potential financial benefits.
3. Expert systems make it possible to capture your unique experience and expertise.

The biggest reason is the third. I have talked to many customers who are potential and now actual users of branches of artificial intelligence, and a common thread has been that they already do something better than their competitors and want to know how they can lever that skill to increase their share of the marketplace.

At Digital we have experts throughout the company and we hope to be able to focus their expertise on satisfying customers. We came up with a concept called the Knowledge Network (Figure 8.1). On the lower left is the customer, our most critical concern. XSEL (for expert selling assistant) helps sales people configure a system that is guaranteed to be accurate in terms of the components that are needed. XCON is an engineering system which ensures that the configuration is correct. I will discuss these in more detail later.

EXPERT SYSTEMS AT DIGITAL

The figure gives a partial list of the applications that are current and running, with some of the prototypes still under development. XCON is the oldest one, having begun in 1979. Basically, its job is to look at each and every order coming into the company and to ensure that that order is complete and totally accurate, and to provide documentation for manufacturing on how to build it. XSEL takes all the knowledge of XCON and makes it more usable and interactive for a person out in the field. We can dial up on a remote terminal anywhere in the field to connect with a computer back at the office which will come up with a configuration for you. XSITE takes the result of the XSEL session and helps you to place the computer in your computer room, by asking, 'How large is it at the doors, is it a raised floor or a plain floor, etc?'

An intelligent diagnostic tool (IDT) is being used in our Burlington, Vermont, factory to diagnose machines that we believe to be faulty as they pass down the production line. It has been able to capture the expertise of the best field service people and comes up with a diagnosis as fast as the best people, and significantly faster than a person just out of training school.

AISPEAR is another type of diagnostic tool, which tries to look ahead (unlike IDT, which works on a system already diagnosed to have a fault). We first asked engineers whether they can ever tell ahead of time that something is going to fail, say, in a week or two's time. They said yes, but when we asked how, they could only say something like, 'Well, we catch these signals

FIGURE 8.1   The Knowledge Network

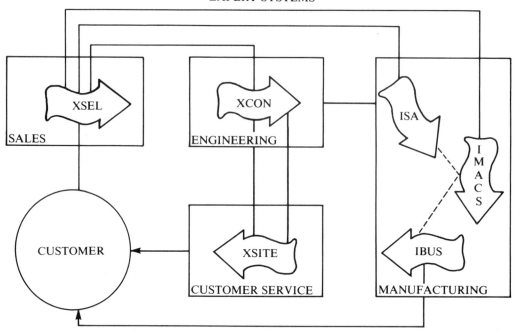

from different places and put them all together somehow in our minds and decide that, say, a tape drive is going to fail a week from now.' More often than not, these people were correct. So we tried to capture that expertise, to pick up electronically or otherwise the same signals and inputs as they did and bring them together, and sure enough we were able to. AISPEAR today is helping our field service people to do predictive as opposed to panic maintenance.

The troubleshooting consultant (NTC) works amongst our many computer-connected networks. We have over one thousand computers connected worldwide over a variety of different networks, ranging from a piece of wire to satellite links. It is very understandable that the network might go down now and again, and we wanted to figure out how we could correct the fault and get back up as fast as possible. In this case we also had a number of expert diagnosticians working in the network troubleshooting area, and so we tried again to capture their expertise and put it to use. The result is a consultant which works on-line with the troubleshooter: information is given to the computer, which responds with advice to investigate a particular board, for example.

TEACHVMS is a consultant of a totally different nature. We have customers who have bought our DEC-20 computers and are migrating to our VAX line. They are used to working on the 20 but find it difficult to move onto a VAX, having learnt different syntax and semantics for the commands. In order to help them, we wrote TEACHVMS which will give you the VAX VMS command corresponding to the one used on the DEC-20: for example, 'connect' is the VMS command corresponding to the 'set host' command on the DEC-20 for connecting two computers. TEACHVMS has been given free to many of our customers.

The prototypes are expert systems that are under development: they are not yet completed and may not ever be (because we always watch out that they maintain a cost-benefit ratio and do the job originally intended). IMACS is being used in our New Hampshire factory to try to coordinate seven different factory systems within one assembly plant, as if it were a senior production scheduler or even plant manager. The seven systems are all computerized and work really well, but they don't talk to another as well as they could. Our goal here was to try to get them to connect in a more or less heuristic or rule-of-thumb fashion, the way a plant manager would, and also to be able to tune the system (for example, to push very hard for revenue one quarter, or for profits, or to increase throughputs or output). IMACS allows you to tune the factory for the maximum gain that you wish.

ISA looks at the seemingly simple problem of matching orders with the list of available materials. If they match, fine, but mostly they don't, supply and demand being what it is. Customers order what they want when they want and we can never predict exactly what we should have at the right time. If you looked at the office of a typical scheduling person, you would see lots of little notes stuck up on the wall, and when an order comes in and it is matched with what is in stock and it is found that, say, a disk drive is missing, then he would look at those notes and perhaps find one that has been put on one side because it's to a country we can't ship to, maybe, and then 'borrow' its disk drive and leave another note saying 'IOU 1 disk drive 4 months from now'. Perhaps he remembers this note, but anyway the goal of ISA is to capture the rules of thumb used by schedulers and to do a better job of making the maximum use of our available material to meet the demand. ISA is just about to go into production, and I think it will do very well.

The intelligent project management system (IPMS) is to be used in another of our factories to control the evolution of a product from engineering into manufacturing. The traditional technology involves trying to track about 2000 events. It is extremely tedious and when people do it we call it a 'burn-out job' — they do it once, and they are off to find a new job. We are hoping to capture the expertise (and the heartaches and triumphs) of the people who do this. The project management system has to be very flexible, and at the moment it looks quite promising.

XPRESS grew out of a very trying need we had during the development of XSEL. People using XSEL were scattered all over the United States and were dialling up over portable terminals to use XSEL back at our development laboratory. When they had a problem they had to be able to get the information over to us right away. The first thing we tried was electronic mail, but although we got the message right away there wasn't enough of the context. You have probably had experiences of running a program and finding something going wrong in the middle but not knowing what happened — was it the program, did you keyboard it wrongly, was there noise on the line, was it a hardware problem, and so on? XPRESS provides an interactive capability to interrupt a program at any juncture, right where the problem is, and to put in a comment. Behind the scenes, a complete trace of the program and all the keystrokes is kept and sent back to the program developers who then can look at it and try to understand what you were doing and what went wrong. XPRESS also records who sent the message, where he was, what time it was, who it was sent to, and when the answer went back, and so we have some good statistics building up on how long it takes to get an error fixed.

The last one is the long-range planning system (ILRPS), which I am particularly fond of, perhaps because it's the hardest. Its goal is to be a smart spreadsheet. When you use an ordinary spreadsheet, you finish up with a matrix of information, which may look right but may sometimes 'smell' funny, although you can't piece together why. You ask yourself whether you added the second shift bid, whether you bought more materials, whether you contracted out, and so on, and if you find a supporting hypothesis all well and good. With ILRPS, we hope that you as the user could key in those heuristics and that the system would be smart enough to check out the spreadsheet for you the way you would do, not necessarily using hard, cold mathematics.

THREE EXPERT SYSTEMS IN DETAIL

I will now discuss the three most heavily used programs in more detail. XCON, the expert configurer, is used to configure virtually all system orders coming into the company today. It began by configuring VAXs and it has now grown to cover the PDP-11 series as well. We look at every system and completely configure it before its manufacture. We validate the customer order to be sure that all components ordered are correct and complete as stated. If there is something wrong, we tell the customer what we think is wrong, why it is wrong, and how to fix it. Lastly, extremely detailed output is given to the technicians, both those in the factory and those on site who will assemble the system.

One of the benefits we didn't predict relates to the interface between engineering and manufacturing. It seems that the engineers would build a product and toss it over to the manufacturers, who would catch it and say, 'No way — you can't get your hand in there to build it like that', and return it to the engineers. This back and forth took a lot of time and therefore money. XCON now occupies the demilitarized zone in the middle, and catches all the problems before they actually go across. As a result, we have decreased our time to market.

XCON has been in daily use since January 1980. It is extremely accurate, and performs about six times the number of functions that the human technical editors did manually on each order before. XCON has now looked at nearly 80 000 system orders and is about 98 per cent accurate (compared to the estimated 75 per cent accuracy of our human technical editors). So we consider XCON a smashing success.

People often ask what we have saved with this. Well I'm afraid our lawyers stop me talking about all the money, but I can say that we've spent many, many millions of dollars developing this and it has saved a great deal more. In order to continue with a project within the company we have to justify it, as opposed to new product development. In order to measure the benefits we started off looking at some major measurable factors, such as the technical editor population and allowances (that is, what we give away to the customer). In fact, we have the same number of people as in 1980, and their job has actually intensified for now they look at the worst cases rather than each and every one. Allowances have been reduced. Previously, we would not discover that, say, a cable was missing until too late, and then we would give the cable away, send it by air freight, have two service calls, and so on, which all adds up. If, however, we get it right first time then it stays right and we have reduced the number of handlings per order. Also, we have lower installation expenses, because the time to install has been dramatically reduced and so has the number of field service trips required.

In the mid-1970s we had tried twice to perform this same task using conventional software technology (using BASIC on a PDP-11) but had failed. It was quite frustrating thinking that we had captured a rule about configurations and then finding out that it wasn't quite right and not having the software capability to incorporate the change rapidly or to keep up with the volume of data. So in 1978 we began to experiment with Carnegie-Mellon University in what was then the new field of expert systems. Professor John McDermott came up with the first prototype by mid-1979 and within twelve months from the start we had publicly demonstrated the version. Two months later we cut over into actual use in the factory and it has grown ever since. It took about another year for our group to become the primary support for XCON. They had to learn the strange new language called OPS and to learn how to take all the knowledge in by themselves. We began to add the PDP-11s and today XCON has knowledge of over 7000 products.

XSEL was in fact our original goal, although we rather backed into it. Whereas XCON looks at an entire order and knows all of the parts that are going to be ordered at one time, XSEL has only one requirement: you first specify the central processing unit, and then, in any order you like, the line printer, memory, disk drives, and so on. The result from XSEL is a complete and accurate (98 per cent) configuration. Right now XSEL is being used by about one-third of our USA sales force, and we plan to train our European salesmen to use it as well.

There are a lot of problems in assisting sales people. Sales people, with respect, do not have the ability to understand the details of hardware configurations. Some of the older ones are very smart in electronics, but some of the newer ones don't know the details very well. Since many of the orders coming in were incomplete and inconsistent, it was difficult to estimate delivery and very expensive getting the proper data out to the sales people. Now XSEL creates a configuration which can be modified as desired, and you can add spares which are not part of the configuration.

The design strategy is worth explaining, as this was very important. We learned many lessons from XCON which we tried to apply with XSEL. First, you need a knowledge engineer (or group) able to write code in LISP or OPS or PROLOG. The users must be involved in the design: you can't just hand them a package on a platter and expect them to use it. You should put out a prototype for users to work with, to test it out.

Secondly, we have participative software design. This *is* a formal process, but we tried to make the process as informal as possible with our first group of 20 users. I would like to acknowledge the help here of Dr Enid Mumford of Manchester. She has spent a good deal of her professional career trying to help people understand how to change environments in factory automation or to introduce word processing into the office. We picked up on a lot of her work and this helped us immensely in getting going. What we did was take 20 sales people as 'volunteers' to help us. We spent the whole first day on what I call socio-psychological issues, considering whether they as sales people would be comfortable using the system. Some, for example, who didn't know how to type would be unhappy lugging around a portable terminal. Others who thought they knew everything there was to know about computers would not like the 'expert' being the terminal rather than themselves. Another problem, which really upset a couple of them, was that they no longer had the pleasure of walking back into the office to announce they'd got the order, with the whole office literally applauding: now the order is sent electronically over the office network and you never even show up. We addressed these issues for fully eight hours the first day, got over that hurdle and went on to a very successful project.

To summarize, then, in order to do participative design, you should carefully articulate four things: the tasks, the job satisfaction, the organizational needs, and the technical alternatives. Don't make a choice too early about which way to go. And remember to focus on the total, not just on the task.

The last of the trio is XSITE. The problem here was that site information was not really clear and was difficult to come by, and laying out a floor in the computer room is a difficult task. So we allowed the user interactively to enter any information about his computer room. He had two major alternatives: one is to say that he knows what his room is and to ask for the configuration to be fitted in it; the other is to ask for the system to determine the smallest amount of floor space into which the configuration will go. XSITE will handle both those alternatives, including multiple computer rooms, with lots of detail.

THE TROUBLESHOOTING CONSULTANT

Turning now to diagnostics, the network troubleshooting consultant (NTC) is fairly recent but extremely productive. We want to assist in the diagnosis of our network problems for the Ethernet or DECNET level with over 1000 interconnected computers. The task was to diagnose the problem and counsel the person fixing it. It's operational at a number of the sites today. We hope to spread it out eventually to as many people as need it. It addresses problems of a broken DECNET, which is our trade name for our networking software capability.

NTC will list the component suspected to have failed and discuss what may have caused it (noise on the line, perhaps, or faulty installation). It sequentially diagnoses network problems, by which I mean that you specify what you know about the problem and NTC responds with a hypothesis, which you respond to and work your way through the problem as if you were talking with one of the best diagnosticians in the company. We have found that problems can be identified a great deal faster, with helpful suggestions.

Crash diagnosis is something which bothers us a lot: it doesn't happen too often but when it does the volume of data is enormous. Somehow the best diagnosticians are able to look at this massive data and decide what to concentrate on. We have tried to capture that ability. We adopt the expert counselling approach, where you tell the system what you know and then weave a way through the mess together. We try to reduce the level of engineering expertise needed. There are only a few people who are really good at this and they can't be everywhere at once, and so we want to have this capability available to more people all the time.

Expert systems, then, are new tools not only for process control but for many different applications. There are problems which can be solved but take a lot of human expertise. There are people who seem to do much better at some tasks than any computer, but these may not be suitable expert system tasks. I can give you a few hints about when to choose an expert system approach. If you can't write a full formal specification, then develop a prototype and get it into the hands of users — then the specification will become much more obvious. If you think a problem has a solution but you can't uncover it, then maybe expert systems are a nice way to work. Also you may have a problem which you can't avoid, and you have to have a solution developed to the point of usability.

ADVANTAGES AND DISADVANTAGES

Now let's consider some of the negatives, which might influence a manager deciding whether to do this. First, expert systems are memory intensive from a computer perspective, but one of the reasons that AI is coming to the forefront today is that memory is much less expensive. In the early days it was only universities that could afford the luxury of a large computer. But AI is not part of the accepted culture: FORTRAN took 15 years to become an accepted language, so it'll take a little while for ours too.

Expert systems are not general purpose problem solvers. For many years to come I believe that AI's going to be a series of custom-built systems attacking problems one at a time. They're not going to be like payroll systems, where you take out 'Smith' and insert 'Jones' and have a nice, neat solution: it isn't going to be that easy. Also, you have to do a lot of education, from customer seminars to visits. Education is necessary for all levels from management to worker.

It's quite true that the maintenance requirements for expert system work can't be predicted. We began by just guessing how many people it would take to maintain XCON. It turns out that it's a small elite crew, and we're doing very well with that today. Technology is always going to eliminate jobs, and for this reason AI expert systems strike fear into the hearts of people. But it's not going to displace people any more than COBOL did when the first payroll was written.

It is most important, though, not to be oversold. Don't let me or anyone else tell you that AI is the be-all and end-all: it isn't. AI should be looked on as just one more tool to add to your kitbag to solve problems you couldn't solve before.

On the positive side, it works beautifully with things that change. We change XCON about every six weeks or so to have a whole new release coming out very frequently. It may not achieve 100 per cent accuracy, but I don't think it ever will until the problem freezes. As long as you are in a dynamic environment, you must look at the potential gain: we were at 75 per cent correct and we are now at 98 per cent correct, which is a marvellous gain.

Also, we can have an incremental product type of development. This is most important for getting knowledge from the expert. Writing a dry paper specification is quite difficult, and lots of people can't tell you how they work anyway, but give them a prototype and then they'll tell you how it really should work. They're much better at going through examples. Our rule of thumb is that within three months we have a small, even very small, prototype going. Of course, you must have an expert, someone on the staff who is going to tell you about the problem, and you must have management support, which comes if management understands it.

GETTING STARTED

When getting started, there's a demand for new skills, which enables people to mature from one job into another. Most of our expert systems people today were not working on them before and were not trained in AI: we trained them ourselves. There are two kinds of people: knowledge engineers and expert system programmers. A knowledge engineer is a person who can interview the problem expert, get the information out, and then look on the other side and say which branch of AI technology should be chosen. Once started, the expert system programmer should be able to develop and make more robust the original analysis. However, he usually has not had enough experience or training to know which of three or four methodologies to use.

You need a small core group to help on the first application and then to bring in apprentices from remote groups. Don't have what I call a 'DP-shop syndrome', a central organization which everything goes to and which knows all what's going on. Instead, say that you're going to help an organization to get started — they send a person in, you train him, in a year, say, their problem is solved, and he goes back to the organization as the AI expert.

Start up many projects in many areas, with the frame of mind that some of them might fail. You may not have the expertise in your own shop, so don't be afraid to hire consultants, enough to get started and over the hump.

There are a number of small vendors today producing what I call AI program development environments. There are a very limited number of people capable of developing an AI program. So, how can you capture the expertise of world-class AI programmers? To my knowledge, there are major developments under way. These will allow you to sit down and key in some knowledge and information without knowing much about AI and to have the program generate AI applications. This will help all of us to make tremendous strides forward.

THE PATTERN OF DEVELOPMENT

We start off with an informal specification, from which we write our first program (Figure 8.2). We distribute it and get some feedback from the experts, and we continue in that mode, as the system grows and grows. The specification is not totally irrelevant — we didn't really write out the formal specifications for any of our programs until well into their development stage.

At the beginning you actually need to identify a problem (Figure 8.3). Our strategy is to work on problems which are critically important to our operation: we don't do a toy application, just to say we've done some AI. When we've selected something important, we write down a small, hard-headed document — the whole thing for XSEL was two pages long — saying what we are trying to accomplish, the time frames, and the cost.

FIGURE 8.2   The pattern of development

HOW DO EXPERT SYSTEMS WORK?

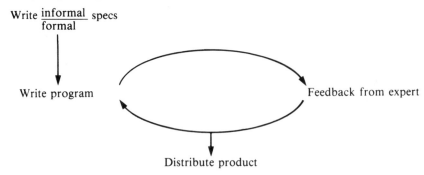

FIGURE 8.3   Stages of development

EXPERT SYSTEMS DEVELOPMENT

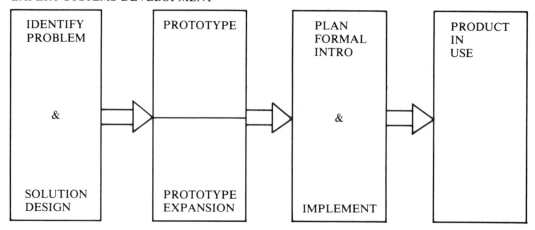

Once the prototype is done, we really push it hard. One has to be thick-skinned about this. People will come back and say 'It doesn't work', but we can't get paranoid and worry that we can't program and the users can't worry that they can't explain themselves. The problem is out in the middle of the table and you both have to work together to solve it.

As you expand the prototype and get nearer to the formal stages, then the lessons you have learned in your data processing shop become extremely important. You begin to worry about how you are going to integrate it. For instance, with XSEL we had to think about using the customer master price list, and other standard files, in conjunction with XSEL. We didn't duplicate or redo any of those, but we worked very closely with the field-order administration people.

The major difference in the end is that it is an ongoing process. There are no post-mortems at the end to help you understand why it failed or didn't fail. The system is growing or evolving. The programs are not smart enough to heal themselves, but they are not static. If you learn something, you don't just sit on it — you put it in. That's why we have a release every six weeks.

Finally, a word on natural language. There are lots of products coming out that are conversational, pretty intelligent, front-ends to a database you might already have. That is going to come to the fore, but also, perhaps a little slower but more important in the long run, we are going to have natural language subroutines which you can incorporate in your current program to make a conventional program much more conversational.

SUMMARY

Many knowledge-based systems are being built around the world. Many of them are quite productive and in day-to-day use. It's a technology that's in its infancy, but beginning to grow. At Digital there are many problems, as we've seen, that resisted conventional solutions which we've been able to solve with this technology and it has already become an important part of our repertoire. Virtually every major group in DEC has an AI effort going on. At the moment there are over 200 people involved in AI work in the Corporation. We need this to help in our complex and changing environment.

When we started with XCON and XSEL we had to do something to get the sales people going, and at the time there was an advertising slogan, 'Digital changes the way the world thinks about computers'. We did our best to take off on that so that 'XCON and XSEL changed the way Digital thinks about programming'. All of this has helped us to become a leading vendor for AI, which was not our original goal. We develop hardware, software and other things to get our customers started.

QUESTIONS

Q. You discussed the financial benefits in terms of Digital, but in what other areas do you think there could be a cost saving? In Digital you've made the organization more efficient, and I can see you could do the same in the private sector. But could you move, for instance, into education?

A. Yes, AI has already come into education through a language called LOGO, developed at the MIT Artificial Intelligence Laboratory. That's one area. As an example of this capturing of rare skills, in a much easier to understand environment than ours, I visited a major food corporation which develops those carbohydrates you have for breakfast and they had two carbohydrate chemists, expert at putting these new formulas together. They wanted to capture that expertise. There are many similar applications in non-computer companies.

Q. You mentioned several times the need to get human expertise from experts. Can you tell me about the sorts of technique that you have for doing that? Is it informal or do you have formalized techniques?

A. To acquire the knowledge from the expert, we usually do it on a fairly informal basis. As often as not, it starts on a case by case basis. With the configurations, we simply took an order and a configuration and showed it to several experts. If they all agreed, then fine; that's a way to start. If they disagreed, as was usually the case, we said, 'Why do you disagree?', and then tried to hash it through until we came to a conclusion. Then each time a new order came through we compared the program's results with what the human experts would have done, and grew our knowledge on a case by case basis. It's very difficult for humans to articulate other than on an anecdotal basis.

Q. I am quite curious about the situation where you have a particular employee with very particular skills, which are his or her marketable quality. If they in fact convey all of those skills that they have to you as a corporation, they lose their marketability. How do you persuade people to cooperate in providing all the information you need, which is in the end for Digital's benefit, but not the individual employee's?

A. An excellent question! Do you want to see the scar I have for that story?

Q. I mean, how far are you up the ladder? How much pressure is exercised by you upon others, or vice versa?

A. I can understand your perspective, but I would respectfully disagree. We ran headlong into what you've just said with XCON. When we first put XCON into development mode, everything was comfortable, with people contributing knowledge happily. When we ran into the brick wall was the first day we said we'd drop the manual system and go live. From that day for the next two weeks, I didn't see another piece of paper — not a thing to show that it was going on at all. So I drove up to the factory, went in the back door, literally, walked out on the shop floor, and looked for the output of XCON. There was none. Finally, someone broke down and said to me that the manager of the technical edit group had told them that if they used XCON . . . He feared exactly what you said — that if he told us everything he knew about editing, he'd be on the street.

Q. But I didn't mean they'd lose their jobs, but their marketability once they want to move on. The skills which they had to enable them to get a job have now been acquired by a computer. They're competing with something which has recorded what they can do.

A. Well, partially true.

Q. But it's a totally different question.

A. OK, let me continue. Perhaps I'll address it. When the manager and I sat down and talked about it, we realized that he was telling us only a very small portion of his knowledge. What was reserved for him and his crew were the worst of the orders. They now had to deal with all the exceptions. They actually became more valuable — it actually upgraded their job. This small group of people has to keep the system 'honest', for they're the final judges of XCON, and to deal with all the situations where XCON fails. It's only 2 per cent but it's a non-trivial amount in volume. So they're more marketable than they were before. What people never lose is their ability to acquire new knowledge. These programs are smart, but as narrow as a pin-head.

Q. So you encourage people to see that there are gateways for them to walk through?

A. Right, and what we did with XSEL (which is why I spent so much time on the 'participative design') was to work through the barriers with the sales people before we even started. Would this reduce their marketability as sales people if they knew *anybody* could key in an order on a terminal? It turned out not to bother them at all, because deep down they thought it was drudge work, looking through forty pounds of catalogue to come up with the right order.

Q. Could I change track and ask about the programming technology involved? All your systems, I understand, are LISP-based. As you know, there's quite a difference in the tradition in the US and in Europe as regards the predominance given to LISP as against PROLOG. Did your knowledge engineers evaluate the potential of PROLOG?

A.   First let me clarify that they're not all in LISP. Some are in a language called OPS, which was originally based on LISP. One of the beauties of LISP is that you can dynamically prototype something else. Currently, we're about half LISP and half OPS. We have looked at PROLOG. For the projects we've tackled, PROLOG didn't fit exactly right. We've continued to run very small internal experiments, but so far it has not proved the right vehicle, for us, anyway. But we are keeping up with it. The Japanese in the Fifth Generation Project adopted PROLOG as their vehicle of choice, but I hear lately that a number of their PROLOG functions are becoming more like LISP over time, because it didn't have sufficient flexibility for certain problem characteristics. I think that in the long run PROLOG will be needed for a certain class of problems which are more mathematically oriented.

FURTHER READING

Bachant, J. and McDermott, J. (1984) R1 revisited: four years in the trenches, *AI Magazine*, Vol.5, No.3, pp 21–32. (*Note*: R1 is a previous or alternative name for XCON)

Forgy, C.L. (1981) OPS5 user's manual. Technical Report, Department of Computer Science, Carnegie-Mellon University

Hayes-Roth, F., Waterman, D.A. and Lenat, D.B. (1983) *Building Expert Systems*, Addison-Wesley, Reading, Mass

McDermott, J. (1982) R1: a rule-based configurer of computer systems, *Artificial Intelligence*, Vol.19, pp 39–88

Polit, S. (1985) R1 and beyond: AI technology transfer at DEC, *AI Magazine*, Vol.6, No.4, pp 76–78

9
IMAGE UNDERSTANDING
JOHN FRISBY
UNIVERSITY OF SHEFFIELD

INTRODUCTION

One of the earliest applications of computers was the processing of visual data, and that field has now become an enormous one, spreading over many and varied tasks. For example, it is concerned with such things as automatic inspection — detecting cracks in printed circuit boards and milk bottles, flaws in castings, screening of medical images, automatic processing of cancer smears, and so on. There's also a large application area in remote-sensing where the goal is to process automatically, say, satellite images for the purposes of management and exploration of resources, and, of course, for automatic map-making. The field is also involved in creating aids for the partially sighted — reading machines, 'automatic guide dogs'. Military applications include target acquisition and target tracking. And there's an enormous applications area in the automation of industrial processes; for example, the automatic visual guidance of welders, cutters, and machine tools and the visual control of various assembly tasks. In general there are a lot of applications trying to make computing power more accessible by going beyond the usual keyboard entry of information to allow a visual input.

The whole field is very large, and here I can do no more than introduce you to some parts of it. I have selected my material with two goals in mind. First, to address an audience made up of industrialists and engineers who have little or no prior knowledge of the field. And secondly, to say something about what the Alvey Programme is doing in a sub-section of the field, called *Image Understanding*.

To give myself a linking theme, I've chosen to consider some of the problems of equipping a small automatic assembly workstation in an industrial environment with visual guidance. Imagine that we have the task of designing a computer system capable of taking visual images of a scene (Figure 9.1), and using them to guide the assembly of some parts (Figure 9.2). We see a plate with a peg in it. We want the computer system to put that plate in a particular position, then take another part, the plate with a hole in it, and place it on the peg, and finally put on these two the L-shaped capping piece with an indentation in it — to form the whole assembly.

An extended version of much of the material covered in this lecture together with suggestions for further reading can be found in Part III of a recent Open University publication entitled *Perception and Representation: a Cognitive Approach* by Ilona Roth and John P. Frisby (Open University Press: Milton Keynes; 1986). Thanks are given to the Open University Press for permission to use material in that source to expand here on the contents of the Alvey Lecture, which of course forms the basis of the present paper.

FIGURE 9.1   The task: equipping a workstation with visual guidance

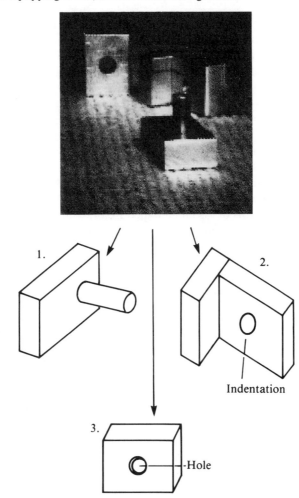

Components

Indentation

Hole

FIGURE 9.2   The final assembly required of the system

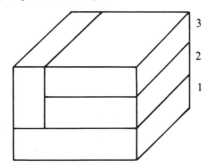

Industrialists will, I hope, forgive me for choosing such a small and simple assembly task. Clearly, a really valuable application would be putting together a brake assembly, or pieces of an electric motor, or something of that sort. But this simple example will serve my purpose of introducing the major difficulties that have been found in giving visual guidance to such tasks in general.

In many industrial situations, it will often be the case that the position of parts as they come to the assembler can be controlled, so that the computer can be told where to expect to 'see' various parts. Now although that may be true for many applications it is also true that it would be very helpful if the computer could be given some means of dealing with misalignments of the parts if they *don't* happen to arrive at the workstation in quite the correct orientations. Or sometimes a part might be missing, or the robot might drop a part while handling it. It would be nice to have the computer able to deal automatically with such situations, and use vision as a basis for taking appropriate corrective actions.

In general, it needs little imagination to see that if we could give the computer system the ability to guide visually the assembly of parts in the flexible way characteristic of humans, then that would be remarkably useful in many industrial situations. But it turns out that giving that kind of flexible visual guidance to even simple assembly tasks is beyond the present state of the art (although some limited forms of visual guidance are presently available). I will review some of the problems that have been found in trying to achieve a flexible *general purpose vision system*.

The first thing to realize is that human vision only *seems* effortless: in fact, it is the end product of an amazingly complex set of computations. Let us go through some of the problems that have to be solved. A basic one is recognizing the parts. We need to identify the plate with the peg, the plate with the hole, and so on. That's a big field in its own right. Also, we need to work out their spatial layout in the scene, and we need to identify certain surfaces for grasping, to find suitable pick-up points for the robot arm. So we need to have concepts available such as 'supporting', 'touching', 'fixed', 'stable'. All these aspects crop up in even our small assembly task involving just three blocks.

Moreover, the required visual guidance needs to be delivered in a reasonably fast time, and it needs to be integrated with information from touch sensors on the robot gripper. And we want the system to be able to cope with the vagaries of natural lighting.

Now, visual guidance of that sort is a very tall order, beyond the competence of any present-day computer vision system. I would like to explain some of the difficulties and the problems that are being worked on.

FROM IMAGES TO SCENE REPRESENTATIONS THAT MAKE SCENE ATTRIBUTES EXPLICIT

To begin at the beginning, let us take a television image of the kind of scene that I have just been describing (Figure 9.3). In the first place we have to get the image into the computer in a form which it can begin to analyze.

The first step is to measure local intensity values all over the image. This is shown (Figure 9.3) for the sample of the image in the inset box. Each number records what is often called an image 'grey level'. Each one is also known as a 'pixel', which is a contraction of PICture ELement. These are the numbers then that comprise 'the computer's image' that it needs to analyze.

The thing to make clear about the grey level image is that it makes explicit only local point-by-point intensity values. By 'explicit information' I mean information available in a form that is immediately useful for subsequent processing. All the interesting things about the scene in Figure 9.3, the things that we so readily see in it, all are only 'implicit' in this array of numbers. For instance, where the parts are, which we so easily see, is not made explicit in the array of pixels. Which parts go together is similarly not evident. We effortlessly see the peg as joined to the lowest block in the image and not attached to the block behind, an important piece of information that needs to be made explicit if we are going to manipulate the blocks sensibly. But that information has to be extracted from the pixel array — it is not already available there.

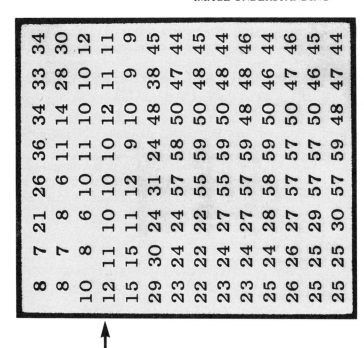

Pixels

FIGURE 9.3 Digitized TV image

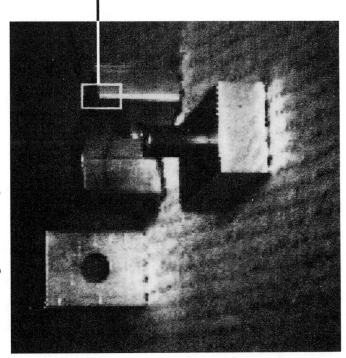

* Only local intensities explicit
* Everything else implicit

And, of course, there are very many other aspects of this scene which need to be made explicit for guiding assembly tasks that are only implicit in the grey level database.

IMAGE UNDERSTANDING NEEDS MULTIPLE REPRESENTATIONS

I will consider the problems of making useful visual information explicit using the general tactics and style of approach that have formed a field often known as *Image understanding*. A distinguishing attribute of the field is the view that it is highly desirable to build up many representations on the way to guiding action.

The first of these representations is a description of intensity changes in the image, because places where intensities change are likely to be where things are happening in the image which are informative about the scene. For instance, edges of objects usually project into the image as intensity changes.

FIGURE 9.4   Representations required for image understanding: 1

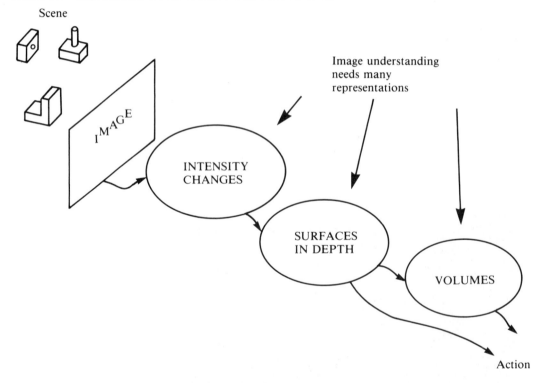

So, making image intensity changes explicit is the typical first step. However, we want to move on from these to representations making explicit the properties of surfaces in the scene, first because we want to be able to grip them, and secondly because we want to be able to plan collision-free trajectories for our robot arm. So we want to know the 3D spatial layout of those surfaces. We also need to represent surfaces because the way surfaces enclose volumes defines the shape of the parts of interest — hence the important task of object recognition can be tackled using descriptions of visible surfaces.

These then are the broad categories of representations that the Image Understanding field has grappled with, and which I shall be discussing. I would like in passing to point out that there is another massive field in the computer vision area, often known as 'Pattern Recognition and Image Processing' (PRIP for short), which is highly valuable, highly industrially relevant, and about which I'll have nothing to say. PRIP's operations are largely confined to the pictorial domain — they work on the image and descriptions of the image intensity changes. PRIP tends to work therefore with effectively two-dimensional objects, such as letters, cells for automatic medical screening, things of that kind. Often its preoccupation is with classification, such as deciding whether a cell is cancerous or not: highly relevant, highly important, well deserving in support, and the Alvey Programme is indeed giving it support under the Man–Machine Interface programme. But I shall be talking about Image Understanding (IU) which is characterized by a concern for multiple representations, making both 3D and 2D entities explicit.

I will begin by introducing some terminology. Figure 9.5 is the same basic picture as Figure 9.4, but notice now the terms 'primal sketch' and '2½D sketch'.

FIGURE 9.5   Representations required for image understanding: 2

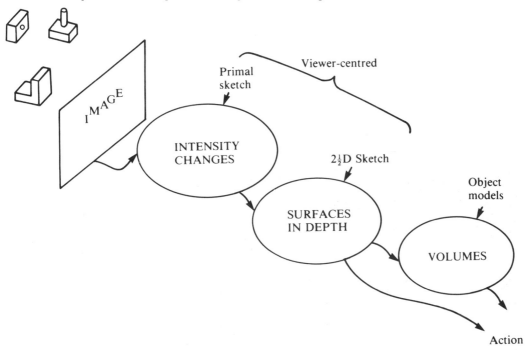

The primal sketch (a phrase coined by a prestigious, but sadly late, member of the IU field called David Marr) describes intensity changes in the image. The 2½D sketch describes the depth structure and other characteristics of visible scene surfaces (e.g. colour, illumination etc.). Both these terms have the word 'sketch' in them to emphasize that they are descriptions taken from the viewpoint of the observer: hence they are said to be 'viewer-centred' representations. The label '2½D' is a way of emphasizing that it deals only with visible surfaces. Clearly, there are surfaces in the scene hidden by the ones we can see, and these are not dealt with in the 2½D sketch — though some of the properties of these hidden surfaces might be available from volume representations dealing with 'object models', once the appropriate object model has been selected, i.e. once the object has been recognized. So, the sequence of representations is:

primal sketch (image domain), then $2\frac{1}{2}$D sketch (scene surfaces domain), then object models (volume representations).

LEVELS OF ANALYSIS

I'd like you to note that I'll be trying to emphasize that, in considering the problems of computing each type of representation, we need to be clear as we go along of different levels of conceptual analysis, a separate concern from levels of representation. The top level of conceptual analysis, *Level 1*, is to do with specifying very clearly the goals of the computation — what exactly we are trying to make explicit — and trying to say what constraints there are for interpreting the usually ambiguous visual information to get the representation required. This level is sometimes called the *computation theory level*. The next level down, *Level 2*, deals with *algorithms* which take advantage of the constraints specified by the computational theory to deliver the representations that we want. An algorithm is a set of procedures which specify in detail a sequence of operations that achieve a given end. The third level of analysis is to do with *hardware*, which I won't be able to discuss here at all.

THE PRIMAL SKETCH

Let's consider then the primal sketch, a description of intensity changes in the image. Let us take that little insert again (Figure 9.6), showing a sample of grey levels — a small subset of the set of the pixels comprising the image. Remember, we are trying to compute symbols that stand for intensity changes, or 'edges', in the image. For instance, there is an edge given by the transition left-to-right of the numbers 24, 27, 57, going from relatively dark to quite bright. We want to be

FIGURE 9.6   The primal sketch

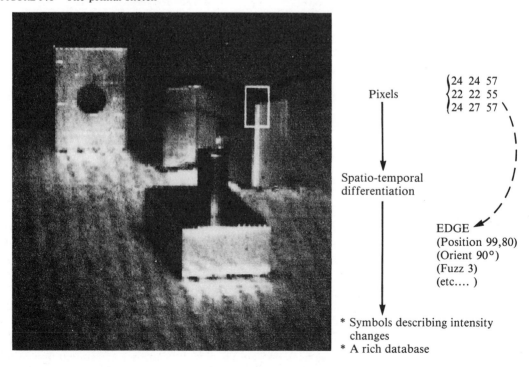

Pixels
$$\begin{cases} 24 \ \ 24 \ \ 57 \\ 22 \ \ 22 \ \ 55 \\ 24 \ \ 27 \ \ 57 \end{cases}$$

Spatio-temporal
differentiation

EDGE
(Position 99,80)
(Orient 90°)
(Fuzz 3)
(etc....)

* Symbols describing intensity
  changes
* A rich database

able to compute a description that tells us that there is an 'edge point' there, in that position, which is part of an intensity change with a vertical orientation. The description should also tell us whether it is a sharp edge or a rather fuzzy one (in fact, this edge is quite sharp), and also give some measure of the contrast of the edge, and various other parameters. The whole set of primal sketch symbols, standing for different types of intensity change — edges, lines, blobs, etc. — form a database for subsequent processing aimed at getting descriptions of scene surfaces and volumes — the things we need to make explicit from the image descriptions of the primal sketch to achieve our goal of guiding actions.

The centre of the stage here is *spatio-temporal differentiation*: 'temporal', because we must remember that we want to be able to deal with images from our scene as they change over time; for example, changes in the images produced by objects moving through the scene, or changes caused by camera movement. Hence, we need to capture edges as they move. Spatio-temporal differentiation is a rather technical topic though and I will not try to deal with it in this brief review. I'm going to assume that we have already got some descriptions of the edges in our image (Figure 9.7). Moreover, as that image is a single snapshot, I will not consider further the problems and benefits of dealing with images changing over time.

FIGURE 9.7   Intensity changes in image

* Digitized TV image   * 'Raw edges'

   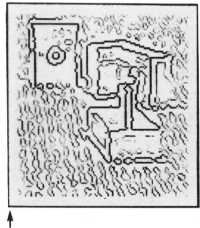

↑   ↑
Only local intensities   Raw primal sketch
explicit, everything   assertions
else implicit

Here then is our image (Figure 9.7), with an illustration, derived in our lab, of some things called *raw edges* that were found in this image. They are called 'raw', because they are the first primitive assertions of things of interest that have been found in the image. They have not been grouped in any way, they are very local, each little point representing a statement that spatio-temporal differentiation has found an intensity transition in a certain position. In the computer will be stored various parameters attached to that point which describe the properties of the edge point.

Now, that is the first step, the first results of our spatio-temporal differentiation. What is to be done with these raw edges? Well, the first thing that has been found necessary is something called 'grouping'. Let's attend to the table-top surface on which the objects are lying. The raw edges here happen to form little irregularly shaped loops, and our human visual system readily sees these structures. But in the raw edge representation, shown in Figure 9.7, that information is only implicit: it now needs to be made explicit. In order to do that we have to group raw edge points together into higher order structures. We can then write into our database some symbols, say 'R' for Region (Figure 9.8). These 'R' symbols serve as a record that a particular cluster of raw edges can be meaningfully grouped together, with the existence of the new 'thing' being logged by the 'R' symbol in the database. Having got out these Regions, we can then look for structures among them. The human eye in this case readily sees the Regions in Figure 9.8 arranged in 'Lines'. We need to get the computer also to find those Line structures and write down symbols for them, e.g. each L (Figure 9.8) represents a 'Line of Regions'.

FIGURE 9.8   The image, with raw edges

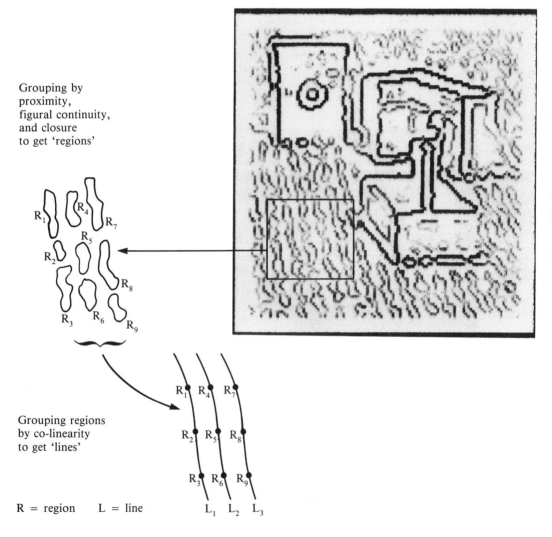

Grouping by proximity, figural continuity, and closure to get 'regions'

Grouping regions by co-linearity to get 'lines'

R = region   L = line

Symbols of this kind have been called 'place tokens' by Marr, because they are tokens standing for structures that can be found in the image at certain places. The business of naming image structures is an example of *The Principle of Explicit Naming*. The idea is, if you want to manipulate anything, give it a name, then you can operate on it, group it, do things with it. The Principle of Explicit Naming is right at the centre of what symbolic computation is all about, and hence right at the heart of the enterprise of Artificial Intelligence.

FIGURE 9.9   Grouping processes

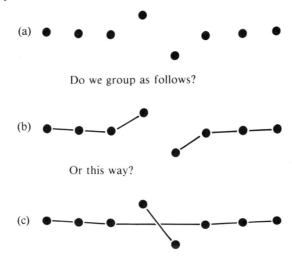

Do we group as follows?

Or this way?

To recap, having got our raw edges, we then try to group them. But in attempting to do that, immediately a deep and classic problem arises, typical of so many vision problems. And that is ambiguity. Suppose the points at the top of Figure 9.9 stood for certain image structures, say like those blobs that I previously described to you: how are we to group them up as forming higher order structures? We could group most of the points to form a horizontally oriented 'Line', and leave the remaining two as out-flyers belonging to a quite different structure, perhaps part of a vertical line of entities crossing over the first. Or, we could form two curved groupings, as shown here (Figure 9.9(b)). Which is it? Well, we need what are called *constraints*. We need some way of guiding (constraining) our choice of what grouping to do. Finding constraints appropriate to a given visual information processing task turns out to be a recurring theme of great importance in Image Understanding. Vision is an undetermined problem in the sense that the image has many possible scenes which could have given rise to it. So knowledge in the form of constraints has to be brought to bear to interpret the image.

The knowledge can be of two broad types: it can be either general knowledge of the visual world — what typical surfaces and surface markings are like, what their typical depth variations are, and so on. Or it can be specific knowledge of particular expected objects: e.g. if we were working in a scene of industrial objects we might be looking for particular entities that can be grouped together in a particular way, because we know about specific properties of the objects to be assembled. Both these types of knowledge have been employed and both found valuable.

The knowledge needed for resolving ambiguities in grouping is usually enshrined in a set of *grouping rules* which specify which sorts of entities are allowed to go together. Consider the example shown here (Figure 9.10); we have an image of raw edges and I've picked out two of them. Each one has a list of parameters that describes them. Notice that each has a position, an orientation, and a contrast. (In Figure 9.10, low contrast edges are shown as grey, high contrast edges as very black.)

FIGURE 9.10 Grouping principles

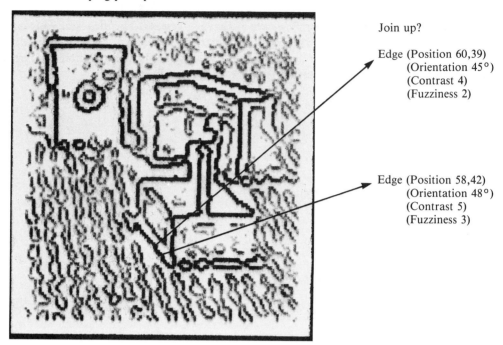

Join up?

Edge (Position 60,39)
(Orientation 45°)
(Contrast 4)
(Fuzziness 2)

Edge (Position 58,42)
(Orientation 48°)
(Contrast 5)
(Fuzziness 3)

Proximity, figural similarity, size, colour, figural continuity, motion, closure ... etc.

The problem is, should these two raw edges be joined together? Your human system immediately sees them as linked up. We have got to find ways of getting our computer to do a similar job. We need to apply a set of grouping rules which embody knowledge of appropriate *grouping principles*. For instance, one grouping principle is 'proximity', which says: try grouping together those things which are near to one another in the image. Another is 'figural similarity': group together things which are alike in their shape properties. In the examples chosen in Figure 9.10, we have figural similarity in orientation; not exact, but nevertheless good enough to satisfy a 'similar orientation' grouping rule, particularly if there are no better potential groupings for the edges in question. Another grouping principle is 'figural continuity': can the elements be linked to form continuous structures, such as long lines or smooth curves, as depicted for the Lines found in Figure 9.8? Yet another principle is 'closure': can a structure be found of elements forming an enclosed region in the image? This principle can be important for finding such entities as the Regions displayed in Figure 9.8.

Motion is also a very important grouping principle. I previously drew attention to the fact that any realistic vision system will need to take advantage of the rich source of information that comprises motion. The human grouping system is very good at grouping together things that have the same movement. The importance of movement is reflected in the fact that almost half of Alvey's IKBS Image Interpretation Research Theme is devoted to capturing movement information from the images and using it to arrive at surface descriptions.

Nevertheless, although movement is important, it is also possible to do very well with static images. Let your eye play over the abstract pattern shown in Figure 9.11. You'll see all sorts of different structures. Sometimes you'll see large circles, sometimes small. Even square clusters of points become visible as you keep looking. You are watching here your own visual system run its own set of grouping processes, pulling together the various parts that it finds in the image that could 'go together', and 'writing down' in some database the structures it finds —

and often changing its mind as it goes along. This is your own visual system doing what I've been describing as 'applying grouping operations'.

FIGURE 9.11   Grouping in human vision

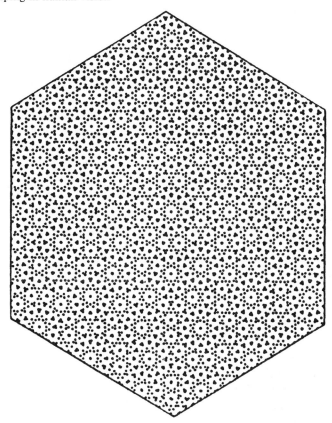

Experience in Image Understanding has shown that it is wise to apply grouping rules using what Marr called *The Principle of Least Commitment*. The idea here is that it is usually very costly to undo things done wrongly, particularly if the error occurs at an early stage in the visual processing hierarchy: hence, at any given stage, do only those things which you are pretty certain about. So in the case of grouping it is best to begin by applying the grouping rules very strictly, by insisting that elements must fit the rules pretty tightly if they are to be grouped together — and if they don't then leave the ambiguity unresolved for the moment. Then, as some of the competing possibilities are taken out by strict applications of the rules, so it becomes possible to employ less stringent demands safely for the remaining elements. In short, it has been found safest to apply grouping rules in a manner which progressively reduces the similarity demanded as the computation proceeds.

Various types of algorithms can be used for grouping purposes but one important general class bears the name *relaxation algorithms*. These have been found useful whenever it is necessary to disambiguate, in a gradual and sensible manner, possible links between a mass of interacting local elements so as to achieve a labelling of those elements (e.g. a label of the type that says 'elements a, k, p . . . all belong to the same entity'). A detailed example of a relaxation algorithm at work will be given later in connection with the stereo correspondence problem.

To recap on where we have got to so far (referring back to Figure 9.5): we start with an image of pixels, we find where the intensity changes are, and then we try to group up tokens representing edge points into higher order structures. This gives us a rich description of the image, called the primal sketch, that forms the database for all subsequent visual processing. The next stage is recovering a description of visible surfaces in the scene, the $2\frac{1}{2}$D sketch.

THE $2\frac{1}{2}$D SKETCH

First of all, why bother with a $2\frac{1}{2}$D sketch? The first reason is that objects are defined by the spatial structure of their surfaces, at least the objects that I'm concerned with here. That is, the sorts of things that we are trying to assemble are defined by the disposition in depth of the surfaces that make them up. So it seems a good idea to make those surfaces explicit, and to look for certain clusters of surface features that define the shape of our objects. The other important reason for computing a $2\frac{1}{2}$D sketch is that the pixel intensity values, the grey levels, muddle up (confound) a whole set of different aspects of the scene. They confound the reflectances of a surface (that is, how much light a surface reflects), with the amount of illumination falling on it. That is, a given pixel value may arise from a dark surface that is strongly illuminated, or from a light surface that is dimly illuminated — exactly the same number could come about in each (very different) situation. Pixel values will also be determined by surface orientation and the distance away of the surface.

In short, depending on the vagaries of particular illuminations or particular arrangements of objects, so pixel intensities for the parts of a given surface patch might be larger or smaller. Hence if we try to operate directly on edge tokens derived from pixels in an attempt to find regions relevant for the purposes of finding objects, and do that without first of all solving for these various properties of surfaces, then we can easily get into trouble. For example, a region represented as a 'thing' in the primal sketch might not correspond directly to part of an object at all, but perhaps be a shadow straddling two quite separate surfaces. Such matters need to be disentangled and this is done by way of computing the $2\frac{1}{2}$D sketch.

Having said that, it is worth remembering that working directly from the primal sketch rather than from a $2\frac{1}{2}$D sketch can work well if you are using two-dimensional patterns (the sort I referred to earlier in the PRIP field — recognizing certain sorts of cells, industrial flaws, cracks in castings etc.) for then you can often find the things of interest working straight off pixels and intensity change descriptions derived from them. But if you are interested in the assembly of the blocks from our sorts of image, then it has been found not to be a good idea to limit the database to those entities. The various surface properties we want are muddled up in the pictorial (image) domain, and they have got to be sorted out in the appropriate domain — that of representations making explicit scene surface properties.

The point here is: we have to work in the right representational domain to find the structures of interest. This is a basic and important realization that has emerged in Image Understanding. It was learnt from brutal experience that we have to be very careful to be always clear about which domain we are in (the image domain, surfaces domain, or volumes domain), and then find representations which suit the particular needs we have.

So those are the underlying reasons we are computing the $2\frac{1}{2}$D sketch. It's a representation describing surfaces, their reflectancies, illuminations, orientations, ranges. The $2\frac{1}{2}$D sketch will also include representations of surface discontinuities, for it is clearly very important to know where a surface ends, where surfaces join with other surfaces, and so on.

Now, there are a whole set of cues implicit in the primal sketch database which we can use for the purpose of getting out surface descriptions. There are shading cues, texture cues, motion cues, contour cues, stereo cues — and others. There's a massive '*shape from . . . .*' literature concerned with ways and means of getting out from one or other of those data sources the surface representations we are after. Research here is in general characterized by finding out what constraints are available for interpreting the ambiguous information available in the primal sketch and developing efficient ways of exploiting those constraints. Since I haven't time to discuss them all, I'm going to deal with just two, *shape from stereo* and *shape from contour*.

SHAPE FROM STEREO

Here (Figure 9.12) we have a scene made up of a square being imaged by two cameras, shown as globes (cf. human eyes), each one looking at the centre of the square. The figure depicts a simplified geometry of stereo projection. If we take the two images, flatten them out and lay them on top of one another, then roughly what you get is shown at the bottom of the figure. Observe that the two images are slightly different. A given corner, for example, is in a slightly different position in one image than it is in the other image; it has both a vertical shift and a horizontal shift in relative position. These differences in position are called *disparities*, and stereo disparities between images have long been known as a valuable source of information about surface shape. Because of their different positions in the head, our own two eyes get slightly different views of the world, and psychological research has demonstrated that those differences are rich in information about the depth structure of surfaces in the scene. So it is a good idea to try to use left–right image differences to help build a computer vision system capable of delivering a $2\frac{1}{2}$D sketch.

FIGURE 9.12   Schematic diagram of vertical and horizontal disparities (much exaggerated in size) for a square fixated with symmetric convergence

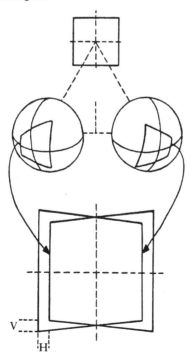

Well, there are various problems in doing this that need to be solved. We need to be able to register the images, that is, get the camera geometry right. Once we have done that, and perhaps

in conjunction with it, we need to find matching points in the two images, which is called solving the *stereo correspondence problem*. Once we know which left–right points go together, we can measure the disparities, both vertically and horizontally, for each point pair. And having got the disparities, we can then interpret them to get $2\frac{1}{2}$D depth features, which are the things we are really after — descriptions giving the structure in depth of scene surfaces.

I'm going to talk about only one aspect of shape-from-stereo — the correspondence problem — by way of illustrating some general points. It's easiest to make clear what's going on here by considering not a stereo image pair of a natural scene, but instead an artificial stereogram. Here (Figure 9.13) we have two noise fields, and if one was presented to your left eye and the other to your right eye, you would (if you had normal binocular vision) be able to see a wavy surface in depth, rather like looking down on a corrugated surface (perhaps some of you will be able to see this by crossing your eyes). These corrugations are orientated horizontally and they vary in

FIGURE 9.13   Correspondence problem

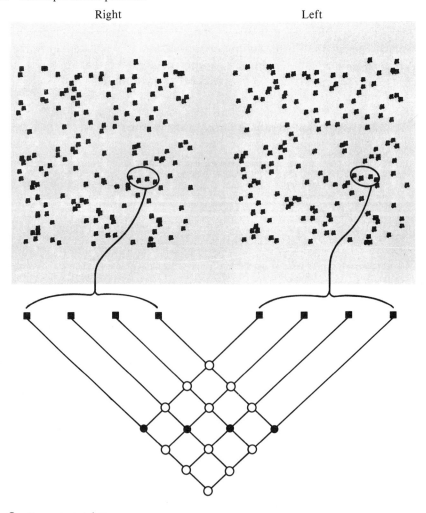

Right   Left

● Correct matches
○ False matches

amplitude from top to bottom. The noise fields could have been organized to display almost any desired pattern in depth, but we happen to have created a ripple in this particular instance. Now imagine trying to program a computer to combine the two images to recover the rippled depth structure. What are the problems to be overcome?

Let's consider just four blobs taken from one little patch of the image and the corresponding four from the matching patch in the other image (Figure 9.13, middle). I've laid them out neatly for the purpose of this demonstration, but I think that you can imagine that in fact they would in general be slightly jittered in their relative positions in the two images, according to the particular depth structure of the underlying surface from which the points arose.

The problem which such a random dot stereogram brings to the fore is: Which dot in the left image goes with which in the right? How is one view to be mapped on to the other? This is the stereo correspondence problem. Obviously, a large ambiguity problem exists, as shown here (Figure 9.13, lower half), which depicts all possible matches between a sample of four dots taken from the right image with four dots taken from the left. Each possible match is shown as a node in a network formed by the intersections of lines drawn from each dot. To understand this network, follow down the line from the left-hand dot from the left image. Each of the possible matches it can form with the four dots from the right image is shown as a circle. The question is: which of these possible matches is the correct one? The same question can be asked for all the other possible matches that can be formed for all the other dots. Now there are in fact 24 possible ways of combining sets of four dots such that each dot is allowed to participate in one and only one match ($4! = 4 \times 3 \times 2 = 24$). The stereo correspondence problem is to choose which combination is the correct one for the particular scene being viewed. That is not easy, especially when it is remembered that sets of four dots have been chosen here only for illustration — much larger sets would often need to be considered by a practical stereo matching system capable of dealing with richly textured surfaces.

For the particular stereogram shown in Figure 9.13, the correct matches for the chosen sample set of four dots are depicted by nodes in the network shown as filled-in circles. They happen to be the correct matches in this case simply because they are the ones that reflect the depth structure of the surface region in question. If the stereogram had been set up to portray some other surface then a different combination of matches would have been 'correct'. Note that all the 'false' matches for the present case are shown in Figure 9.13 by unfilled circles.

Despite the ambiguity in matching left–right image elements, which occurs for stereo image pairs of natural scenes as well as for artificial random dot stereograms, the human visual system nevertheless usually succeeds in combining the two images correctly. How does it do so? It must be using knowledge of the typical nature of scene surfaces and/or knowledge of stereo geometry to provide constraints on allowable matches. To design a stereo correspondence algorithm for a computer vision system capable of achieving stereo performance comparable to that of humans requires identifying those constraints and then using them to design rules for guiding binocular combination. I will illustrate one analysis of this type due to Marr and Poggio who used the following constraints:

1. Compatibility

The goal of the stereo combination process is to say something useful about entities in the scene; hence the primitives extracted from each of the images to be used for matching purposes must correspond to well-defined locations on the physical surfaces being imaged. From this follows *Binocular Combination Rule 1*: elements are allowed to form a potential match if they could have arisen from the same surface marking. What this amounts to is that nodes in the ambiguity diagram (Figure 9.13) can be established only for pairings of left and right image primitives with figurally similar parameters. For the particular stereo pair shown in Figure 9.13, suitable matching primitives would be ones describing small black dots, and as the black dots are here everywhere alike, any primitive could in this case in principle be matched with any other. But suppose the surface depicted by the stereo pair had been grey in colour and speckled with some black and some white dots. Then Binocular Combination Rule 1 would preclude considering matches formed from black/white dot pairings, as these could not arise from the same surface marking in normal stereo projections.

Obviously, the edge points of the raw primal sketch would be another kind of matching primitive that would allow the requirements of Rule 1 to be met for many natural scenes. For example, right and left image edge points could be allowed to form matches if they had roughly the same orientation, same scale (steep or shallow intensity change), and same direction of intensity change (an edge point describing a bright-to-dark intensity change in a given region could be matched with another bright-to-dark one but not with a dark-to-bright edge point). I will show an example of using raw primal sketch edge points in this way later on.

2. Uniqueness

A given point on a physical surface has a unique position in space at any one time. This leads to *Binocular Combination Rule 2*: matches should be selected in such a way that any given matching primitive derived from one image should be allowed to participate in one and only one of the selected matches. To break this rule would be tantamount to allowing a surface marking to be in two places at the same time.

3. Continuity

Because matter is cohesive (it occurs in fairly large chunks — our normal visual world is not a swarm of gnats or a snow storm), the surfaces of objects are generally 'smooth' (compared with their distance from the viewer). In other words, neighbouring points on a surface are likely to be similar in their depths away from the viewer. This provides *Binocular Combination Rule 3*: give preference to matches that have neighbouring matches with similar disparities. That is, choose matches such that, as far as possible, disparities vary smoothly across them, which is why Marr and Poggio called this their Continuity rule.

I have already referred to the fact that it is necessary to understand complex information processing systems at three different levels — computational theory, algorithm, and hardware. The above analysis is at the computational theory level: the next step is to build a practical stereo algorithm which implements the binocular combination rules (recollect that by an algorithm we mean a sequence of operations that achieve a required output representation from a given input representation). Hence attention will be turned now to devising a detailed set of procedures for stereo matching based upon the three rules specified by the computational theory. Once again, the illustration chosen is due to one of Marr and Poggio's stereo algorithms that incorporated the following steps (simplified for present purposes):

1.   Set up a network of nodes representing all possible disparity matches covering the depth range required. Give a value of 1 to each node representing a possible match between figurally similar place tokens derived from the two stereo images. Set all other nodes to a value of zero. Nodes with a value of 1 will hereafter be called 'active'.

2.   For each node in the network, count up how many of its neighbouring nodes at the same disparity are active. In Figure 9.13 these are the active neighbours lying in the same horizontal

row as the node being considered. However, in a practical system the algorithm would need to count active same-disparity neighbours in all directions around the node in question. Call this count the 'same disparity' count.

3.   For each node in the network, count up how many active nodes there are on each line passing through the node being considered. Call this count the 'alternatives' count (because matches on these lines, usually called 'lines of sight', define the set of all possible alternative matches for the image primitives in question).

4.   Subtract the alternatives count from the same disparity count to gain a measure of the 'strength of support' for the match represented by each node.

5.   Define a suitable threshold value for the strength of support needed if a node is to survive as active. Set all nodes that exceed this threshold to a value of 1. Set all nodes with below threshold strength of support to zero.

6.   Repeat Steps 2 to 5 until the network has converged to a stable stage in which few if any nodes change from active to inactive in each repetition (each repetition is known technically as an *iteration*).

7.   Nodes active at the stable endpoint are deemed to be those representing 'correct' binocular matches.

A name often used for this sort of algorithm is *cooperative*, because interactions between many cooperating elements determine the solution. The term 'cooperative algorithm' is often used interchangeably with 'relaxation algorithm'. Algorithms of this general class have been used to implement the kind of grouping rules described earlier, by setting up a network such that the grouping with strongest neighbourhood support satisfying rules of figural continuity, etc., is the one which wins out in the end.

The above algorithm attempts to implement the three binocular combination rules provided by the Marr/Poggio computational theory as follows:

Rule 1 (Compatibility) is embedded in Step 1 in that initially active nodes are restricted to those representing figurally similar matches. Rule 3 (Smoothness) is implemented by the same-disparity count (Step 4) as this ensures that matches with a large number of similar-disparity neighbours will tend to be the strongest and hence survive the threshold cut. Rule 2 (Uniqueness) is implemented in Step 6 by reducing the strength of each candidate match by the alternatives count: doing that tends to suppress all but one match for each image primitive.

Having set out the steps to be followed in the algorithm, the next task is to write a computer program which executes them and see if the algorithm actually does solve the stereo correspondence problem. That would lead to some experimentation in choosing a suitable threshold value (Step 5) and a suitable size for the area over which the same-disparity count is taken (Step 2; it would be foolish to have too large an area as the smoothness constraint upon which this count depends refers to neighbouring points on surfaces as having similar depths, not very distant ones).

In exploring the performance of the algorithm, many issues would arise which are only loosely related, if at all, to the underlying computational theory. For example, in the present case one needs to ask whether the algorithm converges to a stable endpoint without too many time-consuming iterations. Also, one might ask whether simply subtracting the alternatives count is an effective way of insisting on each primitive participating finally in only one of the selected matches (Rule 3). Or one could consider the desirability of allowing possible matches that have been killed off in one iteration to be resuscitated in a subsequent one if their strength of support changed suitably (this is in fact allowed in Marr and Poggio's version of the algorithm). These questions are examples of algorithm level problems that need to be guided by the computational theory, but are usefully kept distinct from the theory itself. After all, if this particular algorithm did not work very well, this would not necessarily imply that the binocular combination rules were themselves inadequate — it could simply be that the algorithm does not take full advantage of them. In fact, partly because he grew to dislike iterative algorithms for various reasons, Marr devised with Poggio a second non-iterative stereo algorithm of a radically different nature from the present one, even though it was based on the same constraints as the first. This example brings out the value of distinguishing between computational theory and algorithm.

So much for the details of the algorithm. What about its implementation in hardware? To illustrate that level of analysis I will describe a hypothetical neural network that might do the job: engineers can think about how they might create a similar scheme in fast parallel electronic hardware.

Imagine replacing each of the abstract nodes of Figure 9.13 (lower half) with a neurone; that is, use a brain cell to represent each of the possible matches, with its activity (e.g. firing rate in nerve impulses per second) coding the strength of support for the match in question. Moreover, imagine the lines in the diagram to be replaced with nerve fibres capable of carrying messages between cells about the current activity of each cell. If the connections these fibres made with each cell were arranged to be *inhibitory* (Figure 9.14) then this hardware implements Step 5 of the algorithm — subtracting the alternatives count. The idea here is that if one cell is 'on' then it has the right to tell all others using one or other of 'its' primitives to 'Be quiet! You can't be right if I am right!'

FIGURE 9.14   Hypothetical neural network

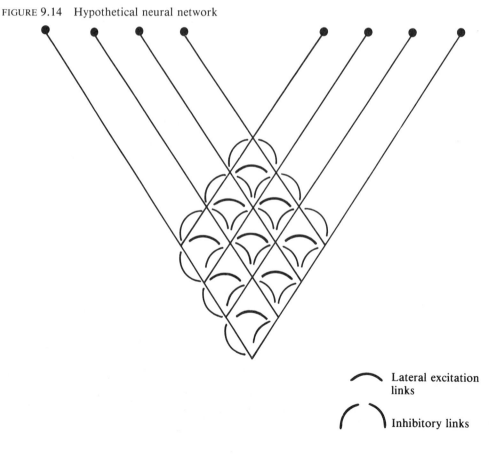

Lateral excitation links

Inhibitory links

Implementing the same disparity count (Step 4) can be easily achieved by putting in some more fibres, this time 'horizontal' ones that link neighbouring same-disparity cells with *excitatory* connections. Here the idea is that cells which are on should say to their same-disparity neighbours: 'I am on, so the chances are that you should be on also, so here is some excitation to help you survive!' The iterative repetitions could be implemented by simply allowing the network of cells to battle it out, as it were, to see which cells survive at the end of the day — that is, after a few tens of milliseconds.

Tests of the Marr–Poggio algorithm just described have shown that it can solve the stereo correspondence problem quite successfully for simple scenes composed of flat surfaces whose orientation is parallel to the line joining the eyes/cameras (i.e. surfaces that are said to lie in 'fronto-parallel' planes). But what of other surfaces, for example surfaces slanting away in depth from the viewer? Using a same-disparity count of active neighbours is then unsuitable, because the neighbours of correct matches in such cases will have few if any same-disparity neighbours — even if the surfaces are smooth and hence in keeping with the continuity constraint. This criticism points up the limited nature of Marr and Poggio's implementation in the present type of algorithm of the constraints identified in their own computational theory.

But one can criticize more deeply and ask whether the continuity constraint is itself really satisfactory. Is it really true to say that the world is generally 'smooth', even if slants are allowed? Many commonplace objects, such as bushes, hair, or tufted carpets, present very jagged surfaces in depth and yet they can be fused very nicely by human stereo vision. Are these just to be regarded as degenerate cases or is there something fundamentally wrong with the theory?

This raises a current controversy in the stereo field which I cannot go into here in detail. I have chosen to describe the Marr–Poggio stereo theory and a particular algorithm based upon it because it serves nicely as an elementary introduction to some key concepts in stereo vision, as well as illustrating the general approach taken in the field of image understanding (searching for good constraints to solve well-formulated problems; distinguishing the different preoccupations of the different levels of analysis — computational theory, algorithm, hardware). But it turns out that the Marr–Poggio algorithm that I have described is not very effective for processing stereo images of most natural scenes, because the surfaces in those scenes do not conform to the continuity constraint as specified by Marr and Poggio. So in Sheffield we have been developing a stereo theory that can cope with a wider range of surfaces, even quite jagged ones. This theory was based on some properties of human stereo vision and it results in a stereo algorithm which imposes a limit on the *disparity gradient* allowed between possible matches if they are to be permitted to exchange facilitatory support. (See Further reading for references giving further details.)

The performance of our algorithm (which we call PMF) is illustrated in Figure 9.15. The upper part of that figure shows a pair of stereo images of our industrial blocks scene (Figure 9.15(a)). Just below them (Figure 9.15(b)) are shown the raw edges extracted from each image, the edge points of which serve as matching primitives for the PMF stereo algorithm (these edge points thus serve the same role as the dots shown in Figure 9.13). The lower part of the figure (Figure 9.15(c)) displays the results obtained by using our disparity gradient stereo algorithm to match up edge points derived from the left and right stereo images. These results are depicted as a *depth map* in which the intensity of each edge point is used to code its measured disparity (the dark-to-feint intensity code depicts depths from near-to-far). As can be seen, points that our own visual system tells us are relatively near are shown dark, those towards the rear of the scene are shown light. So this illustration shows that the depth map is at least a qualitatively good fit to what it should be — the various edge points have been matched up correctly and they have been given the right depth values.

FIGURE 9.15   Constraints of figural similarity

(a) Pair of
stereo images

(b) 'Raw edges'

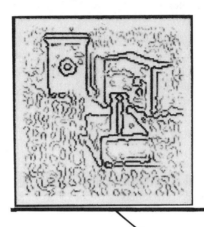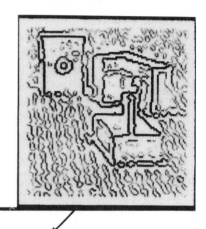

(c) Depth map

Feint = Far
Dark = Near

So, our first step towards a $2\frac{1}{2}$D sketch has been to use stereo to create a depth map: what are we going to do with it? Our particular depth map, made up as it is of raw edge points, is in one respect like the pixels of the original image, in that it is a point-by-point mapping, even though (unlike pixels) each point is labelled with the type of edge that runs through it and with its particular depth value. What we want to do now is to go from this pointillist depth map and build up a $2\frac{1}{2}$D sketch representation using descriptive primitives that capture the depth relationships between points.

What constitutes a good $2\frac{1}{2}$D sketch representation is a question right at the current research frontier, but we think that it will include various 'surface features'. For example, one kind of useful feature (Figure 9.16) would be *corner vertex*, to which would be attached various parameters defining the surfaces that comprise the vertex and where it is located in the scene. Another useful feature would be *concave edge*, formed for example where one of the blocks meets the table top on which it sits (Figure 9.16), with again parameters defining the properties of the surfaces that form the edge and where the edge is. So, what we have to do is derive from the point-by-point depth map various edge and vertex features that define the local depth structure of surfaces, together with descriptions of the surface shapes that form these features. As I say, how to do this is a research question, and it is one that forms a large part of our Alvey work.

FIGURE 9.16   Match corresponding edges

(Ambiguity problem)

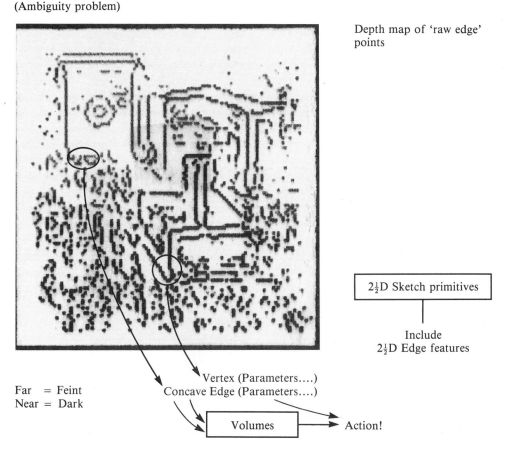

Depth map of 'raw edge' points

$2\frac{1}{2}$D Sketch primitives

Include
$2\frac{1}{2}$D Edge features

Vertex (Parameters....)
Concave Edge (Parameters....)

Far = Feint
Near = Dark

Volumes ⟶ Action!

One aspect of that work that is proving interesting and of value is the use of artificial images created using the new generation of body modellers (e.g. Figure 9.17). These are of value to the research in two respects. First, they provide a good way of checking whether we are getting the right things from our stereo algorithm (or motion algorithm etc.). For instance, it's quite important to test whether a description of a particular depth feature is parameterized correctly. Using an artificial image gives you a good way of doing that, because you know in advance what should be recovered. Secondly, it turns out that many of the data structures used in computer graphics might have relevance to the type of data structures that need to be built up

FIGURE 9.17 CAD/CAM images of blocks

(a)

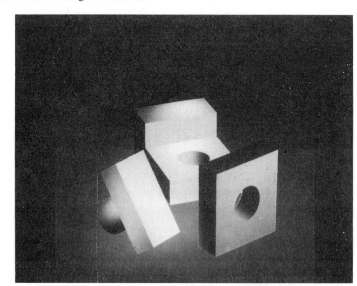

(b)

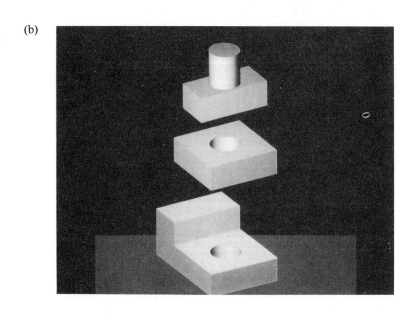

for the $2\frac{1}{2}$D sketch. That is, $2\frac{1}{2}$D descriptions of the depth structure of visible surfaces have certain parallels to what are called 'boundary file representations of solid body modelling schemes'. So, the field of CAD-CAM (computer aided design, computer aided manufacture) is of some relevance to our work in understanding how to build a $2\frac{1}{2}$D sketch.

SHAPE FROM CONTOUR

So much for stereo, what about other cues? It's quite clear that human beings don't need stereo to get out surface information, though it can be useful. Take for example this scene (at the bottom of Figure 9.18). If you look at that with one eye, you can of course immediately see certain properties of the scene: you see a pyramid sitting on a block. Your visual system is readily able to interpret those lines and get out some very good estimations of the depth relationships of the surfaces they depict. This is quite remarkable because the information is so sparse. It is interesting therefore to ask what knowledge is being used to arrive at the depthful interpretation. This question underlies a large and impressive body of work in the Image Understanding area by people like Huffman, Clowes and Waltz, whose approach I'm now going to describe very briefly.

FIGURE 9.18   Waltz's line labelling algorithm (a) Edge types and their associated line labels (b) Dictionary of all possible interpretations of vertices of trihedral solids (c) An example of Waltz-type filtering

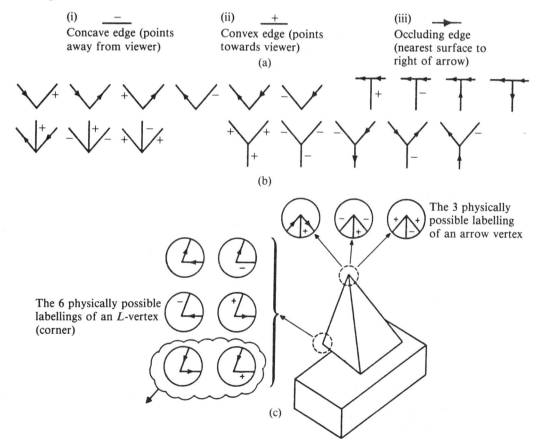

Any particular edge is first of all considered as one of three types: *convex* (pointing towards the viewer), *concave* (pointing away, or *obscuring*. The symbols +, − and > respectively define each type of edge (in the > case, the obscuring surface is by convention deemed to be on the right as one travels down the line in the direction of the arrow). For this simple blocks world, Waltz examined carefully the physics of how blocks world lines project into images and he listed all the possible junction types that can occur. The junctions shown here (top of Figure 9.18) form the complete set of those junction possibilities. This set is said to define the 'junction dictionary' and it can be used to label the lines comprising the drawing of the pyramid sitting on the block (lower half of Figure 9.18) without knowing in advance any correct line labelling at all. Obviously, this is a very useful thing to do, because finding out if, say, a given line derives from a concave or convex edge is just the sort of information we want to make explicit in the $2\frac{1}{2}$D sketch.

The first step is to find, say from the primal sketch database, the junctions that are present and list all possibilities for interpreting each one by consulting the junction dictionary. For example, the arrowhead vertex at the top of the pyramid could be any one of the three arrowhead types shown, as specified by the junction dictionary. In fact, our visual system says that in this particular instance it's the one with outer obscuring edges and central convex edge, but the other possibilities could in principle satisfy that type of arrowhead — if it was considered on its own.

But therein lies the trick: don't consider each junction separately but find labellings for its lines which are consistent with the possible labellings given to the self-same lines at neighbouring junctions. Consider for example the L-shaped corner vertex that is linked to the left-hand descending line of the arrowhead forming the apex of the pyramid. Considered on its own it has six possibilities (shown in Figure 9.18). But you can see that the last two of these require that their upward pointing lines that connect to the arrowhead are obscuring on the opposite side to those for the arrowhead. (Remember, the code for an obscuring line is that the obscuring surface lies to the right along the direction shown by the arrow.) Hence these lines find no possible matches with any of those for the arrowhead. They can thus be immediately eliminated, given the basic strategy of finding mutually consistent line labellings. And it turns out that if a search is made for consistent labellings over the whole image, then certain lines with unambiguous labellings propagate their disambiguating influence right the way through the search space of possibilities. In this way, mutually consistent labellings can usually be arrived at for all lines comprising the image.

Note once again here the distinction between computational theory and algorithm. The theory side of the analysis uses the physics of the projection of 'blocks world' junctions into images to constrain the possible labellings for each junction type. These constraints are then embedded in a search procedure to find mutually consistent labellings given those constraints. The details of how the search is to be conducted is the province of the algorithm level of analysis. It has proved possible to employ here 'relaxation algorithms' to do the job, using an iterative updating of possible labellings as impossibilities are removed at each cycle. Hence the general idea at the algorithm level is rather similar to that employed in the Marr–Poggio stereo algorithm, but now the physical constraints embedded in the algorithm are not to do with surface smoothness or unique matches but with the physics of blocks world junctions. So here again we find it valuable to distinguish carefully between the computational theory and algorithm levels of analysis.

So, shape from contour and shape from stereo are two ways of getting towards the goal of a $2\frac{1}{2}$D sketch. There are many others but I have not time to describe them here. Let's simply take it that we do now have a $2\frac{1}{2}$D sketch, a rich description of the depth structure of visible surfaces, and move on to discuss how it might be used.

OBJECT REPRESENTATIONS

The surface descriptions that comprise the $2\frac{1}{2}$D sketch would be immediately useful for a number of visual tasks. For example, they make explicit information about the depth structure of the scene, which would be useful information for a computer program designed to guide a driverless vehicle. They would also help in planning collision-free trajectories for a robot arm being moved through a pile of objects on a table. And if the surface descriptions were sufficiently rich and the viewpoint good enough, they might be suitable for planning a possible place to grasp a target object without the robot needing to know what the 'thing' is that it is about to pick up. But in general, and certainly for the task of automatic assembly of industrial parts (cf. Figure 9.1), it is desirable to build into a visual system the capability for recognizing the objects with which it has to deal. In this context, recognition means matching an input shape to one of a stored collection of object models. Once recognition has been attained, information stored about the object can be used for planning suitable actions. It is to a consideration of some of the major problems of 3D object recognition that we turn next.

The objects with which we are trying to deal are characterized by the disposition in space of their visible surfaces. Hence, it is natural to consider ways of using the surface descriptions in the $2\frac{1}{2}$D sketch as a database for object recognition. It is worth bearing in mind, however, that a good many current practical industrial 3D object recognition schemes use as their input the kind of information delivered by the primal sketch, not least because the problems of obtaining really good $2\frac{1}{2}$D sketch data are a current research frontier. Even so, promising first steps towards an understanding of how to extract rich surface descriptions have now been taken, and they can be expected to mature into industrially useful schemes over the next few years. In what follows here, I will presume that good $2\frac{1}{2}$D sketch data are available, although most of the general issues that I will discuss about object representations are not critically dependent on that assumption.

So, we want to use symbols in the $2\frac{1}{2}$D sketch representing the properties of visible surfaces in the scene to compute new symbols expressing the shape of the 3D objects that gave rise to them. This 3D shape representation must be capable of being matched to one of a stored collection of 3D object models. Finding a match is our definition of what recognition is. In fact, object recognition is usually attempted in two phases: first, *invocation* of a candidate object model on the basis of some $2\frac{1}{2}$D sketch (or primal sketch) data, followed by checking or *verification* of that hypothesis by testing for the existence of additional visible features which did not contribute to the initial choice but which are predicted from the stored characteristics of the selected model. The initial invocation phase is sometimes described as *bottom-up* or *data-driven*. The verification phase is by contrast often called *top-down* or *concept-driven* (Figure 9.19).

As for the other visual processing tasks we have considered, 3D object recognition amounts to finding valid *constraints*, this time constraints that can guide the search for solutions to three *design choices* that have to be faced in building a 3D shape representation. These design choices are:

(a) What are the *Primitives* that will be used to describe the shape?
(b) What *Coordinate System* will be used to express the spatial relationships between primitives?
(c) What is an appropriate *Organization* of the primitives?

Marr and Nishihara have suggested three criteria that must be met by a 'good' representation of 3D shape. They proposed that these criteria could serve as useful constraints in the search for answers to the design choices. The criteria are:

1. *Accessibility.* Can the representation be computed easily?

FIGURE 9.19   Model invocation and verification

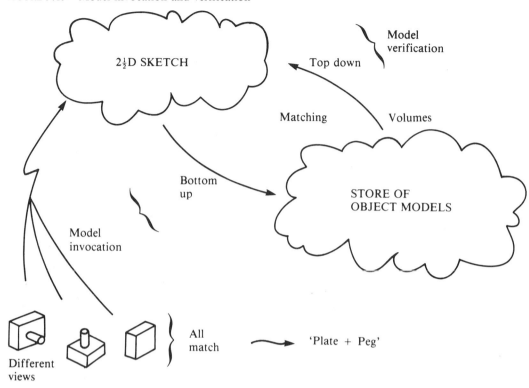

2. *Scope and Uniqueness.* Is the representation suitable for the class of shapes with which it has to deal (appropriate Scope); and do the shapes in that class have *canonical* descriptions in the representation (Uniqueness)? A canonical representation is one in which a particular shape has a single description in the representation; that is, different views of the same object produce the same shape description. For example, the shape of one of the objects we have been considering can be described as 'peg fixed to the centre of a plate'. This description (suitably enriched with various parameters describing the sizes of the peg and the plate, the exact location of their join, etc.) would apply regardless of viewing angle. A representation with this canonical property is obviously advantageous for recognition purposes — there is a single representation for each stored object model to which inputs must be matched. A non-canonical representational scheme, on the other hand, would be one which produced different representations depending on viewing position. For example, a scheme of this type for the 'peg + plate object' might contain a list of separate representations, each one describing the surface features that can be seen from a particular viewpoint. This latter scheme leads to the need for processes capable of solving the problem of matching any given input to just one of a potentially large number of object models. However, this problem may be less formidable than it at first appears, at any rate in certain industrial applications where the number of objects to be recognized is relatively small (see later).

3. *Stability and Sensitivity.* Can the representation be used to capture both the similarities (Stability) and the differences (Sensitivity) between the objects with which it has to deal? These opposing requirements demand a separation of the stable information characterizing the more general and less varying properties of a shape, from information about the subtle differences between shapes in the same basic class. For example, suppose we were confronted with a new version of the 'peg + plate object' in which the peg was slightly bent: we would have little

difficulty in recognizing that this new object had considerable similarities to the old one (Stability) and at the same time we would be able to pick out its differences (Sensitivity). A good general purpose object representation scheme must lend itself naturally to these complementary requirements.

Marr and Nishihara went on to show how these general criteria are helpful in seeking solutions to the three *design choices* to be faced in building a 3D shape representation introduced earlier. We will consider each choice in turn.

PRIMITIVES

What elementary units should be used to describe any given object? These units, called primitives, are analogous to words in a language. Should the 'visual words' for describing objects refer to bits of surface or should they describe explicitly the bits of volume of space occupied by the object?

Consider once more the 'peg + plate'. Surface based primitives could be used to describe a given view of this object as, for example, 'flat round surface patch joined to the edges of a cylindrical surface patch joined to a flat rectangular surface patch joined to . . . . etc.', with parameters attached to each surface patch giving quantitative details on the absolute and/or relative sizes of the surface primitives. This example amounts to describing an object directly in terms of relationships between $2\frac{1}{2}$D sketch entities. Of course, perhaps quite a large number of such views might need to be stored if the object in question needed to be recognized from many different positions (but see later for one way of limiting the number of views needed).

An alternative scheme based on volumetric primitives called *generalized cylinders* is illustrated in Figure 9.20. Here the underlying idea is to find an axis within the volume occupied by each part shape, and then define the surface of the object in terms of a cross-section of a particular shape moved along that axis. The cross-section may vary smoothly in size and shape along the axis, and the axis need not remain straight along its length (think of a banana) — hence the term 'generalized cylinders'.

FIGURE 9.20   Scheme based on generalized cylinders

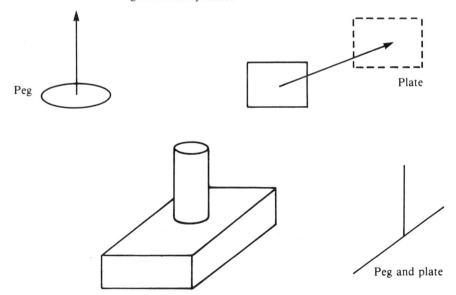

It is easy to envisage how a complex object could in principle be described in terms of a collection of generalized cylinders connected together at certain points. The peg + plate in Figure 9.20 gives only a simple example; more complicated cases can readily be imagined by thinking of stick figure drawings or pipe-cleaner sculptures of familiar animals. Indeed, the fact that the human visual system is so adept at recognizing an object depicted with such an immensely impoverished stimulus as a stick figure was one of the factors that led Marr and Nishihara to take very seriously the idea that our brains do actually compute axis-based volumetric 3D shape representations. Here the argument runs: the reason we can 'see' a stick figure as depicting an object is because the human visual system generates stick-figure-like representations anyway, and so when a stick figure is presented as a stimulus it provides a short-cut, as it were, to the representation it normally has to compute from a very different basis (primal sketch and $2\frac{1}{2}$D sketch primitives).

The criteria that have to be borne in mind in taking the decision to go for surface-based or volumetric primitives are Scope and Uniqueness. Not all objects lend themselves readily to generalized cylinders: a crumpled newspaper was one of Marr and Nishihara's illustrations of a clearly unsuitable object (too many and too poorly defined axes) but it could be that many rather more important and commonplace objects are not well represented using them (would a typewriter be very easy to describe with them, or a telephone?). On the other hand, volumetric primitives make explicit information about the spatial disposition of the parts of an object that would be only implicit in a surface-based representation of the plate + peg object as 'a flat round patch joined to the edges of a cylindrical patch which is joined to a planar patch which is joined . . . etc.'. Because of this, it might prove easier to build canonical representations (meet the Uniqueness criterion) using volumetric primitives. In principle at any rate (but the practical difficulties are considerable!), these allow an object to be represented by a description of the spatial relations of the object's parts which is independent of the angle from which the object is viewed.

COORDINATE SYSTEM

Whatever primitives are chosen, their spatial relationships one to another will be what determines the structure of any given shape description in the representation. To express those spatial relationships requires choosing a coordinate system. That is, a set of axes (x, y, z) with a specified origin need to be chosen for defining a 3D space in which the object's parts can be localized. The immediate question that arises is: should the coordinate system be viewer-centred (e.g. the origin of the coordinate frame set mid-way between the eyes), or should it be object-centred (e.g. its origin located on some part of the object)?

A viewer-centred coordinate system is one which, as its name implies, expresses the spatial disposition of primitives from the viewpoint of the observer. This is easier to compute (more Accessible) but when used for recognition it will obviously be non-canonical (fail the Uniqueness criterion), because it leads to the requirement to store perhaps very many different viewpoint-determined descriptions. Just how many might be required is not clear. Indeed, it is a current research question whether a scheme of this general sort can be made viable by restricting the infinitely large number of possible views to just a few typical or 'characteristic' views of each object that the visual system in question needs to be able to recognize. For example, you rarely need to recognize a car from underneath. That kind of thinking has a long history in the psychological literature on object recognition.

One important idea here is that of the 'view potential' of objects, introduced by Koenderink and van Doorn (1976). They observed that the qualitative character of many views of an object is often the same; that is, they share the same main features even if these features might show some differences in quantitative details (e.g. due to perspective effects). Imagine walking around a detached house, for example, starting at the front. You would initially see the 'front view', which would include such features as the front door, front windows, eaves, perhaps a gable end. As you walked around from that starting point, nothing qualitative would change until a side elevation suddenly came into sight, whereupon a new 'front/side' view would arise comprising all the previous front-view features plus, say, a set of side windows, a side door, etc. Further walking round the house would bring you to a point where the front-view features were lost, leaving the side-view features on their own — the 'side view'. Given such qualitative jumps, the infinity of possible views seen from the ground plane can thus be grouped into only eight classes: front, front/side, side, side/back, back, back/side, side, side/front, as shown in Figure 9.21. Each one is canonical in the sense that a single description of it is computed from the infinity of possible viewpoints which can give rise to it. This realization presents an opportunity for creating a viewer-centred recognition scheme in which the number of views needing to be stored is radically reduced by using a limited number of canonical representations of characteristic views.

FIGURE 9.21   The view potential of a house showing the eight qualitatively different views available from viewing positions on or near the ground plane (after Koenderink and van Doorn)

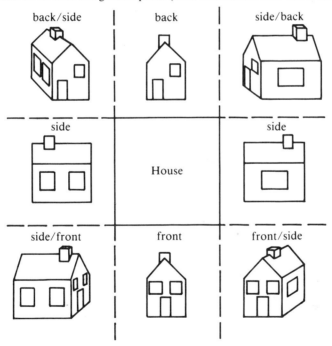

Koenderink and van Doorn employ the apt term 'view potential' to bring out the fact that an object only has a limited number of qualitatively different views. While it may seem more difficult to specify a limited number of such views for less 'regular' objects than houses, the feasibility of this idea is now being explored in various AI labs.

In contrast to the descriptions of surfaces from different view-points, an object-centred coordinate system expresses the relationships between primitives in a framework based upon some property of the object itself. For example, the simple peg + plate axis description illustrated in Figure 9.20 uses the axis of the plate (representing the rectangular block) to define the location of the peg axis (representing the cylinder). It is because the plate axis is fixed by the nature of the object itself, and is therefore independent of viewpoint, that a scheme of this type is described as based on an object-centred coordinate system. The advantage of this kind of scheme is that it is canonical and hence facilitates recognition regardless of the viewer's particular viewpoints. On the other hand, this factor may be offset by the computational difficulties of computing object-centred descriptions.

ORGANIZATION

How should the primitives be organized? Should there be a 'flat' organizational structure, in which each primitive has the same status? Or should there be a hierarchical and modular design, in which primitives at the highest level (or highest module) convey coarse information about the shape, with lower levels giving the details? How the latter scheme might be achieved is illustrated in Figure 9.22, but before considering that figure in detail, note that a hierarchical scheme naturally satisfies the Stability/Sensitivity criterion. This is because similarities at the highest level can deliver the competence to 'see' the sameness between, say, a horse and donkey, or even a horse and tortoise, with lower levels in the hierarchy dealing with their differences.

FIGURE 9.22   Hierarchical organization of generalized cylinders representing human figure

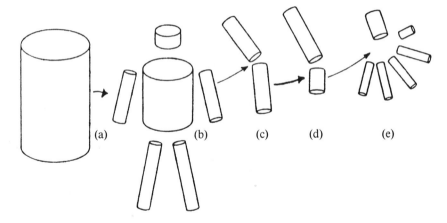

AN EXAMPLE OF AN OBJECT REPRESENTATION

Following on from their account of design choices and criteria, the 3D shape representation scheme proposed by Marr and Nishihara was object-centred, volumetric, modular and hierarchical, and used generalized cylinders as its primitives. An outline of their scheme is described by them as follows:

> First the overall form — the "body" is given an axis. This yields an object-centred coordinate system which can then be used to specify the arrangement of the "arms", "legs", "torso", and "head". The position of each of these is specified by an axis of its own, which in turn serves to define a coordinate system for specifying the arrangement of further subsidiary parts. This gives us a hierarchy of 3D models: we show it extending downward as far as the fingers. The shapes in the figure are drawn as if they were cylindrical, but that is purely for illustrative convenience: it is the axes alone that stand for the volumetric qualities of the shape, much as pipecleaner models can serve to describe various animals. (Marr and Nishihara, 1978)

Marr and Nishihara never reached the point of fully implementing this scheme (see the ACRONYM program of Brooks (1978) for the most advanced version of a generalized cylinders object representation to date). Moreover, Marr and Nishihara discussed the problems of computing generalized cylinders from the primal sketch rather than the $2\frac{1}{2}$D sketch. Although they believed that the $2\frac{1}{2}$D sketch would provide a better basis in principle, knowledge about how to compute surface descriptions of the required type and richness was not then available, and indeed is only slowly becoming available even now.

Note that the stick-figure representation shown in Figure 9.22 provides a list of parts and the spatial relationships existing between them. The latter relationships were called by Marr and Nishihara the 'adjunct relations'. Thus a person and a tail-less horse might be regarded as having the same number of parts (a trunk, four limbs, a neck, and a head) but they would be distinguished by differences in the admissible range of angles at which the component axes connect to the principal axis (as well as being distinguished in terms of the allowable relative sizes of the components, of course).

SUMMARY

Well, that's necessarily had to be a rather hurried introduction to the very large field of *Image Understanding*. What I will do now is try to summarize some of the main features to which I have drawn attention.

Image Understanding starts with the *goal* of using visual information to guide an *action*, in the case used for illustration here, the task of assembling some blocks. Having captured one or more *images* of the *scene* containing the blocks, we found that this goal led to the need to make various properties of the scene *explicit*, using the images as input data. This in turn led to the need for a sequence of *representations*, each dealing with a different *domain*. Each domain had its own set of problems to be solved, and each solution depended on the identification of valid *constraints* that exploited either knowledge of the entities in the scene and the optics of their projection into images, or knowledge about the nature of the task to be undertaken.

The first representation, the *primal sketch*, was concerned with the domain of image descriptions cast in a language of *primitives* such as edge points, edges, lines, and regions. Following a stage of *spatio-temporal differentiation* of the images, *grouping operations* in which were embedded knowledge such as 'edges of objects are usually continuous' played a crucial role here.

The second major class of representations, which together were called the *$2\frac{1}{2}$D sketch*, dealt with descriptions of visible surfaces in the scene. The primitives here were such things as vertices, and concave or convex edges, and the emphasis was on describing the three-dimensional structure of scene surfaces appearing in the current viewpoint. A variety of different *cues* could be used to extract that structure, each requiring a careful analysis of its own appropriate constraints. Two examples were introduced, one dealing with the acquisition of range data from *stereo*, the other with interpreting some of the *contour* cues found in line drawings.

Finally, some of the problems of creating *3D object model representations* were outlined. Various *design choices* for such representations were introduced, namely what *primitives?*, what *coordinate system?*, and what *organization?* These were discussed in the context of constraints arising mainly from the purpose of the model representation — *accessibility, scope and uniqueness*, and *stability and sensitivity*. Some of the pros and cons of *object-centred* and *viewer-centred* model representations were briefly reviewed.

Complex information processing systems need to be understood at a variety of levels, and one important distinction to be emphasized in this summary is the need to be clear about the *level of analysis* being undertaken at any one time. Identifying constraints is at the topmost level — that of *computational theory of the task*. Having completed that analysis, the constraints need to be embedded in *algorithms* — that is, a precise set of steps need to be specified for *processes* operating on an input representation to deliver the desired output representation. Questions at the algorithmic level concern such matters as speed and efficiency. The third level of analysis concerns *hardware*, about which I have had almost nothing to say in this paper but which is a very important matter if artificial vision devices are to be made to run in anything like real-time. Now, all three levels of analysis interact, of course. For example, the design of an algorithm will usually be strongly influenced by the kind of hardware available on which to run it, and vice versa. Nevertheless, experience in Image Understanding to date has shown the need to be very clear at any one time at what level of analysis the issues being addressed lie. Without that clarity, it is easy to spend time building vision systems and end up not knowing quite why they work — or more typically, why and when they fail.

Another theme within Image Understanding is the readiness of its practitioners to seek clues from *biological vision systems*. Understanding vision is a hugely complicated business, a fact not often appreciated by the owners of the best visual systems known to date, human beings, who usually take the apparently effortless delivery of a rich scene description by their eyes and brains so much for granted.

Finally, the potential value of good Image Understanding systems to so many industrial tasks is self-evident. It is for that reason that Alvey is devoting a good deal of support to fundamental research in vision, both via its IKBS and its MMI Directorates.

FURTHER READING AND REFERENCES

An excellent review of Image Understanding is to be found in Brady, M. (1982) Computational Approaches to Image Understanding, *Computing Surveys*, Vol.14, No.1, March 1982. That paper also provides a rich source of references for further reading.

References mentioned in the text are as follows:
Brooks, R.A. (1981) Symbolic reasoning among 3D models and 2D images, *Artificial Intelligence*, Vol.17, pp 285–348
Koenderink, J.J. and van Doorn, A.J. (1977) *How an ambulant observer can construct a model of the environment from the geometrical structure of the visual inflow*. In G. Hauske and E. Butenandt (Eds) (1977) *Kybernetic* 1977, pp 224–47
Marr, D. and Nishihara, H.K. (1978) Representation and recognition of the spatial organisation of three-dimensional shapes, *Proceedings of the Royal Society of London*, Series B 200, pp 269–94
Marr, D. and Poggio, T. (1976) Cooperative computation of stereo disparity, *Science*, Vol.194, pp 283–7
Pollard, S.B., Mayhew, J.E.W. and Frisby, J.P. (1985) PMF: a stereo correspondence algorithm using a disparity gradient limit, *Perception*, Vol.14, in press

10
MACHINE LEARNING
TIM O'SHEA
OPEN UNIVERSITY

I'm going to discuss the importance of learning as a mechanism in IKBS. I'll start off by discussing different types of learning because when you look at learning it turns out to be a very complicated and wide-embracing notion. I shall then illustrate recent work by describing six different machine learning systems that have been implemented in the last ten years. I have chosen them deliberately to indicate a variety of approaches.

I will then describe a piece of work which I think is very important and which is the type of work which IKBS needs very badly — that is the work that Alan Bundy and his colleagues at Edinburgh have done recently. They have gone over the machine learning work and have asked the question, 'Is there some single, common framework that we can use to describe how different machine learning systems work?'

I will then discuss the regular problems that machine learning work shares with the rest of IKBS work. I will also consider some big problems that are really acute in the machine learning area. And then I shall finish, uncharacteristically for me, in a slightly optimistic way by giving some hopeful thoughts about the future direction of machine learning.

It's rather obvious why machine learning is important. One reason that is touted a lot at the moment is what is called the 'knowledge acquisition bottleneck'. All over the world people are beetling away trying to construct expert systems, and one of the problems they immediately encounter is how to get knowledge 'into' the expert system. And people then say, 'Ah, well, if the machine can learn the knowledge then that would solve our problems.' And indeed it would — if the machine could. One of my objectives is to explain why learning in general is much harder than some other blanket AI topics like, for example, understanding or perception.

Machine learning is obviously also important if you are interested in the psychology of learning. It is relevant if you are working in the area of education and training and want to produce a principled piece of computer-assisted instruction or, for that matter, a well-designed textbook.

Machine learning is clearly a critical area for testing representation techniques. If you are making a claim that some representation technique is particularly useful for artificial intelligence, then one of the hard tests that you can subject it to is to use it to represent learning.

The pre-history of learning work — by which I mean the period up to the late 1960s — was largely carried out by people working in cybernetics who were trying to adopt a *tabula rasa* approach. That is, they said: suppose we get a machine and it has nothing in it, and suppose we have some sort of self-organizing principle (and an obvious source of such principles is psychology, and particularly neuropsychology), and suppose we model the great mass of neurons all wired together in the head, and suppose we do something to this great mass (maybe we will simulate evolution or we will offer reinforcement), then the machine will organize itself and learn different things. Probably the most disciplined attempt at this approach was the perceptron, which is a particular device that can be used as a basis for work on pattern recognition. But while it was very elegant it was also sufficiently precise to be amenable to mathematical attack. And two people who are well known in artificial intelligence, Marvin Minsky and Seymour Papert, who are also accomplished mathematicians, lent a great service to both cybernetics and artificial intelligence by taking perceptrons apart. If you want to understand why very simple approaches based on simple uniform representations like the perceptron are almost certainly doomed to failure, then I can't think of a better suggestion than to read their very stimulating book entitled *Perceptrons*.

I will deal with six examples of types of learning (see Figure 10.1). They vary from one extreme to the other: you can learn by rote; by being told something; from analogy; from examples (which is mathematical or scientific induction); from observation; or by discovery and experiment. We have a range from very simple learning by heart to what can be taken to be the equivalent of the scientific method as we know it. Learning is a very complicated thing, and there are all sorts of activities which a machine might do, from acquiring a single fact to acquiring a new theory, that can reasonably be described as learning.

FIGURE 10.1   Examples of types of learning

Six types of learning

Rote learning
By being told
From analogy
From examples (induction)
From observation
From discovery & experiment.

I'm going to offer you one simple model of learning which can be used for thinking about the different examples I shall give, although in fact they will all turn out to be slightly more complicated. In our very simple model (Figure 10.2) we have a learning element, which is a facility inside our machine. The learning element compares the world and our performance in the world. As a result of this comparison it produces a new entry in our knowledge base. The new entry might be a concept or a rule, or it might be something as complicated as a procedure or heuristic. Having acquired our new piece of knowledge, we carry out another piece of performance in the world, and we then learn from that again. That's the simplest model we can have for learning.

The six examples of learning programs I am going to describe have different strategies and learn different things. The range goes from training and reinforcement to discovery. The things being learned are generally non-trivial; for example, tactics for symbolic integration, how to play poker better, or how to understand the plots of Shakespearean plays. Naturally, I will have to simplify greatly. So, as I discuss the six systems, I will say a little bit about their behaviour and about their underlying representational scheme. I will describe what changes in the machine when things are learned and what device is used to carry out these changes. In each case, I'll use

FIGURE 10.2   A simple model of learning

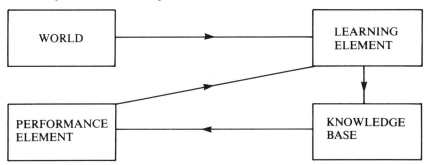

a toy example which, for the most part, will depend on arrangements of children's wooden blocks.

The first example is quite well known and is very important. It's a piece of work done by Pat Winston at MIT in the early 1970s. He was interested in how one might learn concepts, and in particular how one might acquire structural descriptions of concepts. This work is very important in artificial intelligence because it's the first clear example of a symbolic representation approach to learning. Winston represented all his learning symbolically; he wasn't twiddling with parameters or messing about with statistics or dealing with simple self-organizing systems. His approach depends on three things: a training sequence; a set of exemplars of the concept being learned; and the idea of 'near misses'.

My training sequence will have six components: three examples, which I've called Slab-arch, Pillar-arch and Lintel-arch; and three counter-examples, called T-shape, Ruin and Weird-arch (Figure 10.3).

FIGURE 10.3   (a) Slab-arch (b) Pillar-arch (c) Lintel-arch (d) T-shape (e) Ruin (f) Weird-arch

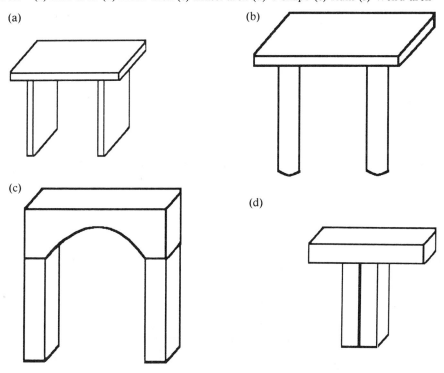

(e)   (f)

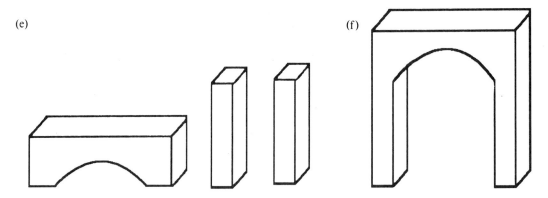

One of the fundamental problems in learning, and one which people working with self-organizing systems tried to avoid, is, how do you describe the different objects? In this case we are going to be dealing with things like slabs, pillars and beams. It's going to make my life easier if I say that slabs, pillars and beams are all examples of sticks. So, what I have done is construct a little hierarchy of the types of objects (Figure 10.4).

FIGURE 10.4   Hierarchy of object types

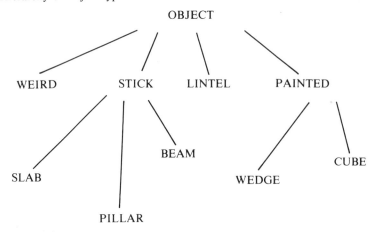

Let us suppose now that we start off with our first example, the Slab-arch. If we use a very simplified version of Winston's approach, we will end up with a description of a Slab-arch as shown (Figure 10.5): two objects A and B supporting an object C, all objects being slabs. So this is an example of an arch. We don't yet know whether, for example, it is important that the objects are slabs, or that object A doesn't marry (i.e. touch) object B.

Let us suppose that we now take the second example, the Pillar-arch. We are told that this is also an example of an arch. That allows us to generalize our conception of an arch, so that we can now say that an arch is a slab supported by sticks, because what pillars have in common with slabs is that they are both sticks. So we have a second version of an arch (Figure 10.6), and this illustrates one of the two fundamental mechanisms in learning, which is generalization.

If we now take our third example, the Lintel-arch, then we are all right with the beams because it turns out from my description of objects that beams, pillars and slabs are all examples of sticks. But we have to generalize to allow our lintel element. So we go back to our symbolic description and change it again to show that an arch is an object supported by two

FIGURE 10.5   First arch structure (Slab-arch)

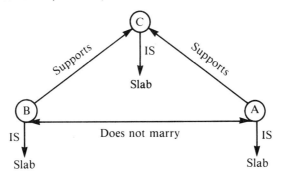

FIGURE 10.6   Arch structure (after Pillar-arch)

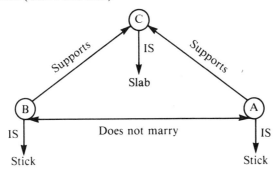

sticks (Figure 10.7). So we have been steadily generalizing our definition of an arch. That then is one of the standard learning processes: start with a specific definition and generalize it.

Now I'm going to provide a counter-example, the T-shape. If we give this to a Winston-style learning machine and say, 'This is not an arch', then the description that we have at the moment

FIGURE 10.7   Arch structure (after Lintel-arch)

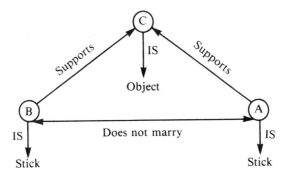

is compared with the description of the T-shape. We find that our description of an arch has to be changed (Figure 10.8) to show that the two objects doing the supporting must not marry (before, we knew that they did not marry, but now we know something a bit stricter — they must not marry).

The second counter-example, the Ruin, is going to give us an important bit of 'archness' which you may not have realized was missing. The Ruin is different from the examples because it does not have a supported object: it is exactly like one of our arches except that the slab is not

FIGURE 10.8   Arch structure (after T-shape)

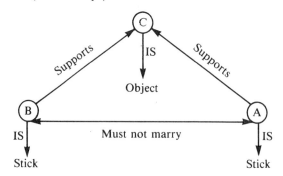

supported. So we now learn that not only must the two objects not marry but they must support the third object (Figure 10.9).

FIGURE 10.9   Arch structure (after Ruin)

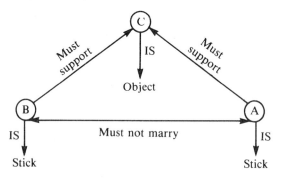

Now to go on to my last counter-example, the Weird-arch. This looks like an arch, quite a nice arch, in fact. But when we try to match it against our description we find that for sure this is not an arch, because our description requires three objects in some sort of relation, but we merely have a single object carved out of wood. So, whatever this is, in terms of our little learning sequence and in terms of our description, it is not an arch. That illustrates a very important thing to consider about symbolic representations: once you commit yourself to an initial vocabulary, an initial description language, and a training sequence, then it is very easy, even in simple examples like this one, to generate counter-examples.

I will now go on to my second main example, which is a system which learns to do integration. It learns essentially by reflecting on its own way of doing integration, and so, in some senses, it is an extremely novel system. It was developed by Tom Mitchell at Rutgers and is called LEX.

It has four main components (Figure 10.10). First, it has a *problem solver*. In this case, the problems it solves are symbolic integrations, and it solves them by heuristic search. The system starts off with an impoverished set of heuristics, with the result that it will eventually solve integrals but not necessarily by the shortest or most economic route.

We than have a *critic* which compares the system's actual solution, which may have lots of blind alleys (such as applying an inappropriate trigonometric transformation), with an ideal solution which it is able to extract from the actual solution. It uses that comparison as a basis for saying here's an example of something the system should not have done because it took the system away from the ideal solution.

These heuristics about what the system should have done are used by a *generalizer* to create a

FIGURE 10.10   Mitchell's LEX

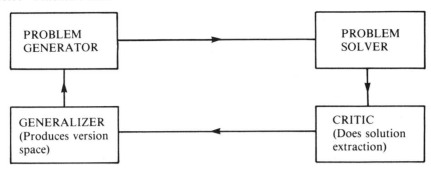

'version space'. This has examples of the most general things that have been used successfully, and examples of the most specific things that have been used successfully.

Once we have worked with the generalizer we go back to the *problem generator* to produce a problem that lies in the space of things that we are not sure that we can solve. We don't want problems that we are guaranteed to solve or not to solve: we want integrals that we will solve, but not in an ideal way.

My toy version of LEX is to learn to build steeples. Suppose I take these two blocks (Figure 10.11) and ask, 'Is that a steeple?', and that I'm told, 'No, it's not a steeple.' Suppose I build the second object (Figure 10.11) and am told, 'Yes, that's a steeple', and that the third and fourth objects are not steeples but the fifth one is. What could I have learned from this?

FIGURE 10.11   Examples for steeple building

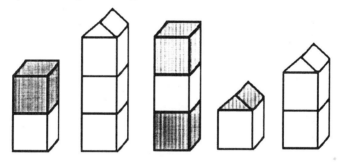

Well, I could have learned two very general rules. One is that to build steeples you should use stacking. There would have been no reason to suppose, if I were just a simple-minded robot starting off with these blocks, that I would initially stack them: I might arrange them along the table rather than up the table. The second general rule is to put a wedge on top. Both of these are over-general rules: neither rule on its own will necessarily give me a steeple. If I just use stacking, I may end up with towers that don't have wedges on them, and if I just top with a wedge then I may end up with things that are too short to be steeples. An example of a specific rule I could get out would be to use three cubes and a wedge. That is a rule which is guaranteed to build me a steeple but it isn't an algorithm that could be used in recognizing all steeples. So that then is Mitchell's approach.

The third approach I will discuss is Ross Quinlan's ID3, which is derived from a piece of psychology work, that of Hunt on concept learning. Quinlan regards learning as constructing classification rules. He says that learning is essentially discrimination: you need to discriminate between one thing and another. He represents classification as a decision tree. The decision tree branches on attributes in the domain; in our example, on things like colour, shape and arrangement.

Where Quinlan's work is superior to all the past work in this area is that he has found a way of constructing a minimum tree. For a given set of attributes, his system looks and says, 'I want to classify things in the most economical way: what is the smallest tree I can build?'

Here (Figure 10.12) is an example of a Quinlan 'steeple tree'. If we look back at our steeple examples (Figure 10.11) we see that there are three that have wedges on top and two that do not. So we can discriminate on 'Do you have a wedge on top or not?'. If the answer is No we can classify the object as not a steeple. Next we can ask 'Are there two blocks?'. If the answer is Yes we can eliminate the other example of a non-steeple. This tree then is a little representation which we can interpret to determine whether a structure is a steeple.

FIGURE 10.12   A steeple tree

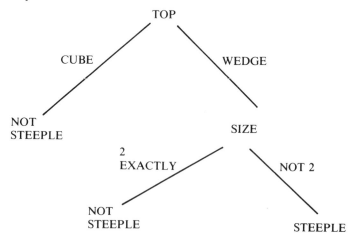

Unfortunately, for this example, it isn't actually the simplest tree I can build. It looks a simple tree, but there is a simpler tree using a different attribute. If you look at the objects again you will notice that our examples of non-steeples have some grey blocks and our examples of steeples have only white blocks. So the simplest tree for our set of examples involves asking the question 'Is it only made of white blocks?' But obviously you don't need to be very sophisticated to have guessed that my notion of steeple doesn't actually depend on colour. In this case, unluckily, an irrelevant attribute, or rather one which later on as we build our tree will turn out to be irrelevant, can be used for the examples given so far. And that is the key problem with Quinlan's approach.

My fourth example is back to Winston — a Winston ten years older, a bit wiser and tackling harder problems. He decided he wanted to tackle the problem of analogy. He used an artificial intelligence representation called frames, which (although nobody's *quite* sure what they are) are large structures with slots that allow you to look at expectancies. Winston's system attempts to generalize these slots in the context of a system that is trying to understand the plots of plays or stories. His frame structure gives you, as it were, a causal structure of how the plot works, and the system tries to generalize some of the slots and transfer any constraints they have.

Let me give a particular example, which is probably an application of artificial intelligence you would not have imagined; a conceptual model for the plot of Macbeth. If we look at it (Figure 10.13) we see the things one would expect to find in an account of Macbeth: loyalty, weakness, murder, influence, and of course Lady Macbeth. At the top we see Macbeth and his murdering of Duncan. Why did Macbeth murder Duncan? Because he wanted to be King. Why did Macbeth want to be King? Because he was persuaded to do so by Lady Macbeth. Why did

FIGURE 10.13   Plot of Macbeth (from Winston)

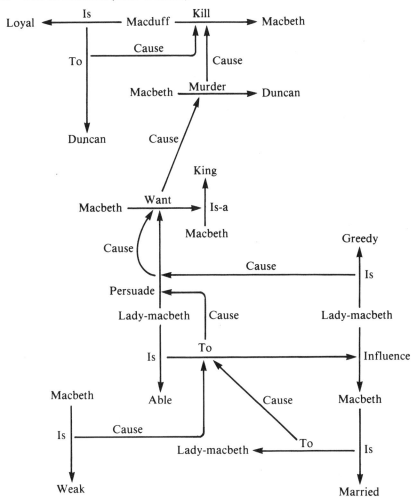

Lady Macbeth persuade him to do that? Because she was greedy. But why did Lady Macbeth have influence over him? For two reasons: she was married to him, and he was weak anyway. So obviously he was a loser and she could get him to go off and murder other people if she wanted to.

Now one of the alarming things about a representation like this is that there are probably many other ways of using the same arrows and the same notations to express the plot of Macbeth. Let us suppose, however, that we have encapsulated Macbeth like this, and that we are interested in why women cause men to murder people. It's an interesting question, so we do a bit of generalization. We end up with this structure (Figure 10.14).

You will notice how Macbeth has been replaced by Noble1, Lady Macbeth has been replaced by Lady1 and Duncan has been replaced by a Generic King. There we have a structure which can allow us to ask questions such as 'How do lady nobles have influence over the men they are married to?' When we see a generalized structure like this, analogy bells immediately start ringing; you all say to yourselves: Ah, ha! Hamlet! Exactly. This allows us to understand the plot of Hamlet, because all we need to do is say Lady1 is Gertrude, Noble1 is Claudius, and make some minor transformations, for example, to change 'is married to' to 'love', and put 'Gertrude's previous husband' in the King slot.

FIGURE 10.14   Plot of Macbeth generalized (from Winston)

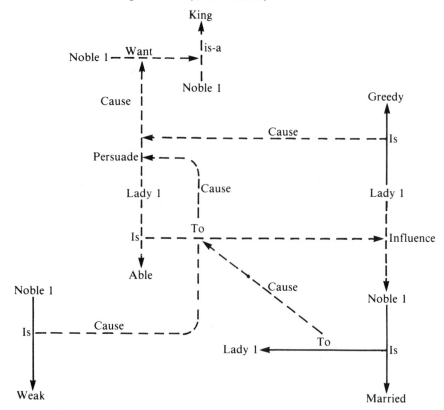

So that's the notion then: take a very specific account of, for example, the plot of Macbeth, generalize it, then go to other things (Shakespearean plays or modern stories) and ask how, doing the minimum damage to the structure, can we get something to map on. For example, in this case, it obviously does less damage to put Gertrude as Lady1 than it does to put her as either the King or Noble1. Then, having found a mapping, we can ask questions like, 'Is it the case that Claudius is weak?' or 'Is he married to Gertrude?' The answer to the second one turns out to be 'No, but he is eventually.'

I will now go on to my personal favourite, a late sixties' program written by Don Waterman. It uses ordered production rules, and what it learns to do is very appealing: it learns to improve its bet decisions at poker. Poker is an inherently more interesting game than chess or checkers (draughts) because it is a game of imperfect information. In chess or checkers both players can see the board and can see each other's moves; in poker, every so often somebody's bluffing or somebody's discarding his cards without his opponents seeing what he was holding that made him behave as he did. So from a game theory point of view it's a much more sophisticated game: you are obliged to have estimates of bluffing.

Waterman's system had a set of production rules that represented a poker-playing strategy. It has a theory of poker which had in it notions like the objective of playing poker is to gain money, you gain money by winning tricks, you win tricks by . . . , and so on. The system would play poker and it would then, as a good player would after playing a game, analyze how it played it and ask from the point of view of its theory what it should have done otherwise.

Instead of going through poker, I will use a very simple, much less interesting game: the steeple game. There are two players, each equipped with cubes and wedges. The object of the game is to build a steeple. Here is one game: I place a cube, you place a cube on that cube, I place a wedge on top — I have won. That gives me a very simple strategy which I can express as two production rules (Figure 10.15). One says, if there is space or a block around put something on it. The second says, if the other guy has produced two cubes put a wedge on it.

FIGURE 10.15   The steeple game

> Rule 1: Space or cube ⟶ place a cube on top
> Rule 2: Two cubes ⟶ cap with a wedge

Now the opponent starts: he puts a cube down, I put a cube on top (happily playing the steeple game according to my rules), he puts a wedge on — he has won. I am distraught. I go back to my theory of steeple playing. My theory tells me that if I can't get a win, get a draw. I then ask the question, backward chaining through my set of production rules, how can I get a draw? The answer is to block the opponent from winning. To do that I could have put a wedge on his cube, forming a house (a well-known example of a non-steeple) so forcing a draw. So returning to my production rules, I now produce a third rule, which I interpose between the other two, to say if there is one block place a wedge on it. So that is what I have learned, and in fact it is very easy to make a production rule system that will learn to play the steeple game. It's not too hard to make a more complicated system that will learn to play poker.

My last example is the most dashing one: it's Doug Lenat's work with a family of programs, the two best-known of which are called AM and EURISKO. Lenat was interested in the process of mathematical discovery, and he started out with a clear commitment to the notion that if your system is to learn anything serious then it is going to need to start with background knowledge. It's like one of those rules for making money: the best way to make a lot of money is to have quite a lot of money. Lenat said that the best way to learn knowledge is to have quite a lot of knowledge already. So he created a system (AM) with a lot of heuristic rules and a whole pile of concepts. In his case he started with 115 mathematical concepts represented much like frames with about 24 slots.

His system has a control mechanism based on an agenda of tasks, and it prefers to do tasks that are heuristically designated as being the most interesting. The system conjectures that this or that might be an interesting thing to do. It has a notion of 'focus of attention', which is roughly that if something has been done recently keep doing it. And he has, in some sense, some innovative heuristics. Here (Figure 10.16) are four of Lenat's heuristics: while in the artificial intelligence sense they are innovative, from the point of view of the philosophy of science they are standard or old hat.

FIGURE 10.16   Lenat's heuristics

> Parsimony
> Regularities
> Extremes
> Inverses

One heuristic is 'parsimony'; that is, if you can find a simple way of combining concepts or a way of reducing your descriptions then do it. Parsimony can be thought of as a form of generalization, one of our learning mechanisms. Another heuristic is to look for regularities. A third is to look at extreme cases, which is a heuristic that is well known in mathematical problem solving and is the type of heuristic described by Polya. Another of Polya's heuristics that Lenat uses is that of 'inverses'; that is, if you have a mathematical function or transformation that is interesting look at its inverse.

Lenat's first system, AM, started off with a description of some fundamental mathematical concepts and then started building up other notions. It built the idea of 'plus', 'partition', 'Cartesian product', 'times', 'exponentiation' and 'divisors' (Figure 10.17). The extra arrows in the diagram represent blind alleys that were entered by applying heuristics.

FIGURE 10.17   Searching for concepts (from Lenat)

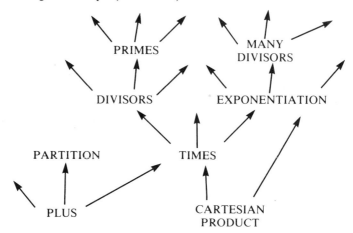

Lenat's system uses a very familiar artificial intelligence method, going by the name known from the General Problem Solver, namely 'generate and test'. It generates a new concept by combining old concepts, or a concept and its inverse, and then tests it. In this case it's tested for its interestingness using the heuristics.

Two particularly interesting things that AM got from its simple concepts were both derived from extreme cases. Coming from the idea of times, it took the inverse to get divisors and then using extreme cases (numbers that have no divisors apart from 1 and themselves) derived the idea of 'prime numbers'. The other example concerned a mathematical concept only recently discovered, in this century, by an Indian mathematician. This was the idea of 'maximally divisible numbers'. Those are the numbers that are in some sense the complementary extreme to primes, as they have many divisors.

Let me go back now to my six studies. Recently, Alan Bundy and some colleagues reviewed various learning systems and tried to provide a unified account of how these systems work. Of the ones I have mentioned, the early Winston work and the work of Mitchell, Quinlan and Waterman can all be very nicely described in Bundy's account. In fact, Bundy's account subsumes many rule learning and concept learning systems. What can't be described in Bundy's account are the two systems that use much more complicated representational schemes and control structures, namely the analogy system of Winston and the discovery system of Lenat.

A slogan which I learnt from Bob Simmons and which can be adapted to every area of artificial intelligence is 'problem solving is like theorem proving is like natural language parsing is like problem solving'. If you look at the different things we have, concept learning is actually like rule learning, for if we have a rule for building arches, so that we know how to manipulate the objects in order to construct an arch, then we can also use that to recognize arches. So I can change from a rule learning system to a concept learning system very simply (in the most extreme case, if I see something that might be an arch, I could destroy it and then try to build it again using my rule for building arches; if I succeed then it was an arch). As we go on, we can see that rule learning turns out to be very much like discovering heuristics, which in turn turns out to be very much like problem solving. In fact, in terms of an artificial intelligence vocabulary, probably the simplest one to use for talking about all the learning systems with reasonable precision is the vocabulary commonly associated with problem solving. We are talking about learning in terms of searching some sort of space, having operators that we can apply in the space. In this case the operators are heuristics and what we are constructing in the space are things like rules or concepts.

The architecture which Alan Bundy and his colleagues propose for learning is basically very simple. He tries to consider everything pretty much as an example of rule learning (we can easily take the concept learning programs and rewrite them as rule learning programs). There are just two components: a 'critic', which looks at our body of rules and says which is the faulty rule; and a 'modifier' which corrects the faulty rule. For example, if we have the rule

H1 and H2 and ... Hn $\longrightarrow$ C

that is, that the hypotheses H1, H2 up to Hn imply some consequent C, then there are two standard ways to correct it: one way is to add a new condition, i.e. to specialize the rule to say that if all those hypotheses and something else then C; the other way is to change the consequent, i.e. to say that the hypotheses do actually describe the situation but we should do something different.

The representation that Bundy uses is called a 'description space', and is actually a generalization of Winston's work described by Richard Young, Gordon Plotkin and Reinhard Linz in a very important paper published only as a one-page abstract for a 1977 conference (which was quite foolish of them!). Richard Young and his colleagues asked, 'Why does Winston's system depend so much on the training sequence? Do you really need "near misses"? What happens if your counter-example of, say, an arch has two things different rather than one thing?' It turned out that Winston was wrong about some of the properties of his learning system. The most important thing he was wrong about was the fact that the sequence of training did not in fact matter. By generalizing Winston's system to allow you to deal with partial descriptions, Young and colleagues showed that it survived perfectly well with different training sequences.

Instead of dealing with a single structure, as Winston had, to represent our current view of what an arch was, we have a space of partial descriptions. Each time we have an example or counter-example, we create something else in our space of descriptions. We have a collection of properties which describe our current most general view of an arch and our current most specific view of an arch. As we run the system, if we take the most general view sometimes we will make errors of commission (that is, we'll do things we shouldn't because we have over-generalized), and if we take the most specific view sometimes we will make errors of omission (that is, we won't say something is an arch when we should).

One way of thinking of description space is as a space that ranges from the most specific version of an arch at the top, through gradually more arch-like features, to right at the bottom our most general version. Starting from scratch, our most general version is any collection of any objects in any arrangements. As we go on, we learn that some features definitely are under the concept and some features definitely are not. For some sorts of attributes people use, this is a very well defined space with two boundaries. As we generalize, the upper boundary is lowered, and as we specialize the lower boundary is raised (Figure 10.8). When the boundaries meet then we know that we've learned the concept successfully and can distinguish between things that are in the concept and things that are not.

This is a very powerful analysis which we can apply to the learning systems that I've

FIGURE 10.18   Description space

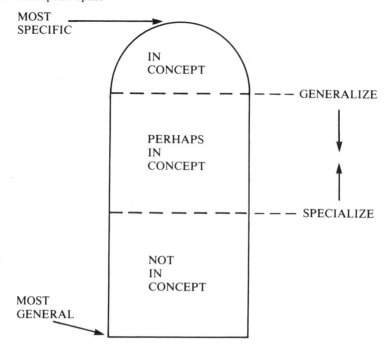

discussed, such as Mitchell's system. We can ask very precise questions, like 'Is this learnable?' and 'Has it been learned for sure?'

Going now into the mechanism of working in the description space, suppose we have a fault, what types of fault might there be? Well, there are basically only two types of fault: factual faults, where an individual rule is false, and control faults, where perhaps the set of rules loops repeatedly. How do we find a fault? By experiment (which is what Waterman's system does), by training (as with Winston's system), or from an ideal trace, i.e. an account of the sequence we really should have followed. Of the three, the ideal trace (which is what Mitchell uses) is the hardest to think about. Suppose you have solved the problem and you have compared your rule trace with an ideal trace. You look at successive transformations until you find the first mismatch: the mismatch rule is an error of commission, where we did the wrong thing in that circumstance. So we need to change that rule.

Elaborating our modification techniques, there are four standard techniques in use. One is ordering, where we rearrange the rules, assuming they are to be used in a linear order. Secondly, we might instantiate a rule; that is, we might bind one of its variables to the surrounding. Thirdly, we might add a condition to the rule. And, lastly, we might update a hypothesis; for example, to put in a new general descriptor (such as sticks, rather than slabs and pillars). For example, if we have the rule

H and G(X) $\longrightarrow$ C

then we can tag that as the first rule or the fourth rule or whatever, we can look at the current value of X and bind that to it, we can add a new condition WW to give

WW and H and G(X) $\longrightarrow$ C

or can change the definition of H or G.

To do this sort of modification, we need to know three things:

1.   The type of instance we are dealing with: whether it is something we did right, a

commission error (something we should not have done in the circumstances), or an omission error (something we should have done but did not).

2. The faulty rule, which we can locate using the ideal trace.

3. The context; that is, what the variables we are dealing with are bound to.

This notion of working in the description space to bring the boundaries together is called 'focusing'. Basically, we are doing two things: we are generalizing correct rules to allow them to try to capture more of the description; and we are discriminating on faulty rules trying to find out why they are faulty. Because we are dealing with a space rather than a single prototype we have got all the past context, in some sense, because they are given by the boundaries of the space we are working with.

In mathematical terms, generalization and discrimination are almost dual. If they were mathematical duals then our life would be enormously easier, but they are not. The reason they are not is that sometimes when you are discriminating you have two things (for example, colour and shape), either of which might be causing your problem but you don't know which, and so you are obliged to make a choice. Generalization does not have that choice problem. In generalizing, you are always saying, well, I will regard red blocks and blue blocks as blocks, or whatever. Generalization does not have the problem of non-determinism but discrimination does.

What problems does focusing have (because from the way I have described focusing it sounds as if we should all rush out and immediately use the Young–Plotkin–Linz approach to learning)? The fierce problem is one that I was just hinting about when I discussed discrimination; that is, if you have a disjunctive concept. If it turns out that the rule you are trying to learn is

(H1 and H2) or (H3 and H2) $\longrightarrow$ C

then you are in trouble, because if the concept is genuinely disjunctive then whichever way you jump to discriminate you will be wrong. If you have disjunction and you try to discriminate, then you over-specialize and actually end up with inconsistencies in your model.

A second endemic problem is noise. If there is any noise, even if only one of your data points is wrong, then using this approach your mathematical reliability goes out of the window, because you over-generalize. With this approach you are not keeping all the data points, all you are keeping is the boundaries. So you won't know retrospectively why you have over-generalized.

What are the solutions? One solution for dealing with disjunction is what is called forking. If you have a disjunctive concept, then you make two copies of the space, one copy for one element that you are interested in, the other for the other element. Now, that leads us to a traditional AI problem, the combinatorial explosion: you only need to break your space in two ten times and you are already dealing with a very large number of spaces.

An alternative solution is to store all the data. Then if you bump into trouble you can go back and re-compute over all the data. In principle, you can yank out a new disjunctive concept like 'wedge or cube' or whatever it is you need. There is one approach to doing that, which is Quinlan's work: all the data is in the Quinlan decision tree. So his classification approach is your solution. Why then should we not use Quinlan's approach? Well, let us compare these two approaches.

In focusing, the great advantage we have is that we know for sure when we've learned something. When we've merged our boundaries in a space then we can say, 'I now have the concept of an arch' or 'I now have the concept of reliably winning king plus knight against king plus bishop'. Using the classification tree you can never tell whether your tree is complete.

However, if you do focusing then there is this very nasty problem with disjunction, and it's not hard to make up legitimate disjunctive concepts where you really would want to describe something with an 'or'. For example, unpunctuality might sometimes be to do with our local transport, or it might be to do with personal unreliability, say.

Another nice thing about focusing is that you have structural rules. You can build rules which can deal with the structures of descriptions or, in Mitchell's case, of problem solving strategies that involve successively applying operators in different domains.

With classification, the big win is that disjunction is guaranteed all right. If there is a disjunctive concept then you get that for free in the branching trees. However, you need all the data, so you are bound to require more memory. We need not worry about the memory load too much, but the other problem is that you can only really deal with simple attributes, which have to be more or less right, as shown by my counter-example. If you have a lot of attributes that are not relevant, but you are learning, how do you know which are the relevant attributes? You may be splitting your tree all over the place on things like colour, flavour, day of the week, weather, and that is doing nothing but just adding an extra memory burden for you.

Overall, in learning we have a trade-off. On the one hand, we can deal with simple representations like trees and simple control structures such as rule order; on the other hand, we can use more complex representations such as frames (as the later Winston does) and control structures like agendas (as Lenat does). The disadvantage of simple representations is obvious: I would be in serious trouble trying to write out the plot of Macbeth with simple ordered production rules. However, the advantage of a simple approach is that you can 'do a Bundy on it'; that is, you can say what a system can reliably do or what it won't do. The problem with the more complex approach is that nobody really knows what a frame or agenda is, so that it is difficult to prove their properties or reason about their limits.

What then are the regular problems that people working in learning have to face? They are:

(a)   the credit assignment problem; that is, working out which rule to give credit to, or to blame;
(b)   disjunction;
(c)   the combinatorial explosion, especially if you are trying to deal with disjunction;
(d)   choice of notation — how you create and add new rules;
(e)   atrophy over time.

If you want to annoy somebody who has built a learning machine, it is actually extremely simple. You ask them for a demonstration and then a week later reappear and ask them what it's learned in the last week. The answer is that these learning machines are bound by their initial language and their initial heuristics. Since Lenat's AM was published a few years ago it has not learned any new mathematical concepts: in some sense, it's been used up.

Those are the regular problems; now let's consider the vicious problems. They are:

(f)   noise, for the real world is full of noise;
(g)   choice of initial vocabulary;
(h)   property inheritance; I used little descriptions that said, for example, Duncan is a King, or pillars are sticks, but property inheritance (to describe the properties of a particular object in terms of more general objects) is a very fraught area;
(i)   the hill-climbing problem;
(j)   the frame problem.

The last two are particularly hard.

For the hill-climbing problem, suppose your learning machine does something and things get a bit worse. It may be that if your learning machine did a second thing then the combination of the two things would result in some massive learning gain. But, in general, learning systems are timid. If they find that things seem to be getting worse at all, then they immediately zoom back to the top of the hill they were last on. That's one of the fundamental reasons why systems like Lenat's or Winston's atrophy: they get stuck with a certain number of things they know because any other change they make actually results in some sort of degradation.

Learning is particularly vulnerable to the frame problem (I should emphasize that this expression was made up before Minsky used 'frame' to refer to a representation). In general, the frame problem refers to a situation where you know something about the world which you start planning on, but the world changes and your view of the world is no longer correct. Suppose our learning system has learned a rule, which it uses to change its behaviour. Let's suppose it learns ten other rules. Now those ten rules may change its behaviour in such a way that the first rule we learned no longer works. For example, I may know one way to tie my shoe laces: if I learn a more sophisticated way it may turn out that if I try to do the simple way as well then the two methods mess one another up.

One standard way to describe the frame problem (made up by Pat Hayes) is to think of a monkey in a situation that monkeys in AI textbooks often find themselves in, where we have a monkey, a box and some bananas and the poor monkey can't get the bananas. Of course,

FIGURE 10.19   Monkey in an AI textbook

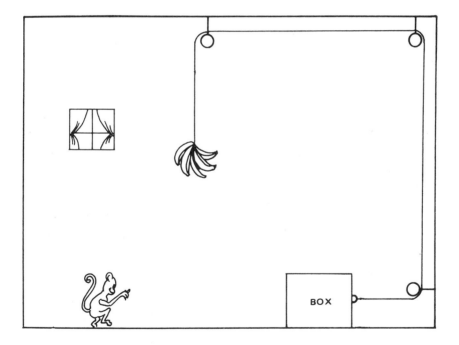

the monkey has read the AI literature, and so does a bit of means-end analysis, to find he can reduce the size difference by pushing the box under the bananas and getting on the box. (If he were an early AI monkey he might get on the box first, then get down again, and then move the box across.) Then, of course, we're home and dry. So the monkey does that, only to discover that the bananas are connected to a rope which, as he pushes the box across, pulls the bananas up. Pushing the box doesn't do any good for the monkey, it is exactly the same distance away from the bananas as before. With a bit of reasoning, we might actually deduce that in this particular circumstance the right thing to do is to push the box away from the bananas. But of course the frame problem may be more severe than that. Maybe the room is located in a space station orbiting the earth, in which case the monkey should just make a little push on the floor and float up and gently catch them.

So, learning is a very difficult area. At the moment, if you want to apply learning in an industrial application, the only realistic advice I can give is to use learning techniques for tuning: build your knowledge-intensive system and then tune away at it.

Let me be hopeful, however: what sorts of technique are we seeing applied? One technique, coming particularly out of the expert systems work, where people have succeeded in building models of some complicated domain, is to use those models to guide your learning. That's happened quite nicely with an expert system called DENDRAL, which has an associated learning component called METADENDRAL. From this point of view, things are going back to front: it's the learning community that's riding on the back of the expert systems community.

Another tactic that you can try to follow, as Waterman did when trying to say what the goal of playing poker is, is to elaborate notions of goals. Mitchell, in his work on solving symbolic integration and other tasks, is now trying explicitly to represent goals separate from the heuristics.

You can also try to create meta-heuristics. Doug Lenat is now working on the problem of getting heuristics which allow us to create new heuristics. In EURISKO he regards the heuristics themselves as a special kind of concept and uses the same techniques of extremes, inverses and parsimony to get new heuristics.

Another very important notion is that of multiple representations; that is, the idea that to learn things in some domains you actually need a number of different representations of the same situation. For example, in the poker-playing situation, you need a representation of strategy and you also need a representation of money.

Another very helpful piece of work is what has been called 'rational reconstruction'. We've seen the rational reconstruction of some expert systems, and now in Bundy's work we are seeing the rational reconstruction of some learning systems. This involves going over the past literature and asking the very important question, 'What can the system do, how is it like other systems, and how is it not?'

Finally, we've seen this knowledge-intensive approach, and people recognizing that Lenat was right: if you want to acquire new knowledge you are going to need a lot of knowledge to start with. So people are adding components to systems, which we can regard as tuning or rule-adjusting.

But we are not going to see in the near future, in industry or science, systems that legitimately do things that we might describe as scientific theorizing. That is obviously much too hard and our representational schemes are much too impoverished to deal with this.

QUESTIONS

Q. I noticed that the discovery style paradigm of Lenat didn't appear to fit into the Bundy type of analysis. Do you have any advice for up-and-coming researchers as to where they might place their bets?

A. I would definitely have advice: be cautious. The safe thing that Lenat did was to use piles and piles of heuristics; the very unsafe thing he did was to deal with representational structures which are really very underspecified. It's very easy for those systems to get entirely out of hand, and also it is very hard to determine why the system learns one concept but not another. My advice would be to stay on the borderline — find a learning system that is quite well understood (a modern example might be Mitchell's system) and try to do something a little bit better. Or alternatively take Lenat's system or Winston's analogy system and take it to pieces to see if there is a simplified account that would give the same effect. But if you regarded Lenat's or Winston's later system as the state of the art you are doomed to misery. It has got to be a question of finding out the properties of those programs and carefully working on the boundary of what we know about for sure.

Q. Is learning all or nothing in the sense that you have implied? I am wondering about your solid arch. Wouldn't it be possible to say that's probably an arch?

A. It wouldn't be possible to say that's probably an arch in the description space I used; arches were an arrangement of three things, with two supporting the third. The notion of introducing probabilities in these areas is always attractive — but it's very dangerous. It is very dangerous because it leads you very easily to over-generalize. That is, if you are not sure what is going on at some stage of the game, you can apply a probability. For example, we could say if a thing has a wedge on then there is a 50 per cent chance that it's a steeple. That would be an unhelpful thing to get into my system too early. It makes more sense to try to look systematically to see if there is a structural description that gets me steeples. The moment you start to apply probabilities, you fuzz the edges: it becomes harder and harder to answer the important question, which is, 'Is this definitely an example?' I would want to be in a position where I could say for certain that my ruin counter-example for an arch was not an arch, and not, after 20 examples, that I was 95 per cent sure that it wasn't an arch. I know some people are more sympathetic to dabbling in statistical methods, but I regard it as a fairly dangerous minor heresy. I would like work in learning to continue for at least another 20 years before one allows people to start introducing probabilities.

FURTHER READING AND REFERENCES

Bundy, A., Silver, B. and Plummer, D. (1985) An analytical comparison of some rule-learning programs, *Artificial Intelligence,* Vol. 27, pp 137–182

Lenat, D.B. (1976) AM: an artificial intelligence approach to discovery in mathematics. Ph.D. dissertation, Stanford University.

Lenat, D.B. (1983) EURISKO: a program that learns new heuristics and domain concepts, *Artificial Intelligence.* Vol. 21, pp 61–98

Buchanan, B.G. and Feigenbaum, E.A. (1978) Dendral and Meta-Dendral: their applications dimension, *Artificial Intelligence,* Vol. 11, pp 5–24

Minsky, M. and Papert, S. (1969) *Perceptrons,* MIT Press, Massachusetts

Mitchell, T.M., Utgoff, P.E. and Banerji, R.B. (1983) *Learning by experimentation: acquiring and refining problem-solving heuristics.* In R.S. Michalski, J.G. Carbonell and T.M. Mitchell (Eds.) (1983) *Machine Learning,* Tioga, Palo Alto

Quinlan, J.R. (1979) *Discovering rules from large collections of examples: a case study.* In D. Michie (Ed.) (1979) *Expert Systems in the Microelectronic Age,* Edinburgh University Press, Edinburgh

Waterman, D.A. (1970) Generalization learning techniques for automating the learning of heuristics, *Artificial Intelligence,* Vol. 1, pp 121–170

Winston, P.H. (1975) *Learning structural descriptions from examples.* In P.H. Winston (Ed.) (1975) *The Psychology of Computer Vision,* McGraw-Hill, New York

Winston, P.H. (1982) Learning new principles from precedents and exercises, *Artificial Intelligence,* Vol. 19, pp 321–350

Young, R.M., Plotkin, G.D. and Linz, R.F. (1977) *Analysis of an extended concept-learning task.* In Proc. Int. Jt. Conf. on Artificial Intelligence, (1977) Morgan Kaufmann, Los Altos, California

11
NATURAL
LANGUAGE PROCESSING
KAREN SPARCK JONES
UNIVERSITY OF CAMBRIDGE

It is very difficult to pitch a short introduction to natural language systems between the daunting and the trivializing, and I am naturally going to have to omit a great deal. Notably, I am not going to be discussing speech at all. But I shall try to give the flavour of the aims of the work in this field, the problems, and the solutions so far. I will consider the following issues: first, what we look for in natural language systems; second, what sort of thing a natural language system is, with a rather basic example; third, what language problems there are to overcome; fourth, what processing ideas and techniques are available; and finally, what the current state of the art is, again via some examples.

WHY NATURAL LANGUAGE SYSTEMS?

So, first of all, what are we looking for in natural language systems? Natural language is an absolutely unrivalled vehicle for the transmission of information: it is very powerful because it is refined and flexible. So it is natural to want a natural language system, first of all to extend our own information processing resources by doing things on our behalf; for example, translating, repackaging messages, summarizing. That is, it is natural to want a system where language processing is the prime function of the whole system. It is also natural to want systems to assist us in our communication with machines, for example monitoring other processes and instructing things like robots; that is, systems where language processing is the function of the interface.

But clearly one needs the same basic language processing capabilities for either of these two functions. And it is clear what the essential characteristics of such language processing systems are. We are talking about systems that can *interpret* an input text, that is, can determine its meaning in a way which is suited to invoking a response from the machine, and correspondingly can *generate* an output text, that is, can formulate a meaningful response and express it in language, where there may be a quite arbitrary amount of concept *manipulation* in between these two processes. As this suggests, one is dealing with a transformation process between word strings and concept structures, or meanings of some sort, or with a process operating in the reverse direction. Language processing is hard because there is in fact no clear boundary between what one thinks of as language operations and what one thinks of as operations on concepts.

I would just like to make a cautionary aside here, which I think is very important, having described language processing systems like this. It is obvious that it is misleading to call a system that simply picks words from text against some sort of reference list a natural language system. It is not really doing anything which could be described as interpretation. But I also personally prefer to talk about language *processing* rather than natural language *understanding,* because we are very far from being able to build systems which understand language in the way that we do. For example, understanding that 'I'm working' means 'be quiet' is something which no current system can do. We may believe that we are moving in an effective way towards understanding natural language understanding systems but we are an extremely long way away from them yet.

WHAT IS A NATURAL LANGUAGE SYSTEM LIKE?

I referred to the basic capabilities of any language processing system: I shall now try to show what supplying these implies. But, of course, any individual system is determined by what kind of role it has, for example if it is an interface system, what particular task it is undertaking (a questioning or query system, for instance), and also what kind of domain it is working in (it may be a query system about the location of car spares). I will try to show how these particular functions, tasks and domains can influence system design. In fact, the challenge of system building is getting the right mix of the general, that is, providing for those things which any language processing system has to do, and the specific, that is, providing for the particular purposes of the individual system.

To show what sort of a thing a natural language system is I shall take a simple, established technology system as a starting point. I shall look at this system's components and architecture, using these to lead into a more detailed discussion. In this I shall be focusing on interpretation rather than on generation, because interpretation is what is most obviously needed.

A SYSTEM EXAMPLE

The comparatively basic system that I am going to take as an example is the LUNAR system developed by Woods. This was a system for asking questions about a database of analyses of moon rocks: when they got the rocks back from the moon they did analyses of them and stored the information about the analyses so that geologists could ask questions about them. LUNAR is an old system, developed in the early 1970s, but it was a good system. It could answer questions like 'I want the average composition of glasses in dust', or 'What samples contain more than 15 ppm barium in plagioclaze?' The system could handle quite complex constructions, in fact more complex than these examples, and was tested in real life by some geologists who seem to have found it reasonably satisfactory.

Figure 11.1 shows the system structure of LUNAR. Essentially, what it did was take a question, feed it into a syntactic processor which produced an intermediate representation of the question, pass this representation on to a semantic processor, to emerge with a formal query which was fed to the actual back-end database search system. Supporting these two processors were syntactic rules and a parser for the syntactic processor, semantic rules and an interpreter for the semantic processor, with underneath both of these a lexicon containing information about individual words.

Looking now at how this system operated, we'll consider first the syntactic processor. The

FIGURE 11.1   The LUNAR system structure

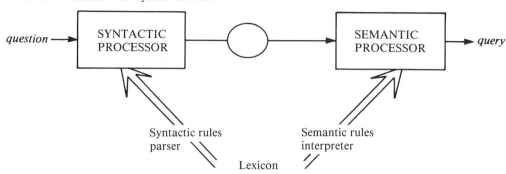

object of the syntactic parser with its grammar rules is to determine the syntactic structure of the sentence; that is to say, what the syntactic categories of the words are and how they are grouped together. In LUNAR this was done by exploiting a so-called augmented transition network. In such a network, parsing involves proceeding from state to state, as you move from one input word in a sentence to another, where conditions are satisfied as you move and structures are built in registers as a result. Those conditions that are satisfied, and the structures that are built, instantiate the grammar of the language. An important point is that satisfying the conditions can involve recursion to a lower level network, and also that the structures built need not in any very obvious way reflect the path through the network following the input word sequence that the system had been presented with. In other words, you can, for example, build the same representation structure for an active and a passive sentence which have very different input word sequences. Amplifying this description (using Figure 11.2(a)), we have a small transition network and you can imagine yourself asking, when you are starting to parse a sentence, let us find a noun phrase; if we can find a noun phrase we can make the first transition. We then look for a verb category word, and then we can either look for a noun phrase or we can just jump according to whether we have an object in the sentence or not, and then we emerge. The noun phrase network (also shown in Figure 11.2(a)) looks for a determiner word like 'the', looks for an adjective which it may or may not find, looks for a noun and then emerges.

A sentence is converted into an intermediate representation in the form of a constituent tree. For example, the sentence 'S23 contains rubidium' will be parsed to produce a constituent tree (shown in Figure 11.2(b)) with a noun phrase subject with a noun which is **S23**, a verb phrase with a verb **contain** and a noun phrase object, with a noun **rubidium.** (Note that the leaves of the tree are internal representations of the original words.)

The semantic processor looks at the syntactic tree that we have built as an intermediate representation to extract what can be described as its propositional content; that is, the concepts that the sentence contains and the meaning relationships between them. The way that the processor does this is by applying semantic patterns to the syntactic sub-structures that are in the tree and translating these into database-relevant commands and predications, building up structures with appropriate quantifiers, such as 'all' or 'each' or 'one'. For example, if we have a constituent tree for the question 'Does S23 contain rubidium?' and we apply rules like those shown (in Figure 11.3) to it, we first look at the sentence node at the top of the tree to see if it is a question, in which case we will output the command TEST. Then we will look at the noun in the subject noun phrase to see if it's a word that stands for the idea of SAMPLE. Then we check whether the verb is 'have' or 'contain' and if the object noun is a member of the semantic class ELEMENT or SAMPLE. These three checks together define a kind of general semantic pattern. If it is satisfied we will output CONTAIN ((N1), (N2)) for whatever N1 and N2 are in

FIGURE 11.2   LUNAR syntax (grossly simplified)

(a)

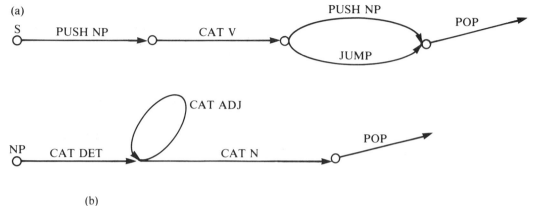

(b)
"S23 contains rubidium"

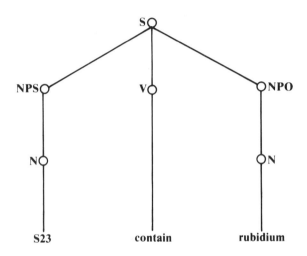

FIGURE 11.3   LUNAR semantics (grossly simplified)

"Does S23 contain rubidium?"

$$S(Q) \longrightarrow TEST$$

$$\left\{\begin{array}{l} NPS/N1 = (SAMPLE) \\ V = have, contain \\ NPO/N2 = (ELEMENT, \\ \qquad\qquad SAMPLE) \end{array}\right\} - CONTAIN\ ((N1),(N2))$$

$$\Longrightarrow \textbf{TEST (CONTAIN (S23, RUBID))}$$

the input sentence. Thus applying the rules to the sentence 'Does S23 contain rubidium?' we will get an output formal structure

TEST (CONTAIN (S23, RUBID))

which is something that can be fired off to the database system and executed. In this way you complete the transition from the input language question to the output database formal query.

LUNAR was a very impressive system for its date (it was finished effectively in 1972), but it embodies certain views of what a natural language processor should be like; that is, views of what the *components* of a processor should be, what the overall *architecture* of a processor should be, and also to some extent views about the *philosophy* of language interpretation and about the *scope* of a language processing system. Thus in LUNAR the parser is a top-down one. The architecture is a sequential one, where you do syntactic processing followed by semantic processing. The underlying philosophy of the system is that the meanings of natural language texts are procedures; for example, the meaning of 'Does S23 contain rubidium?' is 'go away and see if S23 contains rubidium'. And with respect to the scope of the system you notice it was essentially using only linguistic information about the way words can be put together.

These choices were in part influenced by specific system needs; but they can be justified independently as generally valid responses to general language processing problems. However, they were just one set of responses and there are other possible responses. I want to look now at the problems to which one is responding when one is building a natural language system, and then at other responses which have been adopted or put forward to those problems.

WHAT ARE THE PROBLEMS?

One of the most salient characteristics of natural language is ambiguity, and more specifically various forms of ambiguity. We have categorial ambiguity; for instance, the fact that a word like 'likes' can be a noun or a verb. We have word sense ambiguity; for example, the noun 'work' has very many different meanings, such as 'task', 'employment', 'manual labour', 'embroidery', or even 'the froth that you get when you manufacture vinegar'. Then there is structural ambiguity: if I say 'Sam killed the man with the gun', we don't know whether Sam killed with the gun or the man had the gun. There is also referential ambiguity; for example, if I write 'John disliked Bill. He hit him', we are not sure whether 'he' is John or 'he' is Bill and therefore whether 'him' is Bill or 'him' is John. These ambiguity phenomena are global ones in natural language; text interpretation has to resolve them for each particular manifestation that they have in any particular text. They can also take some extremely nasty forms, which are very difficult to deal with, for example compound nouns. If I have a string of nouns like 'metal pot lid', am I talking about the lid of a metal pot or the pot lid which is made of metal? The scope of conjunctions is another problem: if I say 'men and boys who like cricket' do I mean 'men, and boys who like cricket' or do I mean 'men and boys who both like cricket'? Again ellipsis is a form of ambiguity: if we have 'How many were there? Three', then 'There were three' is really what we are saying.

Moreover, the interpretation of an apparently very simple sentence needs a lot of resolution. Take a sentence like 'She told a story with a message'. We may hypothesize that the processor has correctly identified the meaning of this (as indicated in Figure 11.4), namely as 'Karen recited one fable having one moral' and that it's a fable with a moral. In other words, we have eliminated the meaning of 'told' as 'counted', the meaning of 'story' as 'lie', and the meaning of 'message' as 'communication', and we have also decided that 'communication' is not tied to 'count'. That is the kind of thing you have to do even for a very simple sentence.

FIGURE 11.4   Sentence interpretation

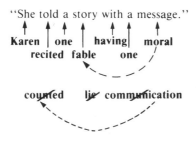

Now you might ask how *we* understand language, given all this complexity, because if you say one is assisted by context, i.e. by what has gone before, then of course how do we sort out what has gone before? The same problem is merely further back. We in fact have very large amounts of information about language, about what words can mean, how they can be put together into larger units, and the ways that these larger units can achieve certain functions. This language information is backed up by very large amounts of information about the world to which language refers, including any particular non-linguistic context the language is being used in at any particular time, and also by information about how one uses language to refer to the world in the process of communication.

But if we have a lot of information, then we're just asking another question: how do we bring these large amounts of information to bear on a particular text in order to select its particular meaning?

In principle one can see that one must operate in some way by predictability or plausibility, by applying the general idea of preferred meaning, by taking the most obvious reading of a text as confirmed by repetition and association, by standard associations between words and concepts. This general idea, which seems an attractive one, is of course an extremely vague one. What you have to do is to see how, in detail, you use all your different sources of knowledge and processes to apply this idea of predictability or plausibility: this is very hard and it is what research in automatic natural language processing is all about.

One way of proceeding, which is currently common practice, is to limit the system's universe of discourse, for example its domain, its purpose, its mode of operation: for instance, does the system take the initiative in interactions with the user? All of these kinds of limitation reduce linguistic variety. Thus with a restricted world you can have words with only one category, or sense, and only certain ways of combining them: for example, with LUNAR you might say we will just have 'rock' as a noun with the meaning 'stone' and forget about it as a kind of sweet. Similarly, dealing with 'analysis of samples with iron' we will make sure that 'iron' and 'samples' go together, because samples having iron (as opposed to analysis having (or via) iron) is a feature of this limited domain.

If you put this kind of limitation on the system it is very much easier to sort out what must be being said. In fact you can get a long way in building systems with specialized domain semantics like this, as LUNAR shows. But once you get beyond really toy systems you will find that the kinds of problem I have just illustrated are still there. For example, suppose I say 'analysis of S23 and S24 for iron': do I mean 'any analysis of S23 but analysis of S24 for iron' or do I mean 'analysis of both S23 and S24 for iron'? That kind of characteristic problem of language can still appear within a restricted domain. So one has to provide mechanisms, even in restricted systems, for dealing with the characteristic problems of language. There is no certainty about what these mechanisms should be like, and there have been a variety of proposals for system design in respect of components, architectures, and also philosophy and scope. In the next section I shall simply indicate some of the possibilities in a necessarily rather summary way.

The crucial issue, where one starts in designing a system, is what kind of meaning representation one wants. This is influenced by what you are going to do with it when you have it; for example, are you going to provoke a robot into action, do some summarizing, or do some translation? What it's like in turn influences what you have to do to get it: for example, if you are going to provoke a robot you have to establish time sequences in your input text rather carefully; if you are doing summarizing you have got to pick up the real gist of the text; if you are going to translate in a literary way you have to preserve the particular way in which things are presented in the input text.

There are very different ideas about the nature of meaning representations. In Figure 11.5 we

FIGURE 11.5   Meaning representations

"A boy hated a girl."

1. **FOR SOME (BOY) FOR SOME (GIRL)**
   (HATE (BOY, GIRL))

2. **((ACTOR (BOY1) $\Longrightarrow$**
   (MFEEL) OBJECT (ANGER)
   TO (GIRL1)) TIME1)

have two possibilities illustrated in an extremely superficial way. One way of representing the meaning of 'A boy hated a girl' would be to say 'for some boy, for some girl, hates boy girl', giving a rather simple kind of propositional representation essentially using the given lexical items. Another way might be to say that 'there is an actor who is a particular boy and he has a mental feeling which is anger towards some particular girl at some particular time'. I deliberately leave these rather sketchy: the example is simply intended to suggest that there can be different ways of representing meaning.

The important point is that we must have an explicit representation of meaning for the system to work on, that can not only be exploited for a direct reaction by the system but can be manipulated so that, for example, it can be integrated into the larger representation of a long dialogue, or filled out with further detail. This may be needed, for instance, in order to provide an answer to a question, as you cannot always answer a question in a simple-minded and direct way. For example (Figure 11.6), suppose I am instructing the system: I start with the command 'Do up the bolt' and then I say 'Fasten it tightly'. To interpret the second sentence the system needs an underlying representation of the fact that something is being acted on which connects 'do up' with 'fasten' and 'it' with 'bolt'. Similarly, if I then ask the question 'Have you finished it?' the system needs to be able to use the fact that if you do something there comes a time when

FIGURE 11.6   Inference

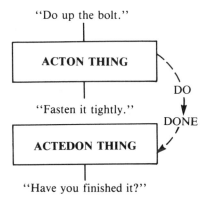

it's done, in order to be able to interpret the idea of finishing it, in this case, finishing doing up the bolt. (This is of course extremely schematic.) In other words, you need a representation which is capable of supporting inference to make connections which are not made explicitly in the text. A language processing system has got to get below the surface words and operate on concepts.

But whatever the specific system needs, if we are building a system for one purpose rather than another, language processing in general uses three sorts of information with corresponding representations for input data. There is *syntax* which you might describe as providing a skeleton, there's *semantics* which puts flesh on the skeleton, and there is *pragmatics* which we can say gives the body a name. Exactly what information of these sorts is needed, and how it should be used, is progressively less well understood as one goes from syntax to pragmatics. In part this is because we have two types of operation, one which we may call pattern-mapping operations, which are direct, while the others are more indirect, inferential operations; and it seems to be the case that as you move from syntax to pragmatics you increasingly call for inference rather than mapping, and inference is much harder to provide than mapping. We do not really know how to do inference, especially inference of the 'common sense' sort that seems to be required.

WHAT APPROACHES ARE THERE?

Given this background, we can now look at the kinds of things that people do. I want to emphasize that this is going to be extremely simplified. I would also like to draw your attention to the fact that the terminology of the trade is very confusing, and that I may use words here that are not necessarily agreed standards. I shall first look at the language processing system components, and then at how they are put together in the overall system architecture.

What processing ideas and techniques are available, then, for the syntactic component? A syntax component has *rules,* it will build *representations,* and its *process* for applying the rules to get the representations is parsing. Some options for each of these three elements of the system's syntactic component are shown in Figure 11.7. There are many theories of what form a

FIGURE 11.7   Approaches to syntax

(a)
Syntax: rules

  e.g. context-sensitive:
   $a \, X \, b \longrightarrow Y$
  context-free:
   $X \longrightarrow Y$

(b)
Syntax: representations
  e.g. constituent tree:

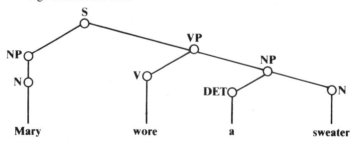

Case structure:

    wore ——— LOCUS Mary
       ——— THEME a sweater

(c)
Syntax: processes

  e.g. top down parsing:
   $S \longrightarrow NP \longrightarrow DET... + N$

  bottom up parsing
   $DET + N \longrightarrow NP... \longrightarrow S$

syntactic grammar should take and also of what the grammar for a particular language should be like. I cannot enter into any detail here. The LUNAR system, for example, used context-sensitive rules, that is it only translated constituent X into Y in some context, here (in Figure 11.7(a)) specified by *a* and *b*. You could have a simpler context-free grammar which simply said, whenever you encounter X in your input text turn it into Y. You can have different types of representation; for example, as you saw with LUNAR, you get a constituent tree (illustrated in Figure 11.7(b) for 'Mary wore a sweater') which tells us we have a noun phrase and a verb phrase containing a verb and another noun phrase. Or you could have a sort of a dependency structure of the verb with case-related items, for example there is a verb **wore** with a **LOCUS** which is **Mary,** the main topic, and a **THEME** which is a **sweater.** This is a quite different type of representation.

One is also concerned in a processing environment with what the parser is like, which applies the rules to the input text. This is a very important question, particularly from a practical point of view. In LUNAR we had a top-down parser; essentially the parser started by saying: Hey, we're sorting out a sentence, one of the things you can start a sentence with is a noun phrase, then if you look for a noun phrase you can begin with a determiner. So we're predicting that we'll get a determiner like 'the' or 'a' and so we set out to see if the first word of the input sentence is indeed a determiner. Then we look for a noun, and so on (see Figure 11.7(c)). An alternative strategy is bottom up, where you see whether the words you are given can be combined to make a valid constituent. So, for example, you might put a determiner and a noun together to make a noun phrase, and so on, building up to get a whole sentence. As you will get many alternatives, you can either go ahead and see what you can do, although you may have to backtrack if you come unstuck, or alternatively you can pursue all your possibilities in parallel.

Some forms of grammar lend themselves to particular parsing approaches. For example, a transition network is obviously best used top down, but equally there seem to be problems with any particular form of grammar in that it is very difficult to handle some phenomena: for example, it is very difficult to handle conjunctions with a transition network like the LUNAR one. But the more general problem with syntax is the fact that category and structure possibilities allow very many alternatives, so there is an essential non-determinism. For example, if you have a prepositional phrase, along with a subject, a verb and an object, should the prepositional phrase be attached to the verb or to the object? You have this problem of having to deal with many possible alternatives either by a backtracking or a parallel processing strategy. There have been some suggestions recently that you can get a more deterministic approach by limited look ahead; if I've got a Y there three words ahead then that implies I must have an X here. But you've still got local ambiguity and in the limit you need some semantic information as well as syntax to give you complete resolution.

It seems clear to many that you should take more account of semantics, because syntax in some sense provides only a very weak kind of information: it does not tell you very much about the meaning of a sentence or text. One way of taking more account of semantics is essentially by putting semantics into your syntax: instead of talking about nouns and verbs (as shown in Figure 11.7) you talk about semantic classes of nouns, such as ship types if you're dealing with movements of ships in a naval environment. Similarly, you do not have just verbs but you have particular verbs which are relevant to that domain, like those for forms of ship motion.

These strategies using a so-called semantic or sub-language grammar can be very effective in limited domains. But it is important to recognize that you do need the kind of information that syntax, as conventionally understood, gives you. Suppose you have a relative clause as in 'Find the ship which is proceeding to Port Said'. This is a standard syntactic concept that you need to use to connect the description of the ship with the ship itself. But, more importantly, you need to take account of regular syntax as you seek less limited language processors. Equally, you need to think about semantics in its own right.

Turning now to the semantic component, what sorts of possibilities are there for its rules, for the representations it produces and for the way it processes or parses its input (to extend the word 'parse' somewhat)?

The semantic component is the crucial contributor to meaning representation. It has the essential role in the transformation of the linguistic input to the conceptual output with which the system is going to do further work. You can think of semantics like syntax, as ambiguity resolution: which of the possible senses of the word are the operative ones in this piece of text? Which of the possible ways in which these words can be related in meaning are the ones that are operational in this text?

The key idea supporting semantic processing is generalization via features, or primitives, which are used to categorize words and message structures, where message structures essentially characterize the kinds of things that can be said. These message structures can take various forms: in LUNAR they took the form of general patterns, such as HUMANS LIKE FOOD (in Figure 11.8(a)), which can underlie a great many individual sentences and can be exploited as a

FIGURE 11.8   Approaches to semantics

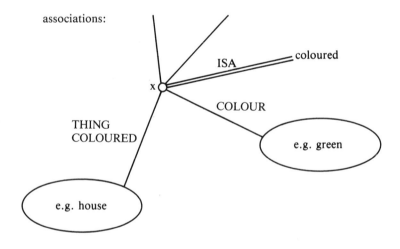

(a)
Semantics: rules

e.g. patterns:
HUMAN LIKE FOOD ⟶

associations:

ISA ———— coloured

x

COLOUR

THING
COLOURED

e.g. green

e.g. house

(b)
Semantics: representations

e.g.logic
**exists   X (mineral (X) &
              exports (Zambia, X))**

Semantic role:

**(exports <CAUSE HAVE>
   AGENT Zambia <WHERE PART>
   OBJECT minerals <STUFF>**

general pattern to interpret individual sentences like 'Auntie likes cake', 'The little boy likes chocolate', and so on. Or you can have your rules in the form of implicit patterns, contained in a sort of association network indicating the connections between words. The idea here (illustrated very schematically in Figure 11.8(a)) is that X is a node for the word 'coloured', which is connected with other words for things that can be coloured like 'house' and also with words for specific colours like 'green'. So although you may not have any explicit pattern you use those connections to help you to determine the relationships between words in individual sentences like 'They have a green house'.

The output representations that the semantic processor builds can be in the form of LUNAR-style logic structures (using the word 'logic' fairly loosely), with rather simple elements. For example, if we have the sentence 'Zambia exports minerals', we could have a logic style representation (shown in Figure 11.8(b)) which says that there **exists** an **X** and **X** is a **mineral,** and **exports Zambia X.** An alternative kind of representation is a sort of semantic role structure with a rather richer explicit representation of the relations between the words, and with semantic features on the words: thus (in Figure 11.8(b)) we have **exports,** which **CAUSEs** something to **HAVE,** and **exports** has an **AGENT** which is **Zambia** which is some sort of **WHERE PART,** i.e. a place, and an **OBJECT** which is **minerals,** and minerals are a kind of **STUFF.** As this suggests, you can have very different types of semantic representation and, as with syntax, the kind of representation you get may or may not be very closely related to the way in which it was got.

Semantic processing can be thought of in a way similar to syntactic parsing, as top-down pattern imposition or as bottom-up node travelling, i.e. a sort of propagation procedure looking for connections in the network. But I do not think it is really useful to talk about semantic processing independently as it is rather closely related to syntax, and so is better considered later under the heading of system architecture.

Syntax and semantics can do a lot for one, but they cannot do everything. The meaning of the word 'this' is typically determined by the real world: if I say 'this' there is nothing in the word itself which tells you what I am pointing to. And more generally, as I said, it is clear that one needs a lot of information about the types of world, and individual worlds, that underpin language information.

What is awkward is that there are no particular text phenomena that call necessarily for what I have rather broadly called pragmatic information. It is more that pragmatic information may be needed anywhere to support the operations of the semantic processor, for example in pronoun resolution to find the referent of a pronoun, in interpreting a compound noun to decide whether we are talking about metal lids of pots or lids of metal pots. Pragmatic information tends to be especially important in making a coherent interpretation of longer texts, connecting pronoun references backward into the text, for example, or in processing dialogue to take account of things like the communicative intent of the speaker and the general course of the interaction.

Looking now at the pragmatic component, i.e. at its rule, representation and processing elements, then, as I said earlier, pragmatics is rather ill-understood and so my remarks will be a bit more sketchy. Referring back to LUNAR, there were no explicit pragmatics in LUNAR. It was a sufficiently simple application for pragmatics to be essentially subsumed under semantics in the guise of those patterns saying, for example, that samples contain minerals: that was actually a fact about the moon rocks world, but it was buried in language rules. But you can see pragmatic information more explicitly in the idea of frames or scripts, which are essentially stereotyped object or event structures. For example you might have a script for demonstrations (as illustrated in Figure 11.9(a)). The first event in a demonstration is that people arrive at a

FIGURE 11.9   Approaches to pragmatics

(a)
Pragmatics: rules

e.g. scripts:
DEMONSTRATION
    E1 PEOPLE ARRIVE LOCATION
    E2 PEOPLE MARCH
    ‥‥‥‥‥

networks:

inference:

precondition
    EVENT ⟶ STATE
    X give Y to Z ⟶ X had Y
motivation
    EVENT ⟶ STATE
    X took Y ⟶ X wanted Y

(b)
pragmatics: representations

e.g. frame instance:
TRIP: FLIGHT = BA123
PASSENGER = J. Smith

net segment:

passenger1 NAME J. Smith

location, the second event is that people march, and so on. These are, of course, general patterns and they will subsume many individual ways of describing the details of demonstrations in particular texts that express that general event in particular ways. You can also express pragmatic information in the form of some sort of fact network, for example (Figure 11.9(a)), showing that employees have names and managers and departments, and managers also have names and employees and departments, and so on.

The particular point to be emphasized in connection with pragmatics is that though you can get a long way in finding particular pieces of information relevant to text interpretation by exploiting these kinds of structure, they may not give you everything. It may be the case that you cannot rely, if you are looking for a particular piece of information to help you, for example to interpret a pronoun, upon the context of a particular slot supplied by a script. Suppose you are at this event in this demonstration: you may not be able to rely on having been told, or even to assume, that you have had people arriving beforehand as specified in the script, but may have to establish the fact explicitly. Or in travelling through a fixed network, you may have to derive an explicit chain of inferences to actually construct a connection in a particular case.

Another form of pragmatic information is thus general inference rules, i.e. ones not tied to domain contexts. For example, one such general inference rule is that if you have an event you can infer a prior state, e.g. if X gave Y to Z, what you can infer is X had Y or he couldn't have given it to Z (Figure 11.9(a)). Similarly, a motivation inference can lead you from an event to a prior state, e.g. from X took Y one can assume that X wanted Y. These are the kinds of thing you in fact have to know, or to be able to derive, so that you can answer questions about why somebody did something. For example, you need to be able to make inferences on the interpretation of the story if, for instance, you are asked 'Why did Jack and Jill go up the hill?'

You can think, as in the previous cases, of the apparatus one has got as a grammar, although I think you have to do it very loosely here. Again, in pragmatics, you may get representations which are quite closely related to the means by which they were got: for example (as Figure 11.9(b) shows), you may have frame instantiations or network fragments; alternatively, you might get something quite different. Thus, imagining interpreting requests to an air flight booking system, you instantiate the frame as a specific trip with **FLIGHT BA 123** and **PASSENGER J.Smith.** Or, similarly, you might think of a pragmatic representation as instantiating some sort of network fact relationship between passengers and their names, e.g. (Figure 11.9(b)) we have a particular passenger, **passenger1,** with the **NAME J.Smith.** Alternatively, you can simply use pragmatic information to help you to fill out the kind of semantic representation I discussed before.

Pragmatic processing is very complex because it relates to the other system components, and so it is not really very pointful to talk about it independently of syntax and semantics; indeed, it leads naturally to the question of system architecture. I have discussed the system's individual components and now we have got to think about how you put these components together. The components are building blocks, but in fact how they're related in a system is at least as important as what they are like individually.

Given our processing boxes, therefore, the question now is: if you want to transform a text into a representation, how do you apply those boxes, what kind of order or combination do you apply them to the text to get the representation? The problem is that in reality all forms of information, syntactic, semantic, and pragmatic, are applicable at all points as you advance through the text, and you would minimize uncertainty about what the text's meaning is if you could bring all these forms of information to bear together in a kind of continued process of hypothesis creation and confirmation. System architecture really is a major issue.

LUNAR used a very simple sort of staged or sequential organization. If you had some pragmatics as well, you would first do some syntactic interpretation, maybe for a whole sentence, then you would do some semantics on the sentence, and then you would do some pragmatics on it. This organization has the advantage of modularity: you can build independent components and apply them in a nice clean way. The strategy can be acceptable if you have limited domains or limited tasks, but it is not very efficient in general because you can build a lot of intermediate structures, for example alternative syntactic representations, many of which will subsequently have to be thrown away, and this seems a bit futile. The alternative strategy is a kind of combined processing, bringing all the system's components to bear at once.

But of course you still have to drive this, there has got to be something that triggers off specific processes, and there are in fact essentially two alternative ways of doing this. You can drive everything lexically in a bottom-up way, finding the best interpretation for the word in hand, given all the sources of information. Thus you can imagine yourself, having got only as far 'the block' in the text 'The block ...', even bringing pragmatics to bear on interpreting these two words, by going out into the world that you're looking at and checking that there is in fact just one block. That would bring pragmatics to bear very early on before you've even looked at the rest of the sentence. The alternative strategy is essentially to drive processing by exploiting a global framework like the pragmatic framework. For example, if you know we're in TRIP and we've got to fill the TIME slot in the frame for TRIP, then let's see if we can find the word 'hours' in the text: that's driving things top down. In general, these more powerful top-down presuppositional strategies, assuming that you know what you are looking for, are very effective for limited applications, but of course they're dangerously inflexible, for they insist that you must be looking for some particular sort of thing. However, even in that kind of strategy you are still taking account of other component information, and the real problem in system architectures is how you manage the interaction between the various components or types of information. System architecture is very difficult and is very far from properly understood.

WHAT SORT OF SYSTEMS HAVE WE?

You might ask, in the light of this awful difficulty and complexity of language processing, how one succeeds in doing absolutely anything at all. Have people succeeded in building any systems above the level of the totally trivial? Research in language processing has been successful in that we have got some helpful ideas, and have got some useful apparatus with which non-trivial systems have been built. That is to say, the basic ideas which I have only been able to present very simplistically have proved capable of handling (some of) the real complexity of real text. I will very briefly now show you some real systems, to illustrate the type of task being tackled, the nature of the system being exploited, and the level of performance reached.

First of all, let's look at a more or less commercial system, Cognitive Systems' EXPLORER for interpreting requests for oil exploration maps (illustrated in Figure 11.10). These maps are

FIGURE 11.10   Cognitive Systems' EXPLORER (from Lehnert and Shwartz, 1983)

COGNITIVE SYSTEMS:

(a) Show me a map of all tight
    wells drilled before May 1,
    1980 but since May 1, 1970 by
    texaco that show oil deeper
    than 2000', are themselves
    deeper than 5000', are now
    operated by shell, are wildcat
    wells where the operator repor-
    ted a drilling problem, and
    have mechanical logs, drill
    stem tests, and a commercial
    oil analysis, that were drilled
    within the area defined by
    latitude 30 deg 20 min 30 sec
    to 31:20:30 and 80-81. scale
    2000 fest.

    By FEST, do you mean FEET (Y or N)

    Y

(b) `User requests a POSTED MAP`
    `latitude 30.34167 - 31.34167`
    `longitude 80 - 81`
    `output medium: PAPER`
    `output device: PHOTODOT`
    `filters:`
    `DRILLING DEPTH > 5000 FEET`
    `COMPLETION DATE > = 5/1/1970`
    `COMPLETION DATE < 5/1/1980`
    `OIL ANALYSIS AVAILABLE`
    `DRILL STEM TESTS PERFORMED`
    `MECHANICAL LOG FILE WELL`
    `DRILLING PROBLEM`
    `WILDCAT WELL`
    `SHELL CURRENT OPERATOR`
    `WELL SHOW OF OIL > 2000'`
    `TEXACO ORIGINAL OPERATOR`
    `TIGHT HOLE WELL`
    `scale of 1" = 2000.0'`

amazingly complicated objects, derived from a database and generated dynamically as actual physical maps. Referring to the kinds of ideas we have been talking about, EXPLORER exploits word-driven parsing, combining syntactic and semantic information, along with scripts relevant to this domain of oil maps, to produce an instantiated script as the request representation. For example, the system can take the long complicated input text shown (in Figure 11.10(a)) and, after suggesting that there was a misspelling or 'fest' for 'feet', actually construct the interpretation as a filling in of the slots in a script or frame (Figure 11.10(b)). So the user is requesting a map for wells with a drilling depth of so and so, drilled between certain dates and operated by Shell in an area between a certain latitude and longitude, and so on, to be output on paper by a photo-dot device: these are all essentially the features which are used to search the database to get the map source and print it.

What the system has proved capable of doing is taking this really quite complicated input text request and turning it into a specification, using standard concepts which the underlying database system handling oil well exploration data knows about. The system is claimed to be very robust and to have quite helpful interaction to clarify uncertainties in the question. Superficially, if you look at a very complicated input text like that illustrated, the system looks extremely attractive, but in fact it's very inflexible: it assumes that the user knows what kinds of map there are and that he will ask for them in a pretty obvious sort of way. The system just knows about these maps and about nothing else.

The second up-front system is Mitre Corporation's KNOBS system (illustrated in Figure 11.11). This is rather more complex because it is for both questioning, which is an application rather like the one I have just discussed, and planning, in a military context. KNOBS uses a whole range of resources of the kind I have mentioned, including word-based parsing, case

FIGURE 11.11 Mitre Corporation's KNOBS (from Pazzani and Engelman, 1983)

MITRE:

U: Send 4 aircraft from the
   109tfw to strike BE70501
   at 0900.

S: What aircraft do you want
   to use?

U: What aircraft are in the
   109TFW?

S: The 109tfw has F-4Cs.
   Would you like to use
   F-4Cs for the aircraft?

U: No, F-4Gs.

S: The 109TFW does not contain F-4Gs.

U: Fly the F-4Gs out of the
   126TFW at Ramstein.

frames, and scripts. It also has inference rules to fill out and connect items. It produces a kind of completely full and explicit case frame as a representation, which is not shown to you here: what I am giving here is the kind of interaction that interpreting inputs can lead to. In the illustration we have the user asking for four aircraft to be sent from the 109 tactical fighter wing to strike so and so at nine hours, the system asking what aircraft do you want to use, the user saying, what aircraft are in the 109 tactical fighter wing, and so on. Essentially, each of the inputs from the user is contributing to a dialogue-derived problem representation, where the processing is supported by a whole lot of script information about what planning bombing missions is about, which generates the responses and constructs the plan.

The third example system is New York University's system for formatting text such as medical records, organizing material under standard headings so that it can be accessed later for information. The system uses a very powerful syntactic parser along with domain specific semantic or sub-language grammar information. It additionally uses quite sophisticated techniques to extract implicit matter, for example filling out explicit time sequences which are often only indicated very indirectly by cues like past tense on verbs and so on. The illustration (Figure 11.12(a)) shows some input text in the somewhat telegraphic style typical of medical reports: 'Patient 1st had sickle cell anaemia diagnosed at age 2 years …' etc. The representation (shown in Figure 11.12(b)) is essentially picking up the various content items in this text and assigning them to record headings like patient, treatment, patient's state, time, and so on. For

FIGURE 11.12   New York University's system (from Sager, 1978)

NYU:

(a) Patient 1st had sickle cell
anaemia diagnosed at age 2
years when he complained of
leg pain. He was worked up
and diagnosis was made. He
was asymptomatic until age 5
when he was admitted to
Bellevue Hospital with chest
pains. He was hospitalised
for a month and released.

(b)

CONJ			WHEN
PATIENT		PATIENT	HE
TREATMENT			
INST			
V-MD		1ST HAD	
		DIAG-	
		NOSED	
PAT STATE			
V-PAT			COM-
			PLAINED
			OF
BODY PT			LEG
NORM			
SYMPT			PAIN
DIAG		SICKLE	
		CELL	
		ANEMIA	
TIME			
P1			
#			
UNIT			
P2		AT	
REF. PT		AGE	(AGE
		2 YRS	2 YRS)

example, the processing of the first sentence says that the kind of medical verb which is associated with the patient is that he was diagnosed, and that the diagnosis was that he had sickle cell anaemia and that the time was at age 2 years; we then go on with the second part of that sentence identifying 'he' as the patient and then there's a patient verb, which is he complained of leg pain, leg is the body part, pain is the symptom, and that was also of course at age 2 years: that's filled in some explicit time information. Notice that the representation, though normalizing, still essentially uses the input text words. The results of the processing are used for such purposes as question answering. Linguistically, it is a really sophisticated system for a very difficult task, as interpreting ill-formed text is very hard indeed.

Finally, of these up-front systems, which you will notice are all coming from the United States, we have the Irvine NOMAD system for translating scruffy text — rather like the medical records I have just shown you — into proper text. The specific application is to naval messages. Like KNOBS, NOMAD uses word-based expectation parsing combined with scripts about the domain and inference to fill out the gaps. The text here (Figure 11.13(a)) seems very much scruffier than the medical material because what happens in these kinds of context is that you have telex operators making up all kinds of abbreviations *ad hoc* and hoping that the recipients of the message will be able to interpret them in context; and of course that is something that is very hard for a language processing system. So we have a text like 'Periscope sighted by

FIGURE 11.13   Irvine's NOMAD (from Granger *et al.*, 1983)

IRVINE:

(a) PERISCOPE SIGHTED BY
CONSTELLATION ABT 2000
YDS OFF PORT QTR, AND
HS HELO VECTRED TO
DATUM. GREEN FLARES
SIGHTED AFTER VISUAL
ON PERISCOPE. HS GAIN-
ED ACTIVE CTC AND CON-
DUCTED TWO ATTACKS.

(b) The Constellation identified
an enemy submarine that was at
225 degrees 2000 miles from
their location. A helicopter-
squadron pursued the enemy submarine. The helicopter-squadron
identified some green flares.
By using an active sonar, the
helicopter-squadron identified
the enemy submarine, and they
fired twice at the enemy submarine.

Constellation abt 2000 yds off Port Qtr.' and so forth. NOMAD paraphrases this text (see Figure 11.13(b)) to produce well-formed sentences * and to fill out the input substantially, for example in interpreting 'HS gained active CTC and conducted two attacks'. But note that this is only one of two paraphrases given, as NOMAD cannot choose between 'The helicopter-squadron' and 'The Constellation' as the subject of 'identified'.

Just so as to avoid inducing too much depression from the fact that everything appears to be going on in the United States, I would like to conclude, briefly, with three much more modest projects from the UK. They have actually been done in Cambridge, but I am basically using them because I happen to know about them in more detail than some other projects. But I must emphasize they are more experimental than the projects mentioned so far.

The first system is a database question system, which uses not only domain-specific semantics but also more general semantics relating to the ordinary world. What this system does is illustrated (in Figure 11.14(a)) by the question 'Who are the green parts suppliers?' The system

FIGURE 11.14   Cambridge database query

CAMBRIDGE:

(a) WHO ARE THE GREEN PARTS
SUPPLIERS?

Who are the inexperienced
suppliers of parts?

Who are the suppliers of
green parts?

(b) Range of (Q1-v3,Q1-v2,Q1-v1) is
    (Shipments,Supplier,Part)
Retrieve into Terminal
    (key of focus relation)
  where
    (Q1-v1.Pnumber=Q1-v3.Pnumber)
  and
    (Q1-v2.Snumber=Q1.v3.Snumber)
  and
    (Q1-v1.Colour="green")

*The word 'miles' was stated to be a misprint in Granger et al. 1983.

Show me the key of the supp-
liers who make shipments of
parts whose colour is green.

shows how it has interpreted this question by feeding back language paraphrases. The first, perfectly plausible one is 'Who are the inexperienced suppliers of parts?' and the second one is 'Who are the suppliers of green parts?' In the general world we have no means of distinguishing those two. But in the database world to which the question is addressed, there are no inexperienced suppliers of parts, there are only suppliers of green parts, and so eventually we generate a formal database query from this interpretation (Figure 11.14(b)), a horrible piece of gobbledegook that you may well not want to have to make up yourself, which is addressed to the database management system. But, just to show somebody who does not know about the back-end database structure that the system has done this correctly, it feeds out another paraphrase from here, saying 'Show me the key of the suppliers who make shipments of parts whose colour is green'. In a sense, the correct formal query has been constructed by a sort of second stage domain-specific processing applied to the initial non domain-specific interpretation.

The second example (illustrated in Figure 11.15) is for database creation, through a system using an integrated semantic and pragmatic network. One of the aims of the project in building this system was to resolve pronoun references in running text using a semantic/pragmatic network. Thus, given an input like 'Plexir manufactures P9999 which is a computer. It is supplied by Smith' and so forth (Figure 11.15(a)), the system is capable of generating a whole lot of formal database creation entries like those shown in Figure 11.15(b):

(MACHINES/RELATION ((MC/TYPE computer) (MC/MCNUM P9999)))

and so on, more than I have shown here.

FIGURE 11.15   Cambridge database creation (from Alshawi, 1983)

CAMBRIDGE:

(a) **Plexir manufactures P9999 which**
is a computer. It is supplied
by Smith. P1010 is a terminal
that is supplied by Clark.
This one is made by Mikota.
These machines are red.

(b) (MACHINES/RELATION
    ((MC/TYPE computer)
    (MC/MCNUM P9999)))
   (MANUFACTURES/RELATION
    ((M/MNAME Plexir1)
    (M/MCNUM P9999)))

```
(SUPPLIES/RELATION
 ((SMC/SID Smith1)
  (SMC/MCNUM P9999)))
(SUPPLIES/RELATION
 ((SMC/SID Clark1)
  (SMC/MCNUM P1010)))
(MACHINE/RELATION
 ((MC/TYPE terminal1)
  (MC/MCNUM P1010)))
 ---
```

The final example is a story-summarizing system. This combines techniques for dealing with predictable text using standard script-like resources with techniques for coping with unexpected matter, because of course one of the things you are interested in in summarizing is not what is predictable about a story but what is novel about it. One of the problems with scripts is that they are only concerned with what is standard or stereotypical and not with what is unexpected.

Figure 11.16 shows an input story, 'Mary wanted to give Susan a present. She thought Susan would like to have a computer', and so on (notice that the story is about *girls* and computers), followed by the simple summary, 'Mary bought a computer for Susan'. Now you may think

FIGURE 11.16 Cambridge summarizing (from Tait, 1983)

```
CAMBRIDGE:


MARY WANTED TO GIVE SUSAN A
PRESENT. SHE THOUGHT SUSAN
WOULD LIKE TO HAVE A COMPUTER
SO SHE WENT TO THE SHOP WHICH
SOLD THEM. THE COMPUTERS
LOOKED EXCITING. MARY WALKED
OVER TO ONE AND TRIED IT BY
WRITING A LITTLE PROGRAM. SHE
ENJOYED IT AND DECIDED IT
WOULD BE A GOOD PRESENT FOR
SUSAN. SHE PAID FOR IT AND
TOOK IT AWAY WITH HER.


MARY BOUGHT A COMPUTER FOR
SUSAN.
```

that is dead obvious, you may think: How trivial; all this stuff about language processing to generate that Noddy summary. But nothing like that sentence occurs explicitly in the input text, the verb 'buy', for example, is never used. The summary has to be generated out of the text by understanding what its real meaning is.

Given all these illustrations, what is the conclusion to be drawn from them? The examples look very good, but all the current systems are extremely fragile. It is very easy to trip over their limitations. You can come unstuck in fact even with some quite unambitious, very well-defined systems; for example, rather modest systems for doing database questions. But, against that, we now have some solid experience of building useful systems, if only of a more modest kind. More importantly, I would like to finish by saying that given the potential value of natural language processing systems, whether operating on our behalf or together with us as interfaces, it is worth doing a lot more work on how to build them.

FURTHER READING AND REFERENCES

Alshawi, H. (1983) Memory and context mechanisms for automatic text processing. Ph.D. Thesis (Technical Report No. 60, Computer Laboratory), University of Cambridge

Boguraev, B.K. and Sparck Jones, K. (1983) How to drive a database front end using general semantic information. Proceedings of the Conference on Applied Natural Language Processing, pp 81–88

Computational Linguistics (formerly *American Journal of Computational Linguistics*), the journal of the Association for Computational Linguistics; enquiries to Dr D.E. Walker, Bell Communications Research, 445 South St., Morristown NJ 07960, USA.

Granger, R.H. *et al.* (1983) Scruffy text understanding: design and implementation of the NOMAD system. Proceedings of the Conference on Applied Natural Language Processing, pp 104–106

Lehnert, W.G. and Shwartz, S.P. (1983) EXPLORER: a natural language processing system for oil exploration. Proceedings of the Conference on Applied Natural Language Processing, pp 69–72

Pazzani, M.J. and Engelman, C. (1983) Knowledge-based question answering. Proceedings of the Conference on Applied Natural Language Processing, pp 73–80

Proceedings of the Conference on Applied Natural Language Processing (1983), available from the Association for Computational Linguistics, see above.

Ritchie, G. and Thompson, H. (1984) *Natural language processing.* In T. O'Shea and M. Eisenstadt (Eds) (1984) Artificial Intelligence, Harper and Row, New York

Sager, N. (1978) *Natural language information formatting: the automatic conversion of text to a structured data base.* In M. Yovits (Ed.) (1978) Advances in Computers 17, Academic Press, New York

Tait, J.I. (1982) Automatic summarising of English texts. Ph.D. Thesis (Technical Report No 47, Computer Laboratory), University of Cambridge

Tennant, N. (1981) *Natural Language Processing,* Petrocelli, New York

Woods, W.A. (1973) Progress in natural language understanding — an application to lunar geology, *AFIPS Conference Proceedings 42,* pp 441–450

Woods, W.A. (1977) *Lunar rocks in natural English: explorations in natural language question answering.* In A. Zampolli (Ed.) (1977) Linguistic Structures Processing, North Holland, Amsterdam

Woods, W.A. (1978) *Semantics and quantification in natural language question answering.* In M. Yovits (Ed.) (1978) Advances in Computers 17, Academic Press, New York

12

PROVING THE CORRECTNESS OF DIGITAL HARDWARE DESIGNS

HARRY BARROW

ARTIFICIAL INTELLIGENCE LABORATORY, SCHLUMBERGER
PALO ALTO RESEARCH

In the dawn of the silicon era, if an integrated circuit was not so simple that it was obviously correct then one could always build a prototype from transistors or nand-gates and try it out. As technology advanced and integrated circuits became more complex, their correctness was no longer obvious and prototyping became slower and more expensive. So the industry turned to computer modelling or computer simulation of the design in order to check it out. They would represent the system on a digital computer, put in all the possible inputs that a design might be expected to cope with, and check that all the right responses occurred. With the advent of LSI and VLSI and chips, things took a rather nasty turn. Even a fairly simple chip, such as a 16-bit multiplier, can face 4 billion possible input patterns. And if it contains a single 32-bit register, then there are 4 billion different ways it could respond to any one of those patterns.

Clearly, we have reached the point where it is impossible exhaustively to test a design for integrated circuits. Therefore, we have to select some subset of the possible inputs as a collection of test cases. This is an operation which is fraught with difficulty. First, it is really rather tricky to decide whether you have got an adequate set of test patterns that will stimulate all the different parts of the chip in all the different modes of operation. There is a very real chance that you will leave out the critical test that you should have used to detect the fatal design flaw. Indeed, many chips have reached the market place with flaws in their design, rather deep logical flaws of various sorts.

This poses a major problem for the VLSI industry. What possible way out is there, if, first of all, prototyping is impossible and now complete simulation is also impossible?

One might try, as people are currently trying to do, to develop methodologies for design which ensure that the design is 'correct by construction'. That is, you proceed from the specifications and transform them incrementally in some way until you flesh them out into a complete design that you know is correct, because nothing went wrong along the way.

Unfortunately, that approach requires an awful lot of knowledge about design, about electronics, and about the domain of the device (the world in which the device is to work). As yet, we do not have any general purpose 'silicon compilers', as they are called.

But there is another way, which is what I'm going to discuss. Instead of simulating the behaviour of the design with particular cases, can't we try to prove mathematically that the design is correct — that it provides all the right responses for all the given inputs that it might see and all the possible values in its registers?

Some early work was done by Tod Wagner at Stanford University in 1977. He was able to describe very simple low-level designs, built out of a small number of logic elements, in predicate calculus and to use a proof checker to verify his proof that they did in fact do what they were supposed to do. Recently, in 1981, I came across some work (see Figure 12.1) of an old friend of mine, Michael Gordon, who is now at Cambridge. He had been trying to develop a methodology for representing and reasoning about digital hardware. His approach was from the point of view of formal mathematics — in fact, he was using Scott–Strachey denotational semantics as the formalism in which to do his proofs. Initially his proofs were entirely manual, but eventually he used the LCF proof checker to check the correctness and consistency of the proofs that he was doing.

FIGURE 12.1   On proving correctness of hardware

(1) A Very Simple Model of
    Sequential Behaviour of nMOS

(2) A Model of Register Transfer
    Systems with Applications to
    Microcode and VLSI Correctness

by Mike Gordon
Computer Laboratory,
University of Cambridge

I found all this very exciting. I wondered whether it would be possible to use AI techniques to develop a system that could do these proofs automatically, because a designer does not want to know about Scott–Strachey denotational semantics. So the work I'm going to discuss lies very much at the intersection of VLSI and IKBS. It's concerned with developing a design methodology, a representation for designs, and with automating algebraic reasoning so that we can prove things about the design.

I will give a little introductory example to show some of the concepts and techniques that are involved. Then I shall go into the principles and practice behind that example and, indeed, behind proving correctness of hardware in general. I will then deal with a much more complex example to illustrate how the principles and techniques actually work in practice, and I will finish up with a couple of proof problems which you might find interesting.

The key issues that we're concerned with are:

(a) How do you describe the structure and behaviour of a digital system?
(b) How do you make inferences about the behaviour of the system using those descriptions?
(c) How do you implement those inferences on a computer?
(d) How do you make it all convenient and easy for a designer to use?

AN EXAMPLE

Imagine you have a little black box which is a counter or timer (Figure 12.2). Inside there is a register holding a count (a number). The output is the current value of the count, and each time the clock ticks the count is incremented by one — except if the control line on the input goes true, in which case the counter gets loaded with whatever number is coming in the input. We

FIGURE 12.2   A black-box counter

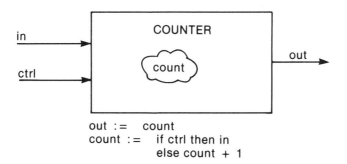

can describe the behaviour of this black box with two equations. One describes the behaviour of the output: the output is the current value of the count. The other describes what happens when the clock ticks: the new value of count becomes if control is true, then whatever is coming in the input, otherwise count + 1.

How do we build one of these things? Well, we propose to build it using three somewhat simpler 'modules', a multiplexer, a register and an incrementer (Figure 12.3). The register is going to hold the current count. The incrementer is going to add one to the count, feed it back into the input of the multiplexer and eventually back into the register, except when control is true, in which case the input gets loaded into the register.

FIGURE 12.3   Implementing the counter

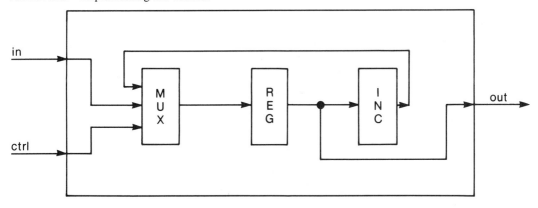

What of the behaviour of these three modules? The multiplexer is fairly simple (Figure 12.4): if the switch (sw) is true then input 1 (in1) gets routed through to the outside, otherwise input 0 (in0). The register has its own internal state, namely its contents. Its output is the current value of the contents and the new value of the contents when the clock ticks is whatever is coming in its input. If you like, this is just delaying the input signal by one clock tick. Finally, the

FIGURE 12.4   Behaviour of the modules

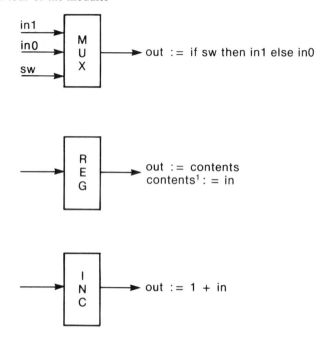

out : = if sw then in1 else in0

out : = contents
contents^1 : = in

out : = 1 + in

incrementer is an extremely simple device: its output is just 1 + whatever is coming in its input.

We now use a program which I have written with the uninspired name of VERIFY. It is written in PROLOG and attempts to prove correctness of designs based on a description of their behaviour in terms of equations and a description of their internal structure. To run VERIFY on our very simple example (Figure 12.5), I say 'verify (counter)', and it says 'attempting to verify counter'. It first tries to verify the components of the counter. This is a

FIGURE 12.5   Running VERIFY on the components of the system

| ?- verify(counter).

>> Attempting to verify counter
Verifying components of counter
  >> Attempting to verify inc
  << inc is primitive
  >> Attempting to verify reg
  << reg is primitive
  >> Attempting to verify mux
  << mux is primitive

Verifying counter as whole

very simple example, for pedagogical purposes: in this case all the components are primitive, that is, they have no internal structure themselves (as far as we are concerned). Primitives are assumed to be correct by VERIFY.

So, after assuming the incrementer, the register and the multiplexer are correct, VERIFY pops up a level and tries to verify the counter as a complete system (Figure 12.6). First, it prints out its own understanding of what it is we've told it this thing does, that is, its specified behaviour. The only things to notice are the output equation:

out : = count

and the state equation:

count : = if ctrl then in else count + 1

FIGURE 12.6   Running VERIFY on the complete system

Specified behavior is:

Module: counter
Inputs: ctrl:boole,
        in:integer
States: count:integer

Output equations:
    out := count

State equations:
    count := if ctrl then in else count+1

Now it is possible for VERIFY to derive, from the structure of that design, from the behaviour of the modules and the way they are interconnected, its own version of the behaviour of the total assembly. So it derives for itself, from the structure, the behaviour shown in Figure 12.7. This in fact looks extremely similar. The problem now is to decide whether those two behaviour

FIGURE 12.7   VERIFY derives the behaviour of the system

Constructed behavior is:

Module: counter
Inputs: ctrl:boole,
        in:integer
States: count:integer

Output equations:
    out := count

State equations:
    count := if ctrl then in else 1+count

descriptions are equivalent. The way we do that is as follows: we got from the specifications,

out = expression1

and we've derived from the structure of the design

out = expression2

We equate those two right-hand sides and try to prove that what we have is now an identity; that is, no matter what values the inputs take, no matter what values the state variables take, this equation

expression1 = expression2

is always true.

The first thing VERIFY does is equate those two equations for the output (Figure 12.8), and lo and behold we get something very simple:

count = count.

That's rather obviously true (I wish life were always that simple!).

FIGURE 12.8   First stage in deciding if the behaviour descriptions are equivalent

Trying to show behaviors are equivalent.
Considering equations for out
We must show that:

count=count

Trivial identity: true

VERIFY then considers the equations describing the new value for the count (Figure 12.9). We have to show that the first expression equals the second expression regardless of the values of ctrl, in and count.

FIGURE 12.9   VERIFY then considers the equations for the new value of 'count'

Considering equations for count
We must show that:

if ctrl then in else count+1
=
if ctrl then in else 1+count

To you and me those expressions are clearly identical: the fact that it says 'count + 1' on one side and '1 + count' on the other doesn't matter at all. But, in fact, this is the crux of the matter. In order to prove that such expressions are in fact equivalent we use a great deal of knowledge about mathematics, and algebra in particular, and that knowledge has to be embedded in VERIFY if it is to work. Well, it does indeed have a great deal of mathematical knowledge. When that knowledge is applied to our simple problem VERIFY proceeds by trying to rewrite the equations so that the left-hand side and the right-hand side turn out to be the same, and then it can rewrite the whole of the equation to true (Figure 12.10) — the 1 is the boolean *true* since we are in the world of electrical engineering. When we have established that this is an identity, all the equations of the two specifications have been shown to be equivalent, and so the counter has been verified.

FIGURE 12.10   VERIFY confirms the design

Trying symbolic manipulation.
Canonicalizing the identity...
Canonical form is:
   1

Identity has been established.

<< counter has been verified.

THE PROBLEM IN GENERAL

Let's now consider the problems that we are faced with in doing this kind of proof. The key problems are, in fact, concerned with the complexity of design, which is of two forms: *structural* complexity and *functional* complexity. By structural complexity I mean the fact that an integrated circuit may contain hundreds of thousands, or millions, of transistors, wires, connections and other components: there are an awful lot of primitive components! By functional complexity I mean that an object that is structurally complex displays an even more complex behaviour. Somehow we have to cope with all this complexity.

So how can we cope? It turns out that there are a few techniques that come to our aid, as we will see. Firstly, we can exploit the inherent hierarchical structure of the design. We can also exploit the inherent replication in the design. We are also going to exploit different ways of viewing what the design does, and different levels of detail in considering the signals that are passing through the integrated circuit. We will do this using algebraic reasoning instead of simulation, and we are also going to use a rather elementary technique that has been given the grand name of memoization; that is, you remember what you've done when you've done it.

Let's consider for a moment the structure of a design. Figure 12.11 is just one very small fragment of a hypothetical integrated circuit. This is what integrated circuit designers are used to dealing with; large, very complex networks of logic elements. But it's very difficult for people to understand this. You actually have to squint at it for a long time and then you start perceiving that there's some sort of regularity here, and gradually you'll start imposing some sort of structure on it.

It is actually a great shame that you have to go to all this work, because during the design process the design is not laid out, God-given, like this at the bottom level. It is in fact a highly structured thing, as shown in Figure 12.12. This is a much better way of describing a design. Looking at the top, this is a top level view of a device called d74. It contains three multipliers and two adders. It's got three inputs and two outputs, and it computes a couple of sums of products. Each of the multipliers is built out of a collection of slices. Each of these slices is built in turn out of three different sorts of thing, one of which is an adder. An adder is built out of three full adder elements, each of which does addition on just one bit from each of the inputs.

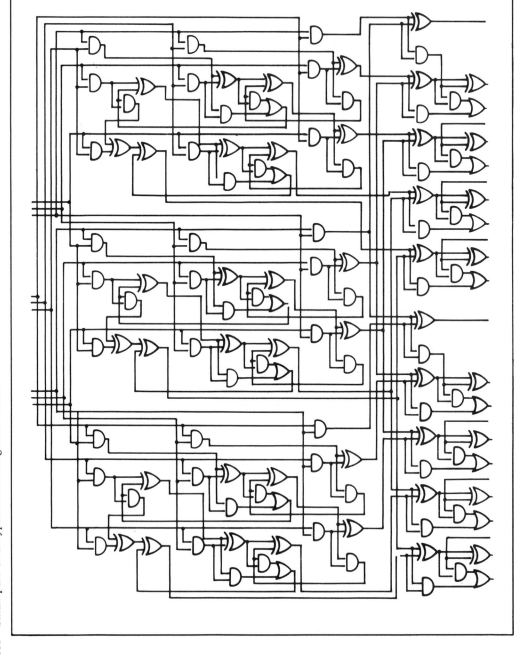

FIGURE 12.11   Small part of a hypothetical integrated circuit

The full adder, in turn, is built out of mux2s, which are built out of nor gates and an inverter. Eventually we get close to the bottom level, where we are building things like an inverter out of individual transistors, connections to ground, and so on. And right at the bottom are the primitives of the design, namely, transistors, connections, ground connections, and pullups.

FIGURE 12.12   The design of a device, called d74

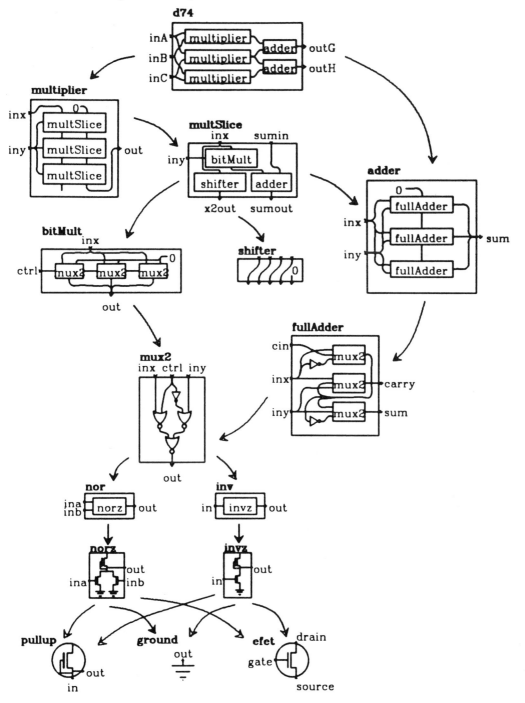

It's much easier to understand the design and what it's doing, looking at that sort of structure. In fact, this hierarchical organization of the design gives us, first, a factorization of the design: it breaks it up naturally into much more manageable pieces instead of that huge monolithic integrated circuit. We can also exploit the fact that pieces of the design are used many times over, for example the multipliers at the top level. What that in turn means is that when we try to prove this design is correct, all we need do is prove once that the multiplier does its job. We don't have to prove it three times because it's used three times in the circuit. So the complexity of the proof goes as the number of different types of module in the design, not the number of different instances of modules or the number of bottom level components — so long as we remember the results we are getting as we get them.

Along with this structural hierarchy there is the signal abstraction hierarchy (see Figure 12.13). At the bottom level, when we're dealing with transistors, we're thinking of the signals really as voltage levels. If we stand back a little from the design, then we really like to think of the signals propagating round as ones and zeros instead. In fact, close to the bottom we think of them as ternary logic signals. When we are considering a design like the network of logic gates we looked at earlier, we're really thinking in terms of boolean logic. Then we might think of the boolean logic as actually implementing operations on bits (binary digits). The bits get composed to perform computations on integers, which in turn one might like to think of as addresses in a computer, or even in terms of objects or data structures with their own characteristics and properties.

FIGURE 12.13   Signal abstraction hierarchy

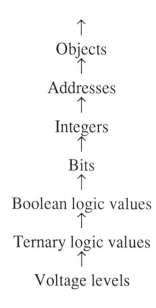

It turns out to be very important to think about the design at as high a level as possible. At the higher levels we are able to describe the behaviour much more succinctly. We are able to invoke semantics at a much higher level, that is, semantics about the domain in which we are computing: facts about numbers, for example. Consequently we can make much bigger steps in doing our proofs.

So much for the hierarchies in a design. I mentioned that a key technique which we were going to use was algebraic reasoning, and the reason for this is that it provides a generalization over those ground level instances. Instead of thinking about four billion patterns of zeros and ones, we can represent what is happening in terms of x's and y's. The symbol doesn't have any particular value — it stands for a whole set of possible values. Consequently, we are bundling a whole lot of possibilities into one symbol and we can reason about a lot of possible situations in the circuit simultaneously. This in turn leads to a great reduction in the number of cases that we have to consider. And, of course, what we are doing has the nature of a proof, something that is going to produce a reliable end product, instead of a set of test cases which may or may not cover everything that can happen in the circuit.

One of the first questions that has to be resolved is how to represent the structure and behaviour of the design. I've already shown you, through the example, a little of how we represent the designs here. We represent a module, a piece of the design, as something that has:

Ports: inputs and outputs;
Parts: internal objects of various sorts, e.g. adders, multipliers, etc.;
Connections: between the parts.

That's its structure.

We represent its behaviour by describing the input, output and state variables that are involved, and we have a set of equations which describes the values of the outputs as functions of the inputs and the current values of the state variables. We have another set of equations which describes new values for the state variables as functions of their old values and the inputs.

In order to proceed further I am going to look at the top level of VERIFY, which as I said is written in PROLOG. The topmost level is a set of three rules that are really pretty simple (see Figure 12.14). If I ask the system to verify a module, the first question it asks is, 'Is that module known to be verified already?'. That will save us a lot of redundant work. Failing that, it asks, 'Is it primitive?', in which case we can assume it is correct. Failing that, if the module is composite, then first we recurse and verify all of the parts, and then we come back and consider the module as a whole, knowing that the parts work, and try to show that the module as a whole is correct.

FIGURE 12.14   VERIFY's topmost level of three rules

```
verify(M) :- verified(M).

verify(M) :- primitive(M).

verify(M) :- composite(M),
             verify_parts(M),
             verify_whole(M).
```

And what is involved in verifying the module as a whole? Well, this also is very straightforward (see Figure 12.15). First, we retrieve the specified behaviour (SB) for this

FIGURE 12.15   Verifying the module

```
verify_whole(M) :-
    spec_behaviour(M,SB),
    imp_behaviour(M,IB),
    equiv_behaviour(SB,IB).
```

module. Secondly, we calculate the behaviour for this module that follows from the way it's been implemented (IB). Then we try to show that the behaviours SB and IB are equivalent.

The last two steps are the key ones, deriving the behaviour from the structure and comparing it to the specified behaviour. Let's consider a very simple module, which we call M, built out of two sub-modules A and B (Figure 12.16). It has an input called data and an output called ans. The behaviour of A is given by the equation

A.out = f(A.in)

i.e. the output of A is some function f of the input of A. Similarly, the output of B is some other function g of the input of B. These two equations describe the behaviour of A and B. There are also three equations which come from the structure, the interconnection of those parts. The first says that the data input of module M is connected to the input of module A. Similarly, the next two equations say that the input of B is the output of A and that the answer out of M is the output of B.

FIGURE 12.16   A module with two sub-modules

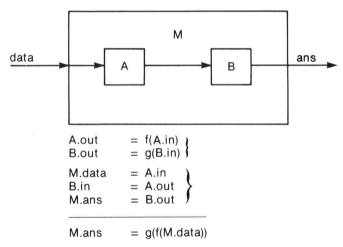

$$A.out \quad = f(A.in)$$
$$B.out \quad = g(B.in)$$

$$M.data \quad = A.in$$
$$B.in \quad = A.out$$
$$M.ans \quad = B.out$$

$$M.ans \quad = g(f(M.data))$$

It's very easy to solve that set of equations, to eliminate all reference to the modules A and B, to come up with the equation

M.ans = g(f(M.data))

This describes the output of the module M as a function of its input. Actually, very simple substitution processes like this will very often enable us to construct equations describing the behaviour of a module. There are some complications when we have loops but these are outside the scope of this paper.

So now the second part of the verification process is trying to prove that the two behaviour descriptions are equivalent. When we think about the sorts of algebraic proof that we often perform, we can broadly categorize three main activities. One is looking for known truths: if we find something that is a known fact we can stop our proof and say yes, we have achieved success. Secondly, the nature of an algebraic proof is, by and large, a sequence of transformations. We start off with some equation and we make a small modification to it, get another equation, another small modification, and so on. We continue this process until hopefully we transform it into something that's known to be true. A third technique we often use in algebraic proofs is case splitting. We come to a point in our proof at which we decide that we have to branch and consider two possibilities, and we then treat them more or less independently.

Let's look at some of these general algebraic processes. What sort of transformations do we typically do? Well, transformations like these (Figure 12.17). The first, '1 + 2' being rewritten as '3', I call the process of evaluation. The second, rewriting 'x and true' to be just 'x', is a process of simplification. Rewriting '(a + b) + c' as 'a + (b + c)' really involves an understanding that ' + ' is an associative operation. Rewriting 'count + 1' as '1 + count' (which is what we needed in the first example) involves understanding that ' + ' is a commutative operation. There are other sorts of transformations which one can do, such as cancelling the 'a' in 'x + a = y + a' to give 'x = y', so that if you have to prove the former, you can reduce it to proving the latter. Finally, there is a more complex operation, in which we rewrite 'fact(n)' as 'n*fact(n − 1)' (if we know that n > 1).

FIGURE 12.17   Transformations

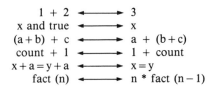

$$1 + 2 \longleftrightarrow 3$$
$$\text{x and true} \longleftrightarrow \text{x}$$
$$(a + b) + c \longleftrightarrow a + (b + c)$$
$$\text{count} + 1 \longleftrightarrow 1 + \text{count}$$
$$x + a = y + a \longleftrightarrow x = y$$
$$\text{fact (n)} \longleftrightarrow n * \text{fact (n − 1)}$$

With all these different types of transformation that we can perform on expressions, a few questions arise. Which of them do we perform when? How do we deal with nasty things like loops? For example, if we rewrite 'a + b' as 'b + a', which is a perfectly reasonable thing to do, how do we avoid doing the same thing again to give us 'a + b' back again, and so on? How can we be sure that what we do to the left-hand side of the equation and what we do to the right-hand side will lead us to the same end result? How, for example, can we be sure that no matter what order we do transformations we get the same result?

The answer, in a nutshell, is by being very careful. You have to apply a certain amount of care to make sure that your transformations are not going to get you into trouble, but you can actually take some fairly straightforward precautions. For example, to help avoid loops we can allow the system to rewrite an expression as long as it's going to put the arguments into, say, lexical order. So the system is not allowed to rewrite 'a + b' as 'b + a'.

The third class of technique I mentioned was case analysis. There are two main classes of case analysis that we're going to use. One is enumeration; that is, considering all the possible values for all the variables involved in an equation. That's actually what we were trying to avoid at the outset, and so we have to use this extremely sparingly. The other sort of case analysis is when you have an expression which is conditional, such as 'if x = 1 then exp1 else exp2'. Both the expressions exp1 and exp2 may involve x. We know that if x = 1 then the first expression is concerned, and wherever x occurs in exp1 we can substitute 1. If we have x = 1 somewhere in exp2 then we know that that can't be true because we only take this branch if x does not equal 1. If we also know that x is a boolean variable, that is, can only be 0 or 1, then we know that in this branch we can substitute 0 for x. So one can perform a little analysis like this on expressions which involve these conditionals.

The general proof strategy for VERIFY is something like this: first, we ask if the expression we are trying to prove is an identity, that is, is obviously true, as it was for the first expression in that simple example; secondly, we ask if the expression is sufficiently simple that we can just brute force our way through all the cases (often the answer is no); and thirdly, failing that, can we use those algebraic operations that I've just described. If for some reason that fails, if VERIFY doesn't, for example, have enough mathematical knowledge, then it will eventually pause and ask for help from the user. I originally intended VERIFY to be an interactive system, but it turned out that by stringing a number of those proof mechanisms together it is possible for VERIFY to deal with a surprisingly broad class of problems. So it only resorts to asking for help very occasionally.

VERIFY IN ACTION

Now let's see VERIFY in action with the design I introduced earlier on (Figure 12.12). To ask VERIFY to prove that this is correct we say please 'verify (d74(2))', d74 being the name of the module and the parameter 2 indicating the number of bits involved: we can have a 2-bit, 3-bit, 10-bit or whatever version (see Figure 12.18). To verify d74 we have to verify the

FIGURE 12.18 Verifying d74

```
yes
| ?- verify(d74(2)).

>> Attempting to verify d74(2)
Verifying components of d74(2)
 >> Attempting to verify multiplier(2)
 Verifying components of multiplier(2)
 >> Attempting to verify multSlice(4)
 Verifying components of multSlice(4)
 >> Attempting to verify adder(4)
 Verifying components of adder(4)
 >> Attempting to verify fullAdder
 Verifying components of fullAdder
 >> Attempting to verify mux2
 Verifying components of mux2
 >> Attempting to verify inv2
 Verifying components of inv2
 >> Attempting to verify inv
 Verifying components of inv
  >> Attempting to verify ground
  << ground is primitive
  >> Attempting to verify join
  << join is primitive
  >> Attempting to verify pullup
  << pullup is primitive
  >> Attempting to verify eFet
  << eFet is primitive
```

multiplier because it was built out of multipliers. To verify the multiplier we have to verify a slice of the multiplier. To do that we have verify an adder, a multiplexer, an inverter, and eventually we get down to the primitives just as we did with the very first example. The primitives (connections to ground, joins of wires, pullups and transistors) we assume to be correct.

Then the proof backs up to consider the inverter (Figure 12.19). This inverter is built out of nmos transistors, which have certain rather interesting idiosyncracies. The transistors behave as switches which can be closed or open and so the behaviour of this inverter is actually represented by fairly complicated equations (see Figure 12.19). If this were an ideal logical inverter the output would be just the not of the input, but it isn't, being built of real transistors, and so the output is the not of the rather messy expression shown: if the input is open circuit then the charge stored on the transistor, otherwise whatever is coming in the input. And the charge stored on the transistor is a state variable, recording the state of the transistor at any particular time and obeying the state equation given.

FIGURE 12.19   Verifying the inverter

Verifying inv as whole

Specified behavior is:

Module: inv
Inputs: in:booleZ
States: charge:boole

Output equations:
    out := not(if in=hiZ then charge else in)

State equations:
    charge := if in=hiZ then charge else in

So that is the specified behaviour — it's what I as the designer said it ought to do. The constructed behaviour, which VERIFY derives from the structure, is as shown in Figure 12.20. We have a much more complicated-looking equation for the output.

VERIFY has to try to equate this to my specification and prove they are identical. VERIFY has to show first (Figure 12.21) that the equation for 'out', which I gave, is equivalent to what it has derived. One of the strategies that one can use in situations like this is to consider all the cases, and since there are only six cases here that is what VERIFY decides to do. In each case the equation can be reduced to true, and this demonstrates that we have in fact got an identity.

Then VERIFY has to show that the specification equation for the stored charge on the transistor equals what is derived from the structure (Figure 12.22). This one happens to be trivially true.

So now we know that the simplest compound object in that design, namely an inverter, actually works. Rather than bore you by dragging you through this design in a huge amount of detail, I'll just consider a couple of edited highlights. One is the multiplexer, which was built, if you recall, as a compound object from three nor-gates and an inverter. Its specification is that the output is if the control signal is true then in1 else in0 (top of Figure 12.23). Since it's built

FIGURE 12.20   The constructed behaviour derived by VERIFY
Constructed behavior is:

Module: inv
Inputs: in:booleZ
States: charge:boole

Output equations:
  out :=
    if if in=hiZ and charge=1 or in=1
      then 0
      else hiZ
      =
     hiZ
    then 1
    else if in=hiZ and charge=1 or in=1
      then 0
      else hiZ

State equations:
  charge := if in=hiZ then charge else in

FIGURE 12.21   Equating behaviours
Trying to show behaviors are equivalent.
Considering equations for out
We must show that:

  not(if in=hiZ then charge else in)
  =
  if if in=hiZ and charge=1 or in=1
    then 0
    else hiZ
    =
    hiZ
  then 1
  else if in=hiZ and charge=1 or in=1
    then 0
    else hiZ

Trying enumeration.
******
Identity has been demonstrated.

FIGURE 12.22   Next stage in the verification

Considering equations for charge
We must show that:

if in=hiZ then charge else in

=

if in=hiZ then charge else in

Trivial identity: true

<< inv has been verified.

FIGURE 12.23   Verifying the multiplexer

Verifying mux2 as whole
Specified behavior is:

Module: mux2
Inputs: ctrl,in1,in0

Output equations:
    out := if ctrl then in1 else in0

Constructed behavior is:

Module: mux2
Inputs: ctrl,in1,in0

Output equations:
    out :=
      not(not(in0 or ctrl)
        or
      not(in1 or not(ctrl)))

from nor-gates and inverters the constructed behaviour derived is the expression shown (bottom of Figure 12.23).

   VERIFY has to show that those two expression are equivalent (Figure 12.24). To show that equating the two right-hand sides gives an identity, it embarks on using what it knows about algebra. First it rewrites the two sides in a standard, canonical form, in which the nots are pushed inside the ors, and the if is pulled to the top of the expression. This expression is not obviously true, and so VERIFY resorts to case analysis. If ctrl is true, then we take the first branch and within it replace all ctrls by true. Then this sub-expression reduces to true. If ctrl is false, then we take the other branch. So we can replace all ctrls in this sub-expression by false, and simplify this, giving true. So the expression reduces to 'if ctrl then true else true', which is always true. We've proved that this is an identity and that sub-module, the multiplexer, has been verified.

FIGURE 12.24   Equating behaviours for the multiplexer

Trying to show behaviors are equivalent.
Considering equations for out
We must show that:

if ctrl then in1 else in0
=
not(not(in0 or ctrl)
      or
      not(in1 or not(ctrl)))

Trying symbolic manipulation.
Canonicalizing the identity...
Canonical form is:

if ctrl
then in1=(in1 or not(ctrl)
                and(in0 or ctrl))
else in0=(in1 or not(ctrl)
                and(in0 or ctrl))

Doing case analysis...
Case analysis yields:
  1

Identity has been established.

<< mux2 has been verified.

The most complex piece of the proof of d74 is actually concerned with verifying the adder. It is very easy to describe an adder: the output is just the sum of the inputs inx, iny (Figure 12.25).

However, the adder is built out of a collection of full-adders. Deriving a description of the behaviour from the structure, gives something that looks really messy (Figure 12.26(a)), something that involves bit 2 of inx, bit 2 of iny, and so on. The poor verifier is faced with the problem of showing that inx + iny equals this expression (Figure 12.26b).

How are we going to do that? First, there are too many cases to do it by enumeration (Figure 12.27). But VERIFY notices that on the right-hand side it's got terms like bit 2 of inx, bit 1 of iny, etc., whereas on the left-hand side it just has inx + iny. So it decides to replace inx and iny by bitwise expansions giving little power series for inx and iny.

FIGURE 12.25   Verifying the adder

Verifying adder(2) as whole
Specified behavior is:

Module: adder(2)
Inputs: iny, inx

Output equations:
out := inx+iny

FIGURE 12.26   Constructing and equating behaviours

(a) Constructed behavior is:

Module: adder(2)
Inputs: iny, inx

Output equations:
out :=
2^3 *
bit(1,bit(2,inx)+bit(2,iny)
    + bit(1,...+...+bit(1,...)))
+ 2^2 *
bit(0,bit(2,inx)+bit(2,iny)
    + bit(1,...+...+bit(1,...)))
+ 2^1 *
bit(0,bit(1,inx)+bit(1,iny)
    + bit(1,bit(0,inx)+bit(0,iny)+0))
+ 2^0*
bit(0,bit(0,inx)+bit(0,iny)+0)

(b) Trying to show behaviors are equivalent.
Considering equations for out
We must show that:

inx+iny
=
2^3 *
bit(1,bit(2,inx)+bit(2,iny)
    + bit(1,...+...+bit(1,...)))

$$+ 2^2 *$$
bit(0,bit(2,inx)+bit(2,iny)
    + bit(1,...+...+bit(1,...)))
$$+ 2^1 *$$
bit(0,bit(1,inx)+bit(1,iny)
    + bit(1,bit(0,inx)+bit(0,iny)+0))
$$+ 2^0 *$$
bit(0,bit(0,inx)+bit(0,iny)+0)

FIGURE 12.27   Bitwise expansions

Domain space too big to enumerate.
Trying symbolic manipulation.
Bit-expanding iny,inx
Bit-expanded form is:
    bit(0,inx)+2^1*bit(1,inx)+2^2*bit(2,inx)
    + (bit(0,iny)+2^1*bit(1,iny)+2^2*bit(2,iny))
    =
$$2^3 *$$
bit(1,bit(2,inx)+bit(2,iny)
    + bit(1,...+...+bit(1,...)))
+
$$2^2 *$$
bit(0,bit(2,inx)+bit(2,iny)
    + bit(1,...+...+bit(1,...)))
+
$$2^1 *$$
bit(0,bit(1,inx)+bit(1,iny)
    + bit(1,bit(0,inx)+bit(0,iny)+0))
+
2^0*bit(0,bit(0,inx)+bit(0,iny)+0)

That's a fairly good start. Now VERIFY tries to rewrite that expression, simplified as much as possible, into a canonical form (Figure 12.28). Whereupon it can go into a small orgy of cancelling and eliminate some of the things that occur on both sides.

The cancellation yields a much simpler expression (Figure 12.29), which has still to be shown to be an identity. It's still too big to do by enumeration but now VERIFY can bring to bear all those transformation rules that it's got built inside it (there are actually about 150 such rules). It tries to rewrite the expression to something that's obviously true, and in fact it succeeds in this and so verifies the adder.

Eventually, the process gets right up to the top of the design, the d74 module itself (Figure 12.30). The specification is given by the two equations for outH and outG. The description of the behaviour derived from its structure is very simple and in fact looks very like the specification. This demonstrates the point that representing the design at as high a level as possible and reasoning about it at as high a level as possible really pays off.

FIGURE 12.28   Canonicalizing and cancelling

Canonicalizing the identity...

Canonical form is:
   bit(0,bit(0,iny)+bit(0,inx))
   + bit(2,iny)*4
   + bit(2,inx)*4
   + bit(1,iny)*2
   + bit(1,inx)*2
   + bit(1,bit(0,iny)+bit(0,inx))*2
   =
   bit(0,iny)+bit(0,inx)
   + bit(2,iny)*4
   + bit(2,inx)*4
   + bit(1,iny)*2
   + bit(1,inx)*2

Cancelling: bit(2,iny)*4
Cancelling: bit(2,inx)*4
Cancelling: bit(1,iny)*2
Cancelling: bit(1,inx)*2

FIGURE 12.29   The adder verified

Cancellation yields the sub-goal:

   bit(1,bit(0,iny)+bit(0,inx))*2
   +
   bit(0,bit(0,iny)+bit(0,inx))
   =
   bit(0,inx)+bit(0,iny)

Domain space too big to enumerate.
Trying symbolic manipulation.
Canonicalizing the identity...
Canonical form is:
   1
Identity has been established.

<< adder(2) has been verified.

FIGURE 12.30   Verification of the whole module

Verifying d74(2) as whole

Specified behavior is:

Module: d74(2)
Inputs: inC, inB, inA

Output equations:
    outH := inA*inC+inB*inC,
    outG := inA*inC+inA*inB

Constructed behavior is:

Module: d74(2)
Inputs: inC, inB, inA

Output equations:
    outH := inA*inC+inC*inB,
    outG := inB*inA+inA*inC

FIGURE 12.31   Verification completed

Trying to show behaviors are equivalent.
Considering equations for outH
We must show that:

inA*inC+inB*inC=inA*inC+inC*inB

Domain space too big to enumerate.
Trying symbolic manipulation.
Canonicalizing the identity...
Canonical form is:
    1
Identity has been established.

Considering equations for outG
We must show that:

inA*inC+inA*inB=inB*inA+inA*inC

Domain space too big to enumerate.
Trying symbolic manipulation.
Canonicalizing the identity...
Canonical form is:
    1

Identity has been established.

<< d74(2) has been verified.

The only difference here is that the terms are in different order. VERIFY deals with the two equations one after the other (Figure 12.31). All that is required with the first equation is to rearrange the terms using the commutativity of + and *, and similarly for the equation for outG. Now it has verified the correctness of the module d74.

The full proof for a 9-bit version of d74 takes something like a hundred pages of output. It involves nine levels in the hierarchical structure, and VERIFY has to prove along the way the correctness of 49 different types of modules — adders, multipliers, and so on. The top level design, if you were to build one, uses 18 400 transistors, and it can accept 34 million different possible input patterns. The proof of correctness of that design goes through in just ten minutes of computer time. The reason is that we achieve success in small doses by breaking up the design into pieces, reasoning at as high a level as possible, and throwing at them a whole battery of different tactics for doing proofs.

A HIGHER LEVEL DESIGN

I think you can see that we can deal with reasonably complex designs. You've seen that we can go right down to the transistor level in reasoning about the design. How far up can we go? Well, here is another rather interesting little example (Figure 12.32).

This is the front panel of a hypothetical computer. It has a program counter with some lights which show its state. There are also some lights which show the state of the accumulator, some switches, and, as on most little computers, a knob and a push button. You can set up a number on the switches, turn the knob to load the program counter, push the button that sets the program counter, turn the knob to run, push the button again and the program starts running at that address.

The computer has an extremely simple instruction set (Figure 12.33). There are only eight instructions: halt, jump to some address, jump if the accumulator is zero, add memory to the accumulator, subtract memory from the accumulator, load the accumulator, store the accumulator, and skip — just a representative set of instructions.

The architecture of the computer is as shown (Figure 12.34). We have inputs from the switches, the knob and the button. We have outputs to the lights (pcout, accout). The computer is built in two parts, a data section and a control section. Looking at the data section (bottom of Figure 12.34), there is a memory address register, a memory, a program counter, an accumulator, an instruction register, and an arithmetic logic unit. All of these are controlled by control signals coming in from the above control section. The control section involves a microcoded instruction set; that is, there is a little ROM holding a set of micro instructions, a microprogram counter and a decoder that decodes each microinstruction into signals on the control lines and the next address for the microprogram to execute.

The microprogram that implements the instruction set of the machine is fairly simple (Figure 12.35). I don't want you to look at the details of this but just to notice that there are about 25 microinstructions to implement the instruction set, each having a 'high' part, which specifies the state of those control lines, and a 'low' part, which specifies the next microprogram address (which is sometimes conditional, such as 'if the button is pushed then goto 1 else goto 0').

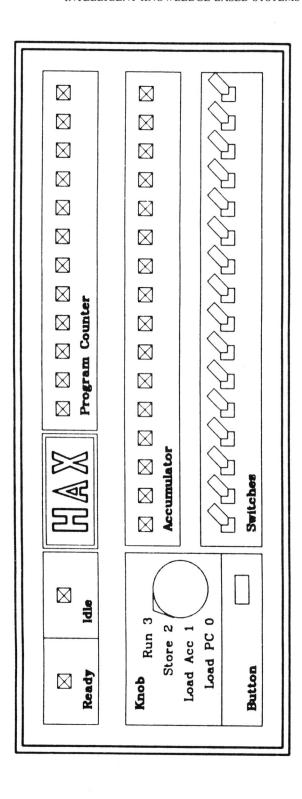

FIGURE 12.32   Front panel of a hypothetical computer

FIGURE 12.33   The instruction set

Instruction set:

000   HALT

001   JMP address

010   JZRO address

011   ADD address

100   SUB address

101   LD address

110   ST address

111   SKIP

FIGURE 12.34   The computer architecture

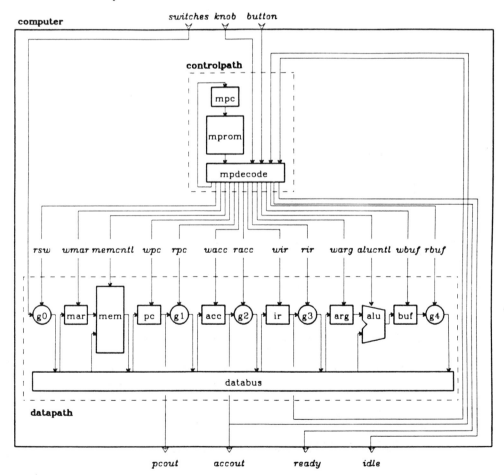

FIGURE 12.35   The microprogram

% Contents of microcode rom

```
romSource(microrom,[
    0:(ready,idle     ;if(button,1,0)),    % loop until button pressed
    1:(0              ;knob+2),            % decode knob position
    2:(rsw,wpc        ; 0),                % switches -> pc
    3:(rsw,wacc; 0),                       % switches -> acc
    4:(rpc,wmar       ; 7),                % pc -> mar
    5:(ready     ;if(button,0,6)),    % begin fetch-decode-execute
    6:(rpc,wmar       ; 8),                % pc -> mar
    7:(racc,write     ; 0),                % acc -> mem(mar)
    8:(read,wir       ; 9),                % mem(mar) -> ir
    9:(0              ;opcode+10),         % decode
    10:(0             ; 0),                % halt
    11:(rir,wpc       ; 5),                % jmp: ir -> pc
    12:(0             ;if(acc=0,11,17)),  % jzro:
    13:(racc,warg     ;19),                % add: acc -> arg
    14:(racc,warg     ;22),                % sub: acc -> arg
    15:(rir,wmar;24),                      % ld: ir -> mar
    16:(rir,wmar;25),                      % st: ir -> mar
    17:(rpc,inc,wbuf  ;18),                % pc+1 -> buf
    18:(rbuf,wpc      ; 5),                % buf -> pc
    19:(rir,wmar;20),                      % ir -> mar
    20:(read,add,wbuf;21),                 % arg+mem(mar) ->buf
    21:(rbuf,wacc     ;17),                % buf -> acc
    22:(rir,wmar;23),                      % ir -> mar
    23:(read,sub,wbuf;21),                 % arg-mem(arg) ->buf
    24:(read,wacc     ;17),                % mem(mar) -> acc
    25:(racc,write    ;17),                % acc -> mem(mar)
    ],
    [idle=0,ready=1,rbuf=2,wbuf=16,warg=5,rir=6,wir=7,racc=8,
    wacc=9,rpc=10,wpc=11,wmar=14,rsw=15,read=12,write=13,
    inc=3,add=4,sub=(3,4)]]).
```

Can we in fact do a proof of the correctness of this little computer? Well, the answer is yes, but it takes something extra that I haven't mentioned until now. The proof actually goes through in two main stages. We use the structure and the specification to prove that if you view the computer at the microinstruction level (that is, if I specify what happens when a microinstruction is executed) then the hardware correctly implements those micro level operations. But now we have to get from the micro level to the instruction level, which is something of a big jump. The computer has to execute a lot of microinstructions to implement one high-level instruction. In order to do the proof we have to symbolically execute microinstructions; that is, we chase down the consequences of executing microinstructions, but manipulating variables not particular values. Then we have to have a proof mechanism that will show that when the micro engine has executed one instruction (i.e. has gone through all the microinstructions that implement one instruction) then those two different levels of description of the machine are equivalent.

We want to show that the state of the computer when it has gone through a sequence of microinstructions is equivalent to the state of the computer when it has gone through the single corresponding instruction at the macro instruction level. We want to show that there is a homomorphism between two behaviour descriptions, one with a lot of detail and one without. To cut a long story short, it is possible to prove that this is indeed correct but it does require a little help from the user. The verifier is slightly cautious and needs to be told to go ahead and consider all the values for a particular variable at several stages in the proof.

But it's interesting that these techniques can span that vast range of description from transistors to complete computers. I think that's very exciting.

ANOTHER EXAMPLE

Here's one last example which again brings something very different. This device (Figure 12.36) is an error-detecting-correcting chip. We have 32 bits of data coming in, from a memory perhaps, plus seven bits of parity code. The idea is that if the data gets corrupted the code is compared with the data to tell which bit got corrupted and to take corrective action.

FIGURE 12.36   Error-detecting-correcting chip

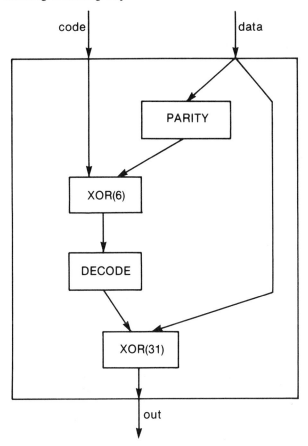

It's implemented by computing a parity code from the 32 bits of input data and comparing that with the incoming parity code using an exclusive-or. The output at this stage should be 0. If it's not, the data has been corrupted and needs to be corrected. The seven-bit signature goes through a decoder which produces a 32-bit word. All the bits of that word are 0 except one, namely the bit that got corrupted. If you exclusive-or that 32-bit word with the incoming data you flip the bad bit and so correct the output.

FIGURE 12.37 Equating behaviours of the chip

```
Trying to show behaviors are equivalent.

Considering equations for out(testEdac,31)

We must show that
```

value(in(testEdac,31))=xor(if(if(value(ctrl(testEdac))=31,not(value(in(testEdac,31))),value(in(testEdac,31)))),and(and(and(xor(xor(x
or(xor(xor(xor(if(value(ctrl(testEdac))=1,not(value(in(testEdac,1))),value(in(testEdac,1))),if(value(ctrl(testEdac))=3,not(value(in(test
Edac,3))),value(in(testEdac,3))),xor(if(value(ctrl(testEdac))=5,not(value(in(testEdac,5))),value(in(testEdac,5))),if(value(ctrl(tes
tEdac))=7,not(value(in(testEdac,7))),value(in(testEdac,7)))),xor(xor(if(value(ctrl(testEdac))=9,not(value(in(testEdac,9))),value(in
(testEdac,9))),if(value(ctrl(testEdac))=11,not(value(in(testEdac,11))),value(in(testEdac,11))),xor(if(value(ctrl(testEdac))=13,not(
value(in(testEdac,11))),value(in(testEdac,13))),if(value(ctrl(testEdac))=15,not(value(in(testEdac,15))),value(in(testEdac,15))))),x
or(xor(xor(if(value(ctrl(testEdac))=17,not(value(in(testEdac,17))),value(in(testEdac,17))),if(value(ctrl(testEdac))=19,not(value(in(
testEdac,19))),value(in(testEdac,19))),xor(if(value(ctrl(testEdac))=21,not(value(in(testEdac,21))),value(in(testEdac,21))),if(value(
ctrl(testEdac))=23,not(value(in(testEdac,23))),value(in(testEdac,23)))),xor(xor(if(value(ctrl(testEdac))=25,not(value(in(testEdac,
25))),value(in(testEdac,25))),if(value(ctrl(testEdac))=27,not(value(in(testEdac,27))),value(in(testEdac,27))),xor(if(value(ctrl(tes
tEdac))=29,not(value(in(testEdac,29))),value(in(testEdac,29))),if(value(ctrl(testEdac))=31,not(value(in(testEdac,31))),value(in(test
Edac,31))))))),xor(xor(xor(xor(value(in(testEdac,1)),value(in(testEdac,3))),xor(value(in(testEdac,5)),value(in(testEdac,7))),xor(xo
r(value(in(testEdac,9)),value(in(testEdac,11))),xor(value(in(testEdac,13)),value(in(testEdac,15))),xor(xor(xor(value(in(testEdac,1
7)),value(in(testEdac,19))),xor(value(in(testEdac,21)),value(in(testEdac,23)))),xor(xor(value(in(testEdac,25)),value(in(testEdac,27
))),xor(value(in(testEdac,29)),value(in(testEdac,31)))))),xor(xor(xor(if(value(ctrl(testEdac))=2,not(value(in(testEdac,2))),
value(in(testEdac,2))),if(value(ctrl(testEdac))=3,not(value(in(testEdac,3))),value(in(testEdac,3))),xor(if(value(ctrl(testEdac))=6,
not(value(in(testEdac,6))),value(in(testEdac,6))),if(value(ctrl(testEdac))=7,not(value(in(testEdac,7))),value(in(testEdac,7))))),xor
(xor(if(value(ctrl(testEdac))=10,not(value(in(testEdac,10))),value(in(testEdac,10))),if(value(ctrl(testEdac))=11,not(value(in(testEd
ac,11))),value(in(testEdac,11))),xor(if(value(ctrl(testEdac))=14,not(value(in(testEdac,14))),value(in(testEdac,14))),if(value(ctrl(
testEdac))=15,not(value(in(testEdac,15))),value(in(testEdac,15)))),xor(xor(xor(if(value(ctrl(testEdac))=18,not(value(in(testEdac,1
8))),value(in(testEdac,18))),if(value(ctrl(testEdac))=19,not(value(in(testEdac,19))),value(in(testEdac,19))),xor(if(value(ctrl(test
Edac))=22,not(value(in(testEdac,22))),value(in(testEdac,22))),if(value(ctrl(testEdac))=23,not(value(in(testEdac,23))),value(in(testF
dac,23))))),xor(xor(if(value(ctrl(testEdac))=26,not(value(in(testEdac,26))),value(in(testEdac,26))),if(value(ctrl(testEdac))=27,not(
value(in(testEdac,27))),value(in(testEdac,27))),xor(if(value(ctrl(testEdac))=30,not(value(in(testEdac,30))),value(in(testEdac,30)))
,if(value(ctrl(testEdac))=31,not(value(in(testEdac,31))),value(in(testEdac,31)))))),xor(xor(xor(xor(value(in(testEdac,2)),value(in(
testEdac,3))),xor(value(in(testEdac,6)),value(in(testEdac,7))),xor(value(in(testEdac,10)),value(in(testEdac,11))),xor(value(in(
testEdac,14)),value(in(testEdac,15))),xor(xor(xor(value(in(testEdac,18)),value(in(testEdac,19))),xor(value(in(testEdac,22)),value(
in(testEdac,23))),xor(xor(value(in(testEdac,26)),value(in(testFdac,27))),xor(value(in(testFdac,30)),value(in(testEdac,31)))))),an
d(xor(xor(xor(xor(if(value(ctrl(testEdac))=4,not(value(in(testEdac,4))),value(in(testEdac,4))),if(value(ctrl(testEdac))=5,not(value(
in(testEdac,5))),value(in(testEdac,5))),xor(if(value(ctrl(testEdac))=6,not(value(in(testEdac,6))),value(in(testEdac,6))),if(val
ue(ctrl(testEdac))=7,not(value(in(testEdac,7))),value(in(testEdac,7)))),xor(xor(if(value(ctrl(testEdac))=12,not(value(in(testEdac,1
2))),value(in(testEdac,12))),if(value(ctrl(testEdac))=13,not(value(in(testEdac,13))),value(in(testEdac,13))),xor(if(value(ctrl(test
Edac))=14,not(value(in(testEdac,14))),value(in(testEdac,14))),if(value(ctrl(testEdac))=15,not(value(in(testEdac,15))),value(in(testE
dac,15)))),xor(xor(xor(if(value(ctrl(testEdac))=20,not(value(in(testEdac,20))),value(in(testEdac,20))),if(value(ctrl(testEdac))=21
,not(value(in(testEdac,21))),value(in(testEdac,21))),xor(if(value(ctrl(testEdac))=22,not(value(in(testEdac,22))),value(in(testEdac,
22))),if(value(ctrl(testEdac))=23,not(value(in(testEdac,23))),value(in(testEdac,23)))),xor(xor(if(value(ctrl(testEdac))=28,not(valu
e(in(testEdac,28))),value(in(testEdac,28))),if(value(ctrl(testEdac))=29,not(value(in(testEdac,29))),value(in(testEdac,29))),xor(if(
value(ctrl(testEdac))=30,not(value(in(testEdac,30))),value(in(testEdac,30))),if(value(ctrl(testEdac))=31,not(value(in(testEdac,31))
,value(in(testEdac,31))))),xor(xor(xor(xor(value(in(testEdac,4)),value(in(testEdac,5))),xor(value(in(testEdac,6)),value(in(testEda
c,7))),xor(xor(value(in(testEdac,12)),value(in(testEdac,13))),xor(value(in(testEdac,14)),value(in(testEdac,15)))),xor(xor(xor(valu
e(in(testEdac,20)),value(in(testEdac,21))),value(in(testEdac,22)),value(in(testEdac,23))),xor(xor(value(in(testEdac,28)),value(
in(testEdac,29))),value(in(testEdac,30)))),if(value(ctrl(testEdac))=31,not(value(in(testEdac,31))),value(in(testEdac,31))))),and(valu
e(in(testEdac,30)),value(in(testEdac,4))),if(value(ctrl(testEdac))=1,not(value(in(testEdac,1))),value(in(testEdac,1))),xor(if(value
(ctrl(testEdac))=2,not(value(in(testEdac,2))),value(in(testEdac,2))),if(value(ctrl(testEdac))=3,not(value(in(testEdac,3))),value(in(
testEdac,3))))),xor(xor(if(value(ctrl(testEdac))=4,not(value(in(testEdac,4))),value(in(testEdac,4))),if(value(ctrl(testEdac))=5,not(
value(in(testEdac,5))),value(in(testEdac,5))),xor(if(value(ctrl(testEdac))=6,not(value(in(testEdac,6))),value(in(testEdac,6))),if(v
alue(ctrl(testEdac))=7,not(value(in(testEdac,7))),value(in(testEdac,7)))),xor(xor(if(value(ctrl(testEdac))=8,not(value(in(testEdac,
8))),value(in(testEdac,8))),if(value(ctrl(testEdac))=9,not(value(in(testEdac,9))),value(in(testEdac,9))),xor(if(value(ctrl(tes
tEdac))=10,not(value(in(testEdac,10))),value(in(testEdac,10))),if(value(ctrl(testEdac))=11,not(value(in(testEdac,11))),value(in(test
Edac,11)))),xor(xor(if(value(ctrl(testEdac))=12,not(value(in(testEdac,12))),value(in(testEdac,12))),if(value(ctrl(testEdac))=13,not
(value(in(testEdac,13))),value(in(testEdac,13))),xor(if(value(ctrl(testEdac))=14,not(value(in(testEdac,14))),value(in(testEdac,14))
),if(value(ctrl(testEdac))=15,not(value(in(testEdac,15))),value(in(testEdac,15)))),xor(xor(xor(if(value(ctrl(testEdac))=24,not(va
lue(in(testEdac,24))),value(in(testEdac,24))),if(value(ctrl(testEdac))=25,not(value(in(testEdac,25))),value(in(testEdac,25))),xor(i
f(value(ctrl(testEdac))=26,not(value(in(testEdac,26))),value(in(testEdac,26))),if(value(ctrl(testEdac))=27,not(value(in(testEdac,27
))),value(in(testEdac,27))),xor(xor(if(value(ctrl(testEdac))=28,not(value(in(testEdac,28))),value(in(testEdac,28))),if(value(ctrl(t
estEdac))=29,not(value(in(testEdac,29))),value(in(testEdac,29))),xor(if(value(ctrl(testEdac))=30,not(value(in(testEdac,30))),value(
in(testEdac,30))),if(value(ctrl(testEdac))=31,not(value(in(testEdac,31))),value(in(testEdac,31))))),xor(xor(xor(xor(xor(value(in(t
estEdac,4)),value(in(testEdac,5))),xor(value(in(testEdac,6)),value(in(testEdac,7))),xor(xor(value(in(testEdac,12)),value(in(testEdac
,13))),value(in(testEdac,14)),value(in(testEdac,15))),xor(xor(xor(value(in(testEdac,24)),value(in(testEdac,25))),value(in(testEdac
c,15)))))),xor(xor(xor(value(in(testEdac,24)),value(in(testEdac,25))),value(in(testEdac,25))),value(in(testEdac,27))),xor(xor(va
lue(in(testEdac,28)),value(in(testEdac,29))),xor(value(in(testEdac,30)),value(in(testEdac,31)))),and(and(xor(xor(xor(xor(xor(if
(value(ctrl(testEdac))=0,not(value(in(testEdac,0))),value(in(testEdac,0))),if(value(ctrl(testEdac))=1,not(value(in(testEdac,1))),val
ue(in(testEdac,1)))),xor(if(value(ctrl(testEdac))=2,not(value(in(testEdac,2))),value(in(testEdac,2))),if(value(ctrl(testEdac))=3,not
(value(in(testEdac,3))),value(in(testEdac,3))),xor(xor(if(value(ctrl(testEdac))=4,not(value(in(testEdac,4))),value(in(testEdac,4))
),if(value(ctrl(testEdac))=5,not(value(in(testEdac,5))),value(in(testEdac,5))),xor(if(value(ctrl(testEdac))=6,not(value(in(testEdac,
6))),value(in(testEdac,6))),if(value(ctrl(testEdac))=7,not(value(in(testEdac,7))),value(in(testEdac,7)))),xor(xor(xor(if(value(ctrl(
testEdac))=16,not(value(in(testEdac,16))),value(in(testEdac,16))),if(value(ctrl(testEdac))=17,not(value(in(testEdac,17))),value(
ue(in(testEdac,17))),xor(if(value(ctrl(testEdac))=18,not(value(in(testEdac,18))),value(in(testEdac,18))),if(value(ctrl(testEdac))=1
9,not(value(in(testEdac,19))),value(in(testEdac,19))),xor(xor(if(value(ctrl(testEdac))=20,not(value(in(testEdac,20))),value(in(tes
tEdac,20))),if(value(ctrl(testEdac))=21,not(value(in(testEdac,21))),value(in(testEdac,21))),xor(if(value(ctrl(testEdac))=22,not(val
ue(in(testEdac,22))),value(in(testEdac,22))),if(value(ctrl(testEdac))=23,not(value(in(testEdac,23)))),value(in(testEdac,23)))),xor(
xor(xor(if(value(ctrl(testEdac))=24,not(value(in(testEdac,24))),value(in(testEdac,24))),if(value(ctrl(testEdac))=25,not(value(in(tes
tEdac,25))),value(in(testEdac,25))),xor(if(value(ctrl(testEdac))=26,not(value(in(testEdac,26))),value(in(testEdac,26))),if(value(ct
rl(testEdac))=27,not(value(in(testEdac,27))),value(in(testEdac,27))),xor(xor(if(value(ctrl(testEdac))=28,not(value(in(testEdac,28
))),value(in(testEdac,28))),if(value(ctrl(testEdac))=29,not(value(in(testEdac,29))),value(in(testEdac,29))),xor(if(value(ctrl(testE
dac))=30,not(value(in(testEdac,30))),value(in(testEdac,30))),if(value(ctrl(testEdac))=31,not(value(in(testEdac,31))),value(in(testEda
c,31))))))),xor(xor(xor(xor(value(in(testEdac,0)),value(in(testEdac,1))),value(in(testEdac,2)),value(in(testEdac,3)))),xor(xor(
value(in(testEdac,4)),value(in(testEdac,5))),xor(value(in(testEdac,6)),value(in(testEdac,7)))),xor(xor(xor(value(in(testEdac,16
))),value(in(testEdac,17))),value(in(testEdac,18)),value(in(testEdac,19))),xor(value(in(testEdac,20)),value(in(testEdac,21))
),xor(value(in(testEdac,22)),value(in(testEdac,23))),xor(xor(xor(value(in(testEdac,24)),value(in(testEdac,25))),value(in(testEda
c,31))))),xor(xor(xor(xor(if(value(ctrl(testEdac))=8,not(value(in(testEdac,8))),value(in(testEdac,8))),if(value(ctrl(testEdac)
))=9,not(value(in(testEdac,9))),value(in(testEdac,9))),xor(if(value(ctrl(testEdac))=10,not(value(in(testEdac,10))),value(in(testEda
c,10))),if(value(ctrl(testEdac))=11,not(value(in(testEdac,11))),value(in(testEdac,11))),xor(xor(if(value(ctrl(testEdac))=12,not(va
lue(in(testEdac,12))),value(in(testEdac,12))),if(value(ctrl(testEdac))=13,not(value(in(testEdac,13))),value(in(testEdac,13))),xor(i
f(value(ctrl(testEdac))=14,not(value(in(testEdac,14))),value(in(testEdac,14))),if(value(ctrl(testEdac))=15,not(value(in(testEdac,15
))),value(in(testEdac,15))),xor(xor(if(value(ctrl(testEdac))=16,not(value(in(testEdac,16))),value(in(testEdac,16))),if(value(ctrl(t
estEdac))=17,not(value(in(testEdac,17))),value(in(testEdac,17))),xor(if(value(ctrl(testEdac))=18,not(value(in(testEdac,18))),value(
in(testEdac,18))),if(value(ctrl(testEdac))=19,not(value(in(testEdac,19))),value(in(testEdac,19)))),xor(xor(if(value(ctrl(testEdac))=
20,not(value(in(testEdac,20))),value(in(testEdac,20))),if(value(ctrl(testEdac))=21,not(value(in(testEdac,21))),value(in(testEdac,21
))),xor(if(value(ctrl(testEdac))=22,not(value(in(testEdac,22))),value(in(testEdac,22))),if(value(ctrl(testEdac))=23,not(value(in(te
stEdac,21))),xor(if(value(ctrl(testEdac))=22,not(value(in(testEdac,22))),value(in(testEdac,22))),if(value(ctrl(testEdac))=23,not(va
lue(in(testEdac,23))),value(in(testEdac,23))),xor(xor(if(value(ctrl(testEdac))=24,not(value(in(testEdac,24))),value(in(testEd
ac,24))),if(value(ctrl(testEdac))=25,not(value(in(testEdac,25))),value(in(testEdac,25))),xor(if(value(ctrl(testEdac))=26,not(value(
in(testEdac,26))),value(in(testEdac,26))),if(value(ctrl(testEdac))=27,not(value(in(testEdac,27))),value(in(testEdac,27)))),xor(xor(
if(value(ctrl(testEdac))=28,not(value(in(testEdac,28))),value(in(testEdac,28))),if(value(ctrl(testEdac))=29,not(value(in(testEdac,29
))),value(in(testEdac,29))),xor(if(value(ctrl(testEdac))=30,not(value(in(testEdac,30))),value(in(testEdac,30))),if(value(ctrl(testE
dac))=31,not(value(in(testEdac,31))),value(in(testEdac,31)))))),xor(xor(xor(value(in(testEdac,8)),value(in(testEdac,9))),value(in(
alue(in(testEdac,10)),value(in(testEdac,11))),xor(value(in(testEdac,12)),value(in(testEdac,13))),xor(value(in(testEdac,14)),val
ue(in(testEdac,15)))),xor(xor(value(in(testEdac,16)),value(in(testEdac,17))),xor(value(in(testEdac,18)),value(in(testEdac,1
9)))),xor(xor(value(in(testEdac,20)),value(in(testEdac,21))),xor(value(in(testEdac,22)),value(in(testEdac,23))),xor(xor(value(
in(testEdac,24)),value(in(testEdac,25))),xor(value(in(testEdac,26)),value(in(testEdac,27))),xor(xor(value(in(testEdac,28)),value(
in(testEdac,29))),xor(value(in(testEdac,30)),value(in(testEdac,31))))))),xor(xor(xor(xor(xor(if(value(ctrl(testEdac))=0,not(value(in
(testEdac,0))),value(in(testEdac,0))),if(value(ctrl(testEdac))=1,not(value(in(testEdac,1))),value(in(testEdac,1)))),xor(if(value(ctr
l(testEdac))=2,not(value(in(testEdac,2))),value(in(testEdac,2))),if(value(ctrl(testEdac))=3,not(value(in(testEdac,3))),value(in(testE
dac,3))),xor(xor(if(value(ctrl(testEdac))=4,not(value(in(testEdac,4))),value(in(testEdac,4))),if(value(ctrl(testEdac))=5,not(value(i
n(testEdac,5))),value(in(testEdac,5))),xor(if(value(ctrl(testEdac))=6,not(value(in(testEdac,6))),value(in(testEdac,6))),if(value(ctr
l(testEdac))=7,not(value(in(testEdac,7))),value(in(testEdac,7))),xor(xor(if(value(ctrl(testEdac))=8,not(value(in(testEdac,8))),value
(in(testEdac,8))),if(value(ctrl(testEdac))=9,not(value(in(testEdac,9))),value(in(testEdac,9))),xor(if(value(ctrl(testEdac))=10,not(
value(in(testEdac,10))),value(in(testEdac,10))),if(value(ctrl(testEdac))=11,not(value(in(testEdac,11))),value(in(testEdac,11)))),if(
value(ctrl(testEdac))=14,not(value(in(testEdac,14))),value(in(testEdac,14))),xor(xor(if(value(ctrl(testEdac))=16,not(value(in(testEdac,16))),value(in
(testEdac,16))),value(in(testEdac,16))),if(value(ctrl(testEdac))=19,not(value(in(testEdac,19))),value(in(testEdac,19))),xor(if(val
ue(ctrl(testEdac))=21,not(value(in(testEdac,21))),value(in(testEdac,21))),if(value(ctrl(testEdac))=22,not(value(in(testEdac,22))),va
lue(in(testEdac,25)))),xor(xor(if(value(ctrl(testEdac))=25,not(value(in(testEdac,25))),value(in(testEdac,25))),if(value(ctrl(testEd
ac))=26,not(value(in(testEdac,26))),value(in(testEdac,26))),xor(if(value(ctrl(testEdac))=29,not(value(in(testEdac,28))),value(in(te
stEdac,28))),if(value(ctrl(testEdac))=31,not(value(in(testEdac,31))),value(in(testEdac,31)))),xor(xor(xor(xor(value(in(testEdac,20
))),value(in(testEdac,13)),value(in(testEdac,11))),xor(xor(value(in(testEdac,15)),value(in(testEdac,17))),xor(value(in(testEdac,
21)),value(in(testEdac,22))),xor(xor(value(in(testEdac,25)),value(in(testEdac,26))),xor(value(in(testEdac,28)),value(in(testEdac,31
))))))))

```
Trying symbolic manipulation.

Can not finalize the identity....Execution aborted ]
```

It is quite a job to describe verbally what this thing's doing and it's even worse to describe it in terms of equations. In fact, you end up with descriptions as shown in Figure 12.37 — I don't expect you to read it! This is only a piece of one of the expressions. There are 31 others like that.

How on earth are we going to deal with a design like that? Well, there are some techniques we can use, and I borrowed a nice idea from my friends Boyer and Moore, who have been attempting to prove things about software.

Consider the chip shown in Figure 12.38, with 32 bits of input data. It computes a seven-bit parity code, and also produces corrupted data — but corrupted in a controlled way in that the kth bit has been flipped over.

Now if I add this to the error-detecting-correcting chip to give the design shown (Figure 12.39) then it's very easy to describe what this is doing. It's not doing anything in fact! The input comes in, gets corrupted in a controlled way, the error is detected, corrected and you get the output coming out. So I can easily describe the behaviour of this: in = out.

It's easy to prove that the data generating chip (Figure 12.38) is correct, and so if I can prove that the whole thing performs just the identity function then I can infer that the error-detecting-correcting chip is correct. I can do this in two ways, either by letting it brute force its way through those huge expressions which involve 2000–3000 terms, or by short-circuiting things by giving it two pieces of information, namely:

(i) *define* parity-code (xor(X,Y)) *as*

  xor (parity-code (X), parity-code (Y)),

i.e. the parity code of the exclusive-or of two things is the exclusive-or of their parity codes, and

(ii) *define* decode (parity-code (2^J)) *as* 2^J, i.e. decoding the parity code of 2 to the J gives 2 to the J. With those two simple facts plugged in, VERIFY just romps through that proof of correctness.

FIGURE 12.38   A data generating chip

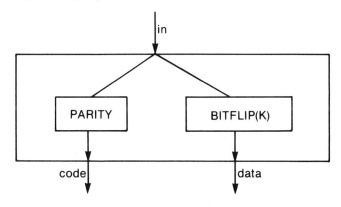

FIGURE 12.39   Combining the two chips

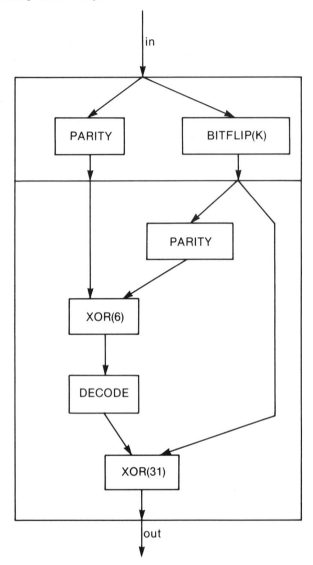

CONCLUSIONS

I hope I haven't given the impression that the whole problem is tied up and that I have a system that can prove the correctness of any design whatsoever. It's still very much at the research stage, but I think it's an exciting enough beginning.

To summarize, the key problems in deciding that designs are correct stem from the complexity of the designs, the structural and the functional complexity. We can exploit the natural structure of the design in trying to circumvent some of these problems. We can compute from the structure a behavioural description of what things are doing, and we can use algebraic proofs and not just enumerative simulation to show that the design is in fact correct. The techniques can span many levels of the design, from transistors to computers, and can actually deal with some designs that are fairly complex. We still have quite a long way to go before this is a usable design tool but I think this is a very interesting beginning. Finally, if you want to know more about this then there's a paper recently published in the journal *Artificial Intelligence*.

FURTHER READING

Barrow, H.G. (1984) VERIFY: a program for proving correctness of digital hardware designs, *Artificial Intelligence* Vol. 24, pp 437–491

Gordon, M. (1983) Proving a computer correct. Tech. Rep. No. 42, Computer Laboratory, Cambridge University.

Stoy, J.E. (1983) *Denotational Semantics: the Scott–Strachey Approach to Programming Language Theory,* MIT Press, Cambridge, Mass.

Wagner, T.T. (1977). Hardware verification. Ph.D. Thesis, Department of Computer Science, Stanford University, Stanford, California

INDEX

$2\frac{1}{2}$D sketch, 127–8, 134–50, 153

ACRONYM, 153
agenda, 165, 170
AI programming,
   environments, 11–12, 26–7
   languages, *see* LISP, POP, PROLOG
AISPEAR, 111–12
algebraic transformations, 208–9
Alvey programme, 12–14, 26, 33, 122,
   127, 154
AM, 165–6, 170
ambiguity diagram, 136–8
ambiguity in language, 179
analogy, 162–4
augmented transition network, 177–8
automatic assembly, 122–4

backward reasoning, 87, 101–2
Bayes' rule, 54
belief model, 54
Bell laboratories airline booking
   system, 6–7
binocular combination, 137–8
body modellers, 144–5
browsing, 101, 105–6

CASNET, 58–60
certainty factor, 41–6, 48, 50, 57
chaining of rules, 43–5

computer-aided design, 144–5
computer-aided instruction, 2, 155
concept learning, 157–62, 166–70
conceptual dependency, 4
condition-driven processing, 68, 74, 77,
   80
conflict resolution, 68, 76–80
conflict set, 78
consequent-driven reasoning, 68, 74–6, 80
continuity constraint, 141
cooperative algorithm, 139
coordinate systems for object
   recognition, 150–52
correctness of hardware designs, 197–227
cost of expert systems, 109, 114, 119
covert term, 62–3
credit assignment problem, 170
critic, 160–61, 167

database, 88
database query, 176, 193–4
data flow diagram, 85–7
decision making, 52–6
decision tree, 161–2, 169
declarative languages, 23, 88
DENDRAL, 172
denotational semantics, 198
depth map, 141–3
disjunctive concepts, 169–70
disparities, 135–41

disparity gradient, 141

EMYCIN, 48–9, 88
EURISKO, 165–6, 172
evaluation of expert systems, 65–6
expert system, 2, 7–13, 36–53, 55–67,
   88–9, 97–121
expert system shell, 48–50, 81–2, 99
explanation, 10, 13, 37, 41, 47, 89, 95,
   101–2
explicit rule ordering, 77
EXPLORER, 188–9

fact memory, 73
Fifth Generation Systems Project, 1, 13,
   83–5, 87, 121
focusing, 169
Fourth Generation program
   generators, 87–8
frame, 11, 94, 162–5, 170
frame problem, 170–71

generalized cylinders, 149–50
grey level image, 124–6
grouping, 129–34

help files, 35
heuristics, 165, 172
hill-climbing problem, 170–71
hybrid systems, 24

ID3, 161–2
IDT, 111
ILRPS, 113
IMACS, 112–13
image interpretation, 12
image processing, 127
image understanding, 1, 7, 28–32, 122–54
inconsistency, 82, 108–9
induction, 100
inference, 12, 55–6, 74–5, 181–2, 186–7
intelligent computer-aided instruction, 12,
   14
intelligent front ends, 12, 94–5
interactive programming, 27–32
INTERLISP, 11, 17
INTERNIST, 58, 60–64, 66
IPMS, 113

ISA, 113

KNOBS, 189–90
knowledge acquisition, 37–8, 95, 100,
   107, 119, 155
knowledge elicitation, see knowledge
   acquisition
knowledge engineer, 117
Knowledge Network, 111–2
knowledge representation, 2–12, 94

language, see natural language
large-scale demonstrators, 12–13
LCF proof checker, 198
learning, 65, 81, 100, see also machine
   learning
legislation, 89–93
LEX, 160–61
LHASA, 97
Lighthill report, 12
line labelling algorithm, 145–6
LISP, 11, 15–27, 50, 84, 101, 109,
   120–21
LISP machines, 26–7
list structures, 17–22
LITHO, 9–11
logic, 55–6, 74–6
logic programming, 76, 83–96
LOGO, 119
LUNAR, 176–80, 183–5, 187

machine learning, 155–74
machine translation, 1–3, 175
Marr–Poggio algorithm, 137–41
medical diagnosis, 36–51, 53–63
METADENDRAL, 172
military programmes, 14
MYCIN, 36–51, 56–7, 76

natural language, 12
   communication, 46–7
   processing, 175–96
   understanding, 3–7, 176
   software, 1–2
noise in learning, 169–70
NOMAD, 192–3
NTC, 112, 115–16

object models,   127–8, 147–53
object-oriented programming,   94
object representations,   147–53
OPS,   77–9, 114, 120
or-tree,   23

parallel processing,   2
participative software design,   115, 120
pattern-matching,   24–6
pattern recognition,   127
perceptron,   156
planning,   12
PMF algorithm,   141–2
POP-11,   15–35
POP-2,   11, 17
POPLOG,   11–12, 26–8, 33–5, 50
pragmatics,   181, 185–7
predicate logic,   11, 21
primal sketch,   127–34, 153
primitives for object recognition,   149–50
principle of explicit naming,   131
principle of least commitment,   132
probabilistic decision making,   53–5
probabilistic learning,   173
procedural languages,   23
production rule,   11, 68
production system,   68–82, 164–5
production system architecture,   73–6
PROLOG,   11, 15–24, 34–5, 56, 76, 84,
      90–92, 101, 109, 120–21, 200, 207
PROLOG workstations,   27
proof checker,   198
PROSPECTOR,   47, 57, 99, 101
prototyping,   15–17, 27, 87, 116–18
PSYCO,   60, 62–4
PUFF,   47, 49

R1,   77, 121
rational reconstruction,   172
raw edges,   129–30

reasoning,   9–10, 41–6, 52–67
recency,   78
recognize-act cycle,   74
refractoriness,   78
relaxation algorithm,   133, 139
RITA,   77–9
rule base,   41–6
rule memory,   73
rule ordering,   77

script,   185–6
semantic network,   57, 60–61
semantic processing,   176–9, 181
semantics,   11, 183–5
shape from contour,   135, 145–6
shape from stereo,   135–45
signal processing hierarchy,   206
software engineering,   12, 15–17, 83–8,
      93–4
spatio-temporal differentiation,   128–9
special case rules,   78
speech synthesis,   1
speech understanding,   1, 6–7
statistical decision making,   52–5, 64–6
stereo correspondence problem,   136–41
story summarizing,   195–6
structured-growth,   11–12
structured program development,   15–17
symbol manipulation,   11, 19–20, 157,
      202–3
syntactic processing,   176–9, 181
syntax,   181–3

TEACHVMS,   112
type-free languages,   11, 24–6

uncertainty,   52–67

VERIFY,   200–27
view potential,   150–51